MASQUERADE

MASQUERADE

Unmasking Dual Diagnosis

RICHARD A. MORIN, M.D.

arnica
PUBLISHING, INC.
Portland, Oregon

Library of Congress Cataloging-in-Publication Data

Morin, Richard A., 1928-
  Masquerade : unmasking dual diagnosis / Richard A. Morin.
  p. ; cm.
  ISBN 0-9726535-9-7 (trade pbk.)
  1. Dual diagnosis--United States. 2. Authors, American--Mental health. 3. Poe,
Edgar Allan, 1809-1849--Mental health. 4. Fitzgerald, F. Scott (Francis Scott), 1896-
1940--Mental health. 5. Berryman, John, 1914-1972--Mental health. 6. Jamison,
Kay R.--Mental health.   I. Title. [DNLM: 1. Poe, Edgar Allan, 1809-1849.
  2. Fitzgerald, F. Scott (Francis Scott), 1896-1940. 3. Berryman, John, 1914-1972.
  4. Jamison, Kay R. 5. Mental Disorders--history. 6. Substance-Related Disorders--
history. 7. Creativeness. 8. Diagnosis, Dual (Psychiatry)--history. 9. Famous
Persons. 10. Intelligence.   WM 270 M858m 2003]

RC564.68.M67 2003
616.89--dc21

                                                                    2003008720

Arnica Publishing, Inc.

620 SW Main, Suite 345 • Portland, OR 97205
Phone: (503) 225-9900 • Fax: (503) 225-9901

Arnica books are available at special discounts when purchased in bulk for premiums and sales
promotions, as well as for fund-raising or educational use. Special editions or book excerpts can
also be created for specification. For details, contact the Sales Director at the address above.

Dedicated to the Honorable S. J. Sheldon without whose intervention in my progressive demise in 1973, this book would never have been written. Through the benevolent coercion of his court adjudication, I experienced an attitude change that saved my life, my family, and my career. Thank you, Judge Sheldon!

CONTENTS

By Anne E. Linton, M.D.

Chief Medical Officer, Betty Ford Clinic

In *Masquerade: Unmasking Dual Diagnosis,* Dr. Morin addresses the lives of three famous authors who were apparently afflicted with two different, yet commonly co-existing diseases: bipolar disorder and alcoholism. Unfortunately, during their lifetimes we did not have good treatments for either disease, much less understand that they actually *had* two diseases.

The fields of psychiatry and addiction medicine have oftentimes looked at these diseases from two different perspectives and have done a good job of treating those with the "single diagnoses"—that of alcoholism and/or drug addiction separate from that of mental illness.

The early physicians who understood the spiritual experience that many alcoholics and drug addicts experienced and used to recover from their addictive disease, often times were limited in their understanding of the medication needs of Dual-Diagnosis patients, for fear they were taking mood-altering substances which could interfere with their sobriety. Thus, many patients with underlying "mood disorders" were encouraged to stop taking their antidepressants and/or mood stabilizers, such as lithium, for fear this was mood altering and would cause a relapse (or may actually be considered a relapse). Unfortunately, many of these patients *would* relapse when they stopped these appropriate treatments for their mood disorder, and then self medicate with alcohol and/or drugs, or worse, commit suicide, or decompensate in terms of their mood disorder, thus keeping them from working their twelve-step spiritual program.

Neurobiology, neurochemistry, and the current state-of-the-art understanding of addiction as a brain disease with behavioral manifestations have helped to clarify the difference between an addictive substance and a substance that is mood *altering,* which is the purpose of the medication in treating mood *disorders.* Carlton Erickson, Ph.D., of the University of Texas and Alan Leshner, Ph.D., formerly of NIDA have stated the following:

"Addiction, by definition, is the continued use of a substance, in spite of negative consequences due to the substance, and is due to impairment in the *mesolimbic dopamine system*, or pleasure pathway of the brain. This is by definition how one determines an addictive substance."

Mood stabilizers, such as lithium and many of the antidepressants, do not activate the mesolimbic dopamine system or "pleasure pathway" of the brain, thus are not "addictive" medications.

The debate continues as to when to medicate patients in early recovery, as many addictive substances cause symptoms that closely mimic many of the mood disorders. As Dr. Morin points out, there is a very systematic way to assess patients, and this helps determine *when* and *if* to treat the underlying mood disorder with medication. This requires a multidisciplinary assessment and a good timeline of symptoms related to substance use as well as family history, and collateral information, all of which go into the decision to medicate or not in early recovery. Many studies have shown that a parallel approach to treating these disorders is the most successful, but the culture of the traditional twelve-step-based, twenty-eight-day treatment program has oftentimes been based on the "no medication" philosophy, and fear of medication. Spirituality and medication are not mutually exclusive as was originally thought. In fact, my experience as an addiction psychiatrist working in various treatment settings, has been that medication, when used appropriately, can actually benefit patients by enabling them to successfully engage in the twelve-step spiritual program, which is the foundation of good, long-term recovery.

With current training programs in both addiction and psychiatry, we can better train psychiatrists to understand addiction, as well as train addiction medicine MDs to understand the Dually-Diagnosed patient. It isn't all or nothing, but rather more of a skillful art to be able to incorporate the two modalities—that of science and spirituality—appropriately. Dr Morin's book provides in-depth case examples of Dual-Diagnosis patients for both the lay person and the health professional.

By James West, M.D.
Outpatient Medical Director, Betty Ford Clinic

It is true that alcoholism appears to be over-represented among gifted people. Of the seven or eight American Nobel laureates in literature, the majority was afflicted with alcoholism and their deaths were attributable to this disease. Dr. Richard Morin addresses the tragedy of dually-disordered victims of alcoholism and bipolar disease in this book.

There seems to be a connection between the creative brilliance in some persons with bipolar (manic-depressive) disorder and alcoholism.

A study conducted by the National Institute of Mental Health found that there is an exceedingly high lifetime prevalence rate, 46 percent, for alcohol abuse and dependence in persons with manic-depressive disorder. A related study found that mania was strongly associated with alcoholism, but major depressive disorder was not.

Until a decade or so in the past, geniuses like Edgar Allan Poe died with this fatal duality of bipolar disease and alcoholism.

Now a combination of therapies exist to save these gifted minds.

Alcoholics Anonymous combined with proven medical treatment for bipolar disease is the path to recovery.

PREFACE

I have studied three famous deceased American authors from a psychiatric and a chemical dependency perspective in an attempt to determine if their traumatic lives resulted from their genius or from a Dual Diagnosis (a coexistent mental disorder and an addiction disorder). These authors struggled to live with their mental disorders, their addiction disorders, and their personality disorders during their short lifetimes that ran more or less consecutively during the two hundred years before there were any specific treatments for their conditions. Some of them lived before there was even an ability to diagnose the psychiatric part of their Dual Diagnosis and before society accepted the other component of their Dual Diagnosis as a disease. I refer to alcoholism and drug addiction that was most commonly called at that time, inebriety.

During the two-hundred-year period that these three authors lived there was a social quandary about whether or not inebriety was due to a moral issue (sin), a legal issue (prohibition), a religious issue (antichrist), or was it just the result of being possessed by some evil, invisible power that needed to be exorcised? There were a few stalwart physicians, such a Benjamin Rush, a signer of our Declaration of Independence in 1776, who insisted that inebriety was a disease at a time when most physicians considered it the effect of demons and related to lax morals and slothfulness. Although there were approximately forty treatment centers for inebriety in the colonial United States, they closed during the prohibition period.

Only in the past decade did the term Dual Diagnosis begin to be seen as a factor that had something to do with treatment and recovery from either or both of its component parts of psychiatric disorders and alcohol and drug addiction. All we knew for sure was that there were some individuals who had a sickness resembling alcoholism and mental illness that did not respond well to treatment for either of these conditions and were constantly involved in a phenomenon of relapse or recidivism that was referred to as the "revolving door." These patients, many of whom I treated as the co-medical director of Brighton Hospital and who I could not understand because they had such poor outcomes from our otherwise successful addiction in-patient treatment program. Because of my disappointment and confusion regarding the revolving door patients, I decided to do formal residency training in psychiatry in 1980–83 to see if I could learn why this was so. At least 50 percent or more of the in-patients I saw and treated while in training seemed to have the same dual afflictions. In fact, in many cases, they were the self-same patients seeking treatment once again for their misery at a state psychiatric hospital. Their revolving door (recurrent relapses) took them to many different types of institutions searching for an answer to their recidivism.

What I learned should have been obvious. It was all but impossible for these individuals to recover unless their physicians recognized that they had a Dual Diagnosis, prescribed proper treatment for both diagnoses, and that the patient understood and accepted that they had two separate, usually unrelated diseases. It was also important that they received treatment for both at essentially the same time, and preferably in the same facility. Generally speaking, what is meant by a Dual Diagnosis is that the individual has both a psychiatric disorder plus an alcohol or substance abuse disorder that coexists concurrently. One disorder may have started before the other, but the final confusing condition is that they co-exist. That may sound simple enough. Denial about an individual's illness is a fairly common phenomenon for a period of time. Some individuals with psychiatric disorders unconsciously deny or are unaware that they suffer from two such disorders for prolonged periods, sometimes indefinitely. The same denial is frequently a factor with alcohol and/or a substance abuse problem. And, just like psychiatric disorders, the denial may be prolonged and sometimes indefinite or interspersed with periods of spontaneous remissions. Furthermore, individuals with this type of Dual Diagnosis are usually oblivious of the fact that their symptoms for each disorder are similar or even identical. In other words, while individuals that have a Dual Diagnosis may be aware of their symptoms (confusion, hallucinations, depression, anxiety, mania, paranoia, sexual dysfunction, insomnia, occupational problems, and marital problems, etc.), they have no concept of what is causing these symptoms. Almost always they think it may be some outside force causing the symptoms but cannot believe that they have a psychiatric disorder or an alcohol or substance abuse disorder. They prefer to think that someone or something else is adversely influencing their lives but not alcohol and not drugs and not mental illness but more likely their boss, wife, husband, children, friends, or even God. They are willing to believe that there is a conspiracy by some unknown enemy and quite possibly the devil. This sharing or mimicking of symptoms between psychiatric disorders and alcohol and drug addiction disorders is why I have chosen the title *Masquerade: Unmasking Dual Diagnosis* for the title of this book.

To illustrate the Dual Diagnosis or *masquerade*, I will include the psychiatric evaluations and psychiatric formulations, as well as the alcohol and addiction histories of the three famous deceased American authors, Edgar Allan Poe, F. Scott Fitzgerald and John Berryman. These men had interesting, brilliant, but failing careers along with their many traumatic life experiences related to their Dual Diagnoses. However, even though all three men did function at a genius level, they never were able to comprehend and admit the relationship between their alcoholism and their manic-depressive disorder (bipolar disorder) or even that they were so afflicted. This was in part due to the pathological denial of these illnesses that is almost universal and is also in part due to the absence of scientific knowledge or treatment for their illnesses that existed during their lifetimes. Another factor that limits insight is the fact that both psychiatric illnesses and addiction illnesses have spontaneous remissions and exacerbations as part of their normal course. John Berryman, relatively late in his life, got introduced to the program of Alcoholics Anonymous and he received some appropriate treatment inadvertently for his undiagnosed manic-depressive disorder but it was too late to reverse some of the complications or prevent the deterioration of his genius or his suicide. Berryman wrote a book called *Recovery* published posthumously about how and why he didn't recover in AA.

The reader will discover from the biographies in this book the how and why of the discovery of these "masquerading" types of Dual Diagnoses. When both conditions are properly diagnosed, it will allow for a much better diagnosis and treatment for these patients and help them start again with more happy, joyous, free, and productive lives that they will be able to share with others. This type of happiness is attainable and happens regularly and frequently to alcoholics and drug addicts who do not have a Dual Diagnosis. In AA they call this phenomenon, "becoming weller than well." But, as I have already stressed for the Dual Diagnosis patient, proper diagnosis and treatment is mandatory or they will be condemned to follow their miserable, deteriorating unsuccessful lives. As the autobiography of a fourth famous American author, Kay Redfield Jamison, abridged in this book will show, treatment of Dual Diagnosis can and usually does result in happy and successful careers. Or, as Dr. James West of the Betty Ford Center succinctly points out in his Foreword to this book, combination therapy can save a gifted mind.

Finally, I do not believe that the discovery of the Dual Diagnosis of any type would have been possible if it were not for the insightful work of a stockbroker by the name of Bill Wilson and a surgeon, Dr. Bob Smith. They met for a fortuitous meeting in Akron, Ohio in 1935 and started their personal recoveries by sharing the miseries of their alcoholism with each other. Slowly, after that meeting of these two struggling men, the program of Alcoholics Anonymous came of age. Soon after, Jack Alexander wrote an article about Alcoholics Anonymous in the March 1, 1941 issue of the *Saturday Evening Post* and the attendance at AA meetings mushroomed. It soon became an international fellowship helping thousands upon thousands of alcoholics recover.

In the 1960s and 1970s many federal and state judges in the United States discovered AA for treatment of their adjudicated alcoholics. This began the first movement away from jails, prisons, poor houses, mental asylums, and hard labor camps, and toward therapy frequently referred to as *benevolent coercion.* On September 5, 1973, one of those judges full of wisdom and compassion, the Honorable S. J. Elden, began to see that there were many different kinds of alcoholics and drug addicts. Through the insights of Judge Elden and his other colleagues, they began to see differences between different types of alcoholics and drug addicts. There were the public inebriates and the "normals" that were simply down and out. But there were also the criminals, the mentally ill, the demented, the traumatic brain injured, the medically ill, the surgically under-recovered, and the personality disordered. It was the Honorable S. J. Elden that I have dedicated this book to because he was the person totally responsible for redirecting my life toward recovery. Many had tried, but Elden was chosen.

As a result of these changes in attitude by society in general and alcoholics and other addicts, in particular the alcoholics, and especially if their families began to see alcoholism as a treatable disease and they had the courage to demand treatment for their alcoholism and other addictions. The biggest innovation in thinking came about when private insurance companies like Blue Cross and Blue Shield started to cover alcoholism and other addictions for detoxification and rehabilitation in acute hospitals and alcohol and drug rehabilitation units. The year was 1975. This courage for alcoholics to do the things they could do to get well was part of their AA program:

SERENITY PRAYER

God Grant me the Serenity
to Accept the Things I Cannot Change
The Courage to Change the Things I Can
And the Wisdom to Know the Difference.

Their general change in attitude from despair to hope was fostered by the personal recoveries of thousands of others, such as Representative Wilbur Mills and his lovely wife, as well as Senator Harold Hughes. This national "flight into health" really escalated when the former First Lady, Betty Ford, shared her personal recovery from alcohol and Valium addiction. One could almost say that with Betty Ford, recovery became fashionable and the illness lost much of its stigma. During this "golden era of recovery" hundreds of thousands of alcoholics and addicts recovered, and many new and old treatment centers opened or expanded. For the first time in the twentieth century, alcoholics could be and were admitted to general medical and surgical hospitals with their true diagnosis, *alcoholism,* without their doctors losing hospital privileges for doing so. In fact, new alcohol rehabilitation units were actually opened in hundreds of acute medical and surgical care hospitals throughout the United States for the first time ever. Never mind that there just happened to be an excess of acute hospital beds at that time. The outlook for the proper diagnosis and treatment for alcoholism and drug addiction was good and it seemed like it would only get better and better during those golden years between 1975 and 1990.

About this time I was finishing my formal training as a resident in psychiatry (1983) and making plans to take the examination for board certification by the American Boards of Psychiatry and Neurology. I would have had to be blind not to recognize that these were the same patients—literally and figuratively speaking—moving back and forth between the different types of treatment centers. These were the patients with a Dual Diagnosis and they, in turn, were the patients that I had decided to do the residency to learn more about in the first place. They were the chronic revolving door patients that had concerned me so much because they were in and out of treatment constantly. I also knew that most of them had a strong desire to stay sober and live normal, happy lives. They just could not do it. There are two solutions to this puzzle:

About 20–40 percent of individuals afflicted with an addictive disorder or a mental disorder actually have *both*. This is to say that they have, at the same time, both an addictive disorder and a mental disorder. They have what has become known as a Dual Diagnosis, or in some cases, a Multiple Diagnosis. People that could help these individuals surround them and try to assist in every way, including their family, friends, employers, their physicians, and, in some cases, law enforcement agencies. Most, if not all of these interested people want to assist in the recovery process, including the patients themselves, but are totally unaware of the possibility of a Dual Diagnosis. As a result, the patients never get both illnesses treated at the same time and therefore usually never get well. This is a tragedy! It does not matter which illness came first, *both illnesses need simultaneous treatment.*

Secondly, most of the symptoms associated with mental disorders are the same symptoms that are associated with alcoholism and the other chemical addictions. Many medical and surgical illnesses, including head trauma, often present with symptoms that are similar or even identical to mental disorders and/or alcohol and drug intoxication, withdrawal, or reversible or irreversible dementia, and amnesia, making the condition even more confusing and difficult to diagnose.

In *Masquerade: Unmasking Dual Diagnosis,* I will address mood disorders and addictions in a rather unique way. To illustrate these *"masquerades"* I will be presenting four biographies of famous people who I believe had either a Dual Diagnosis or Multiple Diagnoses including a mental disorder and an addiction disorder. Each author had difficulty receiving and accepting their Dual Diagnosis and any treatment available to them, with the single exception of Jamison. The reason for the suffering and early demise of the other three was because the psychiatric specialty and alcoholism specialty were in their infancy, and medications and treatments for both were just slowly becoming known. These three men never received adequate treatment for either of their illnesses and they never did recover. They all died prematurely, at least one and probably two by suicide. The fourth famous person, Kay Redfield Jamison, is living during the present time period and has received the current available treatments for her illnesses. Her life story illustrates one success after another. She has written several books, including *An Unquiet Mind,* which describes her illnesses and recovery, and from which I have quoted extensively.

Once again, Benjamin Franklin's sage advice proves true when he said, "To recognize ourselves diseased is half the cure." I would like to paraphrase this famous quotation with great respect to Franklin and say, *To recognize all of our diseases and accept the treatment will lead to a quality recovery.* Kay Redfield Jamison's autobiography abridged in this book is a fine example of that. There is another personal parenthetically related experience I have had that relates directly to the above quotation of Benjamin Franklin. One of the psychiatric examiners during the oral boards for my certification in psychiatry and neurology asked me a very important question that until that time I had never thought much about. He asked, "What is the hardest thing about treating a bipolar (manic-depressive) patient?" I contemplated the question, thinking of all of the bipolar patients I had treated since becoming a psychiatrist, and answered, "Keeping them on their lithium medication." He nodded and smiled and I knew I had just passed the examination and the American Boards of Psychiatry and Neurology would soon certify me. It was March 1988. I had already been certified by the American Society of Addiction Medicine.

That date was a landmark for me. I was in an occupational-induced euphoria, which was a new experience for me. I was hopeful that things in psychiatry and addiction diagnosis and treatment were going to continue to improve and we were headed toward a treatment utopia that would go on and on. Such was not to be the case. Quality psychiatric and addiction treatment is expensive but nowhere near as expensive as poor quality or no treatment. History is once again repeating itself. Whenever the societies of the world have budget crunches, the first groups of patients to have their assistance reduced are invariably the alcoholics, the drug addicts, and the patients with mental illnesses. This is true both in the private insurance sector as well as with the state and federal government. Their cost-cutting methods include rationing care for psychiatric, alcohol, and other addiction patients, especially in-patient care. The progress that had been made in these fields was definitely stymied in some sectors, mainly the disenfranchised and the newly-identified Dual Diagnosis patients and especially those with the masquerading type of Dual Diagnosis. The reader will note this also in the biographies and autobiography of our four authors with manic-depressive disorders. When reading these stories, keep in mind all the ramifications of the patient's diagnoses and treatments, or lack thereof. Imagine what the outcome of the tragic lives of these famous, gifted people would have been had they received proper treatment as did Kay Redfield Jamison. What would their creative abilities have been?

—Richard A. Morin, M.D.

ACKNOWLEDGMENTS

The writing of this book is the culmination of my years as a medical doctor, first as a physician in general practice, then shifting to the treatment of alcoholism and substance abuse that lead to an interest in psychiatry and the diagnosis of dual illnesses.

My first debt of gratitude is to Anne, my wife of fifty-five years, for her love, patience, and encouragement throughout the five years it took to research and write this book.

I thank my friend, Leo McMamara, professor emeritus at the University of Michigan, for his constructive critique with regard to enrichment, clarity, and structure in the completion of this project.

I thank James W. West, M.D., who is my friend, my mentor, and advisor, and whose longtime association with The Betty Ford Center has provided him with the wisdom, insights, and experience to counsel this author through the maze.

I thank Ruth Richards, M.D., Ph.D., professor of psychology, Saybrook Graduate School Associate Clinical Professor, for sharing her work on trauma, motivation, and creativity.

I thank my friend, Ira Marshall, for being extremely generous with his time and understanding in reading and giving honest feedback and suggestions. It was very helpful.

My thanks to Ross Hawkins, my publisher, and Gloria Gonzalez, my editor, and the staff of Arnica Publishing, Inc. Ross, for his cutting–edge expertise in the world of publishing and for having the ability to get it done. Gloria, for her patience, acumen, and counsel in editing this project.

Finally, thanks to the many friends and colleagues who have contributed their accumulated pearls of wisdom.

"Here we find hope, perhaps we can turn psychopathology more frequently toward creative outlets, and even thereby increase health."

—Ruth Richards, M.D.

CHAPTER ONE

Alcoholism and Psychiatry: The Inseparable Dual Diagnoses

Not everyone who suffers from the disease alcoholism has a second mental illness. Likewise, not all people with a mental illness have a comorbid condition of alcoholism or any other chemical addiction. However, almost everyone knows, either from experience or observation, that alcohol and other chemical addictions cause changes in the mood, behavior, and thoughts of its users. All mental illnesses likewise are associated with mood changes, aberrant behaviors, and disorders of thought. I believe that most everyone knows that alcohol and other chemical agents have been involved in the heights and depths of human experience. It has been used, either as a privileged agent in ritual, ceremonial, and social occasions of celebratory and religious intent, or as a legal or illegal recreational substance, and usually with a beneficial or at least a benign result. On the other hand, a smaller but significant number of individuals have subjective and objective experiences from alcohol and other chemicals that can range from great fulfillment and joy to the deplorable instrument of countless instances of human wretchedness, depravity, criminality, catastrophe, insanity, or death. These same phenomena can occur in individuals with mental illness. Yet, these experiences in mood, behavior, and thought can be found to be a natural part of the normal human experience. It is only when the addiction or the mental illness interferes with the ability of that individual to work, love, and play in proper proportions that the individual is deemed by his society as being in need of either treatment or confinement or both.

How is one to determine or diagnose when these individuals have an addiction or a mental illness since their symptoms are often quite similar, if not identical? Of course, if alcohol is the cause of their aberrant behavior, moods, or thoughts, the odor of alcohol on the person's breath may be a clue. Or, if the symptoms vanish after a good night's sleep that may be a clear indication of the adverse effects of alcoholism or addiction early on in the individual's drinking or drugging career. This is reminiscent of the often-told story about Winston Churchill when he was at a palace party and apparently intoxicated. One of the aristocratic ladies of the spinster type noted that Sir Winston was behaving inappropriately. She approached him and said to him, "Sir Winston, you are disgustingly drunk." He replied, "I know your ladyship, but you are disgustingly ugly and I will be sober in the morning."

Sir Winston was correct as far as acute alcoholism is concerned, but chronic alcoholism can cause brain damage and therefore become irreversible. Occasionally the brain damage is reversible as has been shown by CT scans of the brain and serial psychometric tests. Mental illness, such as Korsakoff's psychosis from alcohol, is usually irreversible, but other forms of dementia, such as substance-induced dementia, substance-induced personality disorder, substance-induced delirium, substance-induced mood disorder (depression and/or mania), substance-induced persisting amnesic disorder, substance-induced hallucinations, persisting perception disorder, substance-induced psychotic disorder, and substance-induced loss of executive functioning, can be totally or partially reversible. Many of the symptoms of the above illnesses of addiction can also result in disabilities relative to work, love, and play. These same symptoms can also result from different functional mental illnesses usually classified as affective disorders, psychotic disorders, anxiety (neurotic) disorders, and personality disorders. When these occur in the same individual they can be said to have a Dual Diagnosis. We will discover from studying the biographies of the famous authors in chapters four, five, and six, and the autobiography of the author in the second chapter that the criteria for making a Dual Diagnosis requires a thorough psychiatric and substance abuse history. This will include the developmental or childhood history, the family history, the past medical, surgical history, and the chronological present illnesses that will result in a diagnostic psychiatric formulation and treatment plan. This diagnostic format will be followed for each biography in this book, including the autobiography of the author, but this will not be so in the autobiography of Kay Redfield Jamison, who will give her own symptoms, diagnoses, and treatment plan as she herself describes them in her book, *An Unquiet Mind*.

Of course, alcoholics and drug addicts are prone to have accidents and therefore traumatic brain injuries are a hazard. The head injury can result in classical psychiatric symptoms in a person that did not have psychiatric symptoms or disorders prior to the traumatic brain injury (TBI), that can mimic, or even cause, all of the disorders that can be attributed to addictions and functional psychiatric diagnoses. It is also possible that the TBI may cause a decreased tolerance to alcohol or drugs and therefore the TBI may cause an increased sensitivity and low tolerance to alcohol and/or drugs and in a sense then cause alcoholism or other chemical additions. Therefore it not unusual for the TBI to cause a type of future alcoholism and/or drug addiction that was not present before the accident and is not inherited. It is important to note that either the substance-induced illness or the traumatic brain injuries can precipitate a seizure disorder, which may be associated with a change in personality, pseudo-dementia from depression, depression, post traumatic stress (anxiety) disorder, or a psychosis due to the traumatic brain injury. A thorough description of the concept of Dual Diagnosis or Triple Diagnoses was discussed in the Preface. In this chapter we will deal primarily with the disorders of alcoholism and other drug addictions and some of its mental complications that come under the heading of mood disorders (manic-depressive disorders).

DISEASE OR SIN?

We will begin with the controversy over the use of alcohol in our society. The nation and the world has always been divided between those who view alcohol as the "privileged agent" for use in ritual, ceremony, and social celebration to enhance the human experience with fulfillment and joy and those who view alcohol as a deplorable instrument of countless instances of irresponsibility, crime, lasciviousness, violence, and all types of wayward behavior.

Given the undeniable truth of these two viewpoints, generations of mankind have asked, what is to be done? Some groups and many cults have insisted upon the positive side, singing paeans to the near-divine joys of the spirits of vine and grain in relation to fertility, health, harvest, friendship, and their god or gods. Others have been so transfixed by the horrors associated with drink that they sought to forbid it, prohibit its manufacture, distribution, and consumption through prohibition by law or through the religious dogma of sin.

I have no quarrel with either the Wets or the Drys, and indeed very little interest in alcohol itself because in today's world it comes in many equally dangerous addictions from morphine to marijuana and from Seconal to Valium. Nor will I have much, if anything, to say about what might be called normal drinking (or normal not drinking, for that matter). Even so-called "problem drinking" is of no real concern for this book. This chapter will explore how and why alcohol and other addictive drugs can cause pathological conditions in a certain minority of persons, that mimic or masquerade as a whole array of mental symptoms. The symptoms produced depend upon the addictive substance abused, the quantity consumed, and the susceptibility of that individual to that chemical.

Generations of humans have debated the goodness or badness of alcohol itself or the depravity and hopelessness of narcotics, sedatives, cannabis, and tranquilizer addictions. There has also been a division of opinion as to alcoholism, or habitual drunkenness, or inebriety, or lack of temperance, to give it some of its past labels: is it, for instance, a sin or a sickness? Does it come from weakness of character or from bad luck in the human draw or bad genes from their parents from fate as it were? Is it a moral or medical question? These are momentous questions with huge consequences in regard to real human suffering and healing—whether spiritual or physical—and have hinged upon the answers given at various times and in various ways.

The American Medical Association defines alcoholism as a disease. Alcoholics Anonymous perceives alcoholism as an illness that affects the body, mind, and spirit. In this text the subject will be regarded not as a sin, but as a *sickness*. This should be evident especially since the terms used to describe the condition is "alcoholism," and not "habitual drunkenness," or "possession by demons," or other such terms that suggest a personal weakness or some evil power or possession by a demon.

The disease concept for alcoholism evolved from the pragmatic experiences of the self-help program of Alcoholics Anonymous following failures of other treatments for alcoholism such as religion, psychiatry, sociology, psychology, and criminality approaches. As William James said, "That which works is true." The clergy, physicians, psychiatrists, sociologists, and other professionals found that the disease concept was a viable theory and worked along with the precepts of each of their professions. Alcoholism and drug addiction can now be called the Disease Precept of addictions. It follows the American Medical Association's and the American Society of Addiction Medicine's definition of a disease. Their tenets of a disease state that there frequently is not a known cause. Although there may be a specific agent precipitating the addiction disease it does not cause the disease in all who consume that agent—usually 10–15 percent of the population are susceptible. Genetics may be a factor but there are other inconsistent factors also. As stated in *Dorlund's Medical Dictionary, 24th Edition*, like all other diseases, alcoholism and other chemical addictions are characterized by *a definite morbid process having a characteristic train of symptoms; it may affect the whole body or any of its parts, and its cause, pathology, and prognosis may be known or unknown.* A committee of distinguished addictionologists produced the most recent definition for the American Society of Addiction Medicine (ASAM). Published in the *ASAM News* in March–April 1990, the definition is, in part, as follows:

Alcoholism is a primary, chronic disease...characterized by...impaired control over drinking, preoccupation with alcohol, use of alcohol despite adverse consequences, and distortions in thinking, most notably denial.

The creators of the definition then do something unusual. They define terms. For example, a *primary disease* is not a symptom of some other disease; they define *disease* as disabling and involuntary, associated with a common set of characteristics by which individuals "differ" from the norm and which places them at disadvantage. *Impaired control* means the inability to limit alcohol use. *Denial* includes a range of "psychological maneuvers designed to reduce awareness of the fact that alcohol use is the cause of an individual's problems rather than a solution to these problems."

Other definitions from the past are still viable today. ASAM, for example, defined alcoholism in 1976 as a chronic, progressive, potentially fatal disease, characterized by tolerance, physical dependency, or pathological organ changes caused by alcohol.

For our purposes, alcoholism and other chemical dependencies are defined as *a compulsion to drink alcohol or use other addicting mind-altering substances, causing harm to self or others.* The word *compulsion* puts it in the involuntary, or *disease* category as well as in the *mental disorder* category. All addictions are both in part physiological (medical) and psychiatric (mental) and therefore have a potential to fall into the masquerades of the Dual Diagnosis concept.

It may be a little confusing that the terms *Dual Diagnosis* and *masquerade* imply a distinction between *mental* disorders and *medical* disorders. Especially since many aspects of *addiction* disorders are in fact psychiatric disorders but some aspects of alcoholism and drug dependence are also medical disorders. Examples in the *DSM-IV* of the American Psychiatric Association could be all of the substance-induced psychiatric disorders (changes in mood, anxiety, thought, cognition, and personality), literally speaking. On the other hand, it is good to realize that both medical and psychiatric disorders can mimic each other or another medical or psychiatric disorder. The importance of the Dual Diagnosis concept is that all aspects of both medical diagnoses and psychiatric diagnoses must be considered before assuming the patient's symptoms are from a single diagnosis. This is especially true when there is the probability of primary alcoholism and/or primary drug dependence coexisting with another primary psychiatric diagnosis.

Despite these caveats, the definition of *mental disorder* that was included in *DSM-III* and *DSM-III-R* is still used in the *DSM-IV* because it is as useful as any other available definition and has helped to guide decisions regarding which conditions on the boundary between normality and pathology should be included. In the *DSM-IV*, each of the mental disorders is conceptualized as a significant behavioral or psychological syndrome or pattern that occurs in an individual and that is associated with present distress. For instance a painful symptom or disability can cause impairment in one or more important areas of functioning or a significantly increased risk of suffering death, pain, disability, or an important loss of freedom. In other words, for a psychiatric disorder to be a full-blown disorder, distress, pain, or disability should be present. In addition, this syndrome or pattern must not be merely an expectable and culturally sanctioned response to a particular event. An example would be having a depressed mood after the death of a loved one. To make a diagnosis of a psychiatric disorder, a disability, pain, distress, or an important loss of freedom must be present. Whereas with alcohol and other addictions, the disabling symptoms may be present while the individual is actively using his substance of choice, but with abstinence and rehabilitation he would no longer have a psychiatric illness because he probably would no longer have a disability. Unless, of course, he also has a Dual Diagnosis. With medical diagnoses, on the other hand, disability may or may not be present in order to make a diagnosis. An individual may also have a *personality trait* or a *personality disorder*. According to the *DSM-IV*, "*personality traits* are not disabling or maladaptive but are enduring patterns of perceiving, relating to, and thinking about the environment and oneself in a wide range of social and personal contexts but are never mental disorders." An individual qualifies as having personality disorder when the following applies:

His pattern of inner experience and behavior deviates markedly from the expectations of the individual's culture, is pervasive, inflexible, has an onset in adolescence or early adulthood, is stable over time, and can lead to distress and impairment. Once a personality disorder causes impairment, distress, or disability, it then becomes a mental disorder. An individual is not classified as having a mental disorder or a personality disorder if his response is to a culturally-sanctioned event such as sadness or depression over the recent death (six months) of a loved one or loss of a career. Whatever the cause, it must be currently considered a manifestation of a severe behavioral, psychological, or biological dysfunction in the individual. Neither deviant behavior (e.g., political, religious, or sexual), nor conflicts that are primarily between the individual and society are mental disorders unless the deviance or conflict is a symptom of the individual as described above.

I believe that I have given a satisfactory description on how mental disorders, alcohol and other addiction disorders, personality disorders, medical and surgical disorders, including psychic and physical trauma, as well as some inadvertent side effects of approved treatments for these disorders can all cause disability, distress, and maladaptive behavior. These dysfunctions can become severe enough to prevent the individual's ability to work, love, and play in proper proportions and therefore result in a category that the American

Psychiatric Association calls mental disorders. As I described in the Preface all of these categories may present with many of the same symptoms and can lead to a diagnostic dilemma that I have been referring to as the Dual Diagnosis.

Let us explore some of the questions and understandings, or misunderstandings, relative to what is today called *alcoholism*, a pathological condition occurring in a certain percentage of persons, a minority, who drink, or who are disposed to drink, the beverage alcohol.

Since this book is looking at alcoholism from the point of view of psychiatry, the reader can naturally assume that the subject matter of this book will not consider alcoholism as a sin but as a disease. The disease concept of alcoholism and other chemical addictions had not been widely accepted until after the start of Alcoholics Anonymous in 1935. Before AA, alcoholism was viewed as a sin, poison, character defect, or being possessed by Satan, and these attitudes led to national prohibition of alcohol through the constitutional amendment called the Volstead Act in 1919. From then until its repeal in 1934, the possession of alcohol for consumption other than by prescription was a criminal offense. The passage of the Volstead Act was somewhat surprising since early in the nineteenth century, Benjamin Rush, M. D., a psychiatrist as well as a noted citizen and the most celebrated physician in Revolutionary America, proclaimed inebriety (alcoholism) a disease needing medical treatment. Dr. Rush was a member of the Continental Congress, a signer of the Declaration of Independence, and Physician-General of Washington's Continental Congress. Rush proposed asylums for inebriates in 1830 and it was said that there were forty treatment centers for inebriates in the colonial United States. With the enactment of the Volstead Act, literally all of the asylums for inebriates were closed and from then until about the 1970s inebriates (alcoholics) requiring medical or psychiatric care were committed to the chronic wards of state mental hospitals.

Alcoholism by definition is a chronic, progressive disease, fatal if allowed to run unchecked. It is incurable, but its progress can be arrested. It is characterized by tolerance for high concentrations of alcohol in the brain, and by physical dependency. Early on in the individual's use of alcohol most rookie alcoholics can identify with the magic sense of omnipotence that occurs when they drink—a feeling that everything is just perfect the way it is. It is no wonder that they have a desire or compulsion to repeat those events often. However, as the toxic effect of alcohol changes the brain and the brain's thinking processes, the individual starts having social, legal, occupational, health, marital, medical, and psychiatric problems including sexual dysfunction and insomnia. At this inevitable stage of misery, the drinking may be perpetuated by a desire for oblivion or an escape from reality. At this point the alcoholic or addict has so many social, physical, and mental problems that he seems to have a desire or a need to be invisible and in many cases behaves as if he were—only to find out, on many occasions the next day, that his drunken behavior has added another proverbial nail to his coffin.

The diagnosis of alcoholism has very little to do with the quantities of alcohol consumed or the frequency of that consumption. Alcoholics may drink continuously, never letting the sun go down or the moon rise and set without ingesting some quantity of alcohol; they may confine their drinking to set times and places and with or without drinking companions. They may indulge in spaced binges, with days and weeks and months of abstinence intervening. The results are the same. The physical damage to some body organs may have a relationship to quantity of alcohol consumed but that does not have as much to do with the modern concept of alcoholism. The *sine qua non* of alcoholism is *the loss of control of the individual's behavior when under the influence of alcohol or chemicals* and *the compulsion to use again in spite of adverse consequences.*

Related to this loss of control is the unanswerable question of when the addicted person is going to start drinking, or even more important, when is he going to stop drinking or using drugs once he has taken the first drink or mind-altering chemical.

Finally, we should talk about the important symptom of *denial.* Denial is a progressive symptom that can start with simple lying, then progress to rationalization to explain away painful reality and finally result in its use as an immature defense mechanism (immature coping skill) to ward off external or internal anxiety. With continued drinking the denial can become even more pathological and irreversible as a result of toxic brain damage. The patient can present with the confabulation of dementia (Korsakoff's psychosis) and that is the most severe form of denial and usually referred to as *pathological denial.*

It is because of the signs and symptoms listed above for alcoholism and chemical dependency that there is very little compassion, sympathy, or even empathy extended by most members of society as well as many health professionals, including physicians, nurses, psychologists, and psychiatrists.

In fact, the general attitude of most people who do not suffer from alcoholism, both social drinkers and teetotalers, is that *it is the addict's fault—all they would have to do is drink or drug less.* This traditional, poor advice is typical from family members and health professionals alike, and fits in well with the attitude of the alcoholic or drug addict that subjectively feels and says, "I can stop drinking and drugging any time I want to—I just don't want to yet." This is known as "the conspiracy of silence," a result of the denial that occurs in the family, friends, employers, and health professionals and is an indication of the high but false value that society as a whole places on the recreational drug, alcohol.

The great success of the fellowship known as Alcoholics Anonymous has brought alcoholics to recovery in much greater numbers and with a much greater chance of sustained success than any means known. Their success is due partially (and only partially, since several key features account for its success) in its seizing upon the *disease concept of alcoholism,* and viewing the condition as a sickness. There are two points that should be noted in our present discussion. As we have seen, the concept itself was not new (recall the work of Dr. Benjamin Rush) or original with AA.

First, AA was there when prohibition came to an end and our society apparently had heard enough about the sin of drinking. The increase in the availability and incidence of alcoholism made AA very timely. The second point is that AA embraced the disease concept and the movement became a great success before there was any firmly established proof that alcoholism is indeed a disease. That is to say that AA did not go forward on the basis of scientific research and finding of fact, but on the basis of intuition and personal experience. Alcoholism was deemed an allergy of the body causing an obsession of the mind. Once again, as William James said, "That which works is true!"

In 1957, the American Medical Association finally recognized that alcoholism was a true disease but it was not until the early 1970s that the major health care insurers, such as Blue Cross-Blue Shield of Michigan started paying for detoxification and rehabilitation. However, when the cost skyrocketed and managed care came into vogue, services for alcoholism and chemical addiction were the first to be cut. This is true even though treatment statistics proved that treatment was cost effective—especially for the patient's employers regarding absenteeism and medical expenses for illnesses secondary to alcoholism or chemical dependency.

The way in which the founders of AA, Bill Wilson and Dr. Bob Smith, and the early members came to adopt the disease concept is instructive. In their efforts at recovery, these men were especially indebted for the help and advice of several medical persons. Among them was Dr. William Silkworth, who had trained as a neuropsychiatrist and was physician-in-charge and subsequently medical superintendent of the Charles B. Towns Hospital, which specialized in the treatment of habitual inebriates. Dr. Silkworth was the professional who encouraged Bill Wilson to think of alcoholism as "an allergy of the body and an obsession of the mind." Of Dr. Silkworth, William White writes in *Slaying the Dragon: The History of Addiction and Recovery*:

> Silkworth's suggestion of a constitutional vulnerability which promoted alcoholics to drink—out of necessity rather than choice—became the cornerstone of the modern disease concept of alcoholism. It was Silkworth's belief that this vulnerability was a biologically determined hypersensitivity to alcohol, and that this characteristic was never lost, no matter how long the alcoholic refrained from drinking. To Silkworth, the primary evidence of an allergic response to drinking was an insatiable craving for it that was excited by even the smallest exposure to the substance. He believed that there was only one way for those allergic individuals to avoid an "attack" of alcoholism: complete and enduring abstinence.

Another medical contributor to the evolving notion of the alcoholic as a person with a sickness was Dr. Harry Thiebout, a psychiatrist who, during the 1940s, treated Bill Wilson for recurrent bouts of depression. Dr. Thiebout was the first psychiatrist to offer a modern psychiatric interpretation of addiction that took into account what he regarded as the profound psychological insights contained within the program and objective fact of AA's astounding success in an area where other procedures were marked by much more modest, if any, victories. He characteristically spoke of alcoholism as "a symptom that had assumed disease proportions" and of the disease concept as a "metaphor." Where others might see that term as merely poetic language, Thiebout rightly viewed the metaphor as a profound insight—one that enabled thinking and practice to move along the right lines to treatment that actually worked, and helped alcoholics to recover in advance of research findings that yielded scientific knowledge. In this, Thiebout was at one with the work of the

National Committee for Education on Alcoholism (later known as the National Council on Alcoholism, and later still the National Council on Alcoholism and Chemical Dependence). This body, the brainchild of Dr. Thiebout's patient, Marty Mann, undertook to persuade public opinion that alcoholism is a disease and the alcoholic is a sick person. She believed that the alcoholic could be helped and was worth helping, and that the disease of alcoholism was a matter of public health and therefore a public responsibility. Thiebout's plan worked brilliantly and contributed, along with other favorable social conditions at the time, to the general acceptability of these ideas and widespread social and political commitment to them. This commitment to the alcoholic and the chemically dependent person has waned somewhat in recent years relative to the federal and state government's financial priorities, but it is not dead or even gasping for air, and in time it will be revived.

There is a principle one learns early (or ought to) in clinical medicine and it is, simply stated, that any laboratory test or research conclusion is of value in direct proportion to how much or how little it confirms a clinician's honest medical impression. If the laboratory test or research conclusion doesn't confirm the medical impression, then somebody has made a mistake, and the first suspect is the clinical or research laboratory. This basic philosophy has served me well and has held up throughout my medical and psychiatric career, as a general practitioner for twenty years and then for a further twenty plus years as a psychiatrist specializing in psychiatry, chemical addictions, and traumatic brain injuries. I am not saying that physicians cannot be wrong, but when a presumptive diagnosis is made after thoroughly checking the patient's past history, clinical symptoms, and physical examination, the inconclusive laboratory test result should at least be repeated before the diagnosis is changed. I have found that laboratory tests and prospective and longitudinal studies are of great value if they confirm what has long been suspected over many years. Fortunately, most honest research and most competent laboratory testing do concur with the clinical opinion—most of the time!

Knowledge about the treatment of alcoholism and chemical dependency and other psychiatric diagnoses that mimic or masquerade as alcoholism (Dual Diagnoses) are numerous. *Conflicting data between laboratory findings and physical findings may be your first clue of a Dual Diagnosis.*

One such case that drove this point home for me was a thirty-six-year-old male with a wife and four young children who had uncontrollable headaches.

I referred him to the University of Michigan Hospital and to a world-renowned neurosurgeon there—the very best. The patient had all kinds of x-rays, laboratory tests, and neurological examinations, and all were negative except an elevated spinal fluid protein. It should be noted that elevated spinal fluid proteins are common in-patients with brain tumors. The patient and his family begged the neurosurgeon to do what had to be an exploratory craniotomy to localize the suspected tumor. Finally, the neurosurgeon relented and surgery was done. No tumor was found and the patient died of complications from the surgery. It is especially noteworthy that the patient's mother was a hypochondriac and when she was in her fifties had both breasts amputated to prevent her from developing cancer of the breast.

The program of Alcoholics Anonymous has been in existence for sixty-seven years and has millions of members worldwide; it is emphatic in saying that alcoholism is a disease and that total abstinence from alcohol and similar sedative medication is necessary to produce a remission. Many professionals and lay people alike have tried to disprove these two propositions with no success whatever. For someone with alcoholism, there is no way one can go back to the compulsive behavior and get different results; there is no way an abstinent alcoholic or addict can return to drinking or drugging again without having a relapse to their addiction. It's that simple, it will not happen.

As humans, we have a tendency to forget what we have learned and then have to proceed to learn it all over again every so often—every generation for instance, seeming to believe that this time it will be different. About a half-century ago the Rand Corporation reported research on helping a small group of men, identified as alcoholics, return to social or controlled drinking. What at first was reported as success in due time had to be re-evaluated because the project failed—as it had to. All of those men who had not become totally abstinent through AA, had been jailed or had died. About twenty years later another such project, "Individualized Behavior Therapy for Alcoholics," by M. and L. Sobel (1970) reported success in the same endeavor; this too was shown to have failed with the same identical results. Now, once again, a little before the beginning of the twenty-first century and coinciding with the writing of this book, a large prestigious university in the Midwestern United States, has changed its philosophy about its addiction treatment program to aim at the goal of "responsible," controlled drinking for its patients. Hope springs eternal in the highly-motivated, denial-shrouded, and well-funded breast. As one might have anticipated, the tragedy of death awaited the victim of an auto accident where the driver of the automobile causing the accident was enrolled in this "controlled drinking" treatment philosophy.

The American Society of Addiction Medicine (ASAM) is a group of over 6,000 physicians, representing all surgical and medical specialties, engaged in careers as addictionologists. Most members of this group are themselves in recovery. They are willing to, and indeed do, "bet their lives" that addiction (alcoholism) is a disease and that total abstinence is necessary for remission. They should know. They are working in chemical dependence treatment centers observing and caring for patients, doing research, going to AA meetings for their own recovery, are abstinent from alcohol and all addictive drugs and medications, and are happier and more successful than they ever were using addictive drugs including alcohol. Don't suggest to them that anyone can return from alcoholism to social drinking. They won't be interested. Why return to what they know will be a life of misery and failure when they are living sober, happy, successful, and free lives?

Here we need to examine what I have called and firmly believe to be the most successful "treatment program" for alcoholism and other chemical addictions, the programs of Alcoholics Anonymous and its counterpart for drug addiction, Narcotics Anonymous. Given the centrality of the disease concept to AA and its success, it may come as a big surprise to some readers to learn that nowhere in the first 164 pages of the Book, *Alcoholics Anonymous*, and indeed nowhere at all in the key passages setting forth "the program of recovery," is the word *disease*, or any of its symptoms, mentioned at all.

That is because the Big Book of AA was written in 1935 when the term allergy was in vogue. If the Big Book is ever rewritten it will no doubt change its emphasis from "allergy" to "disease" as that is where AA tradition as well as therapeutic pragmatism now stands.

As yet, the philosophy of this book stands firm in recommending to its readers the well-founded conviction that AA is not only the best single response but that it is the only response in cases of alcoholism and other pure chemical addictions; that is, without complications such as antecedent, or consequent, or co-existent medical or psychiatric conditions affecting or effected by the alcoholism or addictive chemicals, or, in other words that don't have a Dual Diagnosis of masquerading illnesses. The personal experience of thousands upon thousands who have recovered in AA and who, without further or other treatment, would seem to be leading a sober, healthy, and happy life suggests that this is true in many such cases.

One of the attractions of AA for certain persons is precisely that its program of recovery was not based on research findings nor did it proceed from theory to application. Rather, Bill Wilson and Dr. Bob Smith and the other early members first got well through their activity of self-help and sharing, and then proceeded to help others. This was the basis for the well-known "Twelve Steps" set forth in the Big Book, *Alcoholics Anonymous*, and recommended as a program of recovery from their character defects (personality traits or disorders). Not a single one of the Steps say, "Well, we finally shaped up and stopped drinking!" At an early stage of reflection upon an analysis of what they had done, the pioneer group in AA articulated six principles of recovery. They said: "We admitted we were powerless over alcohol; we got honest with another person in confidence; we made amends for harm done to others; we worked with other alcoholics without demands for prestige or money; we prayed to our Higher Power to help us do these things as best we could." The Twelve Steps that evolved from this early formulation, and that are set forth in chapter five ("How It Works") of the Big Book of *Alcoholics Anonymous*, read as follows:

We:

1. Admitted we were powerless over alcohol—that our life had become unmanageable.
2. Came to believe that a Power greater than ourselves could restore us to sanity.
3. Made a decision to turn our will and our lives over to the care of God, as we understood Him.
4. Made a searching and fearless moral inventory of ourselves.
5. Admitted to God, to ourselves, and to another human being the exact nature of our wrongdoings.
6. Were entirely ready to have God remove all these defects of character.
7. Humbly asked Him to remove these shortcomings.
8. Made a list of all the persons we had harmed, and became willing to make amends to them all.
9. Made direct amends to such people wherever possible, except when to do so would injure them or others.

10. Continued to take personal inventory and when we were wrong, promptly admitted it.

11. Sought through prayer and meditation to improve our conscious contact with God *as we understood Him,* praying only for knowledge of His will for us and the power to carry that out.

12. Having had a spiritual awakening as a result of these steps, we tried to carry this message to alcoholics, and to practice these principles in all our affairs.

AA has many characteristic traditions, and clichés, about how to live a sober life. But the Twelve Steps are "suggested as a program of recovery," and set forth the essence of the program. That they are suggested rather than, say, ordered or prescribed is not only a form of wording peculiarly disarming and attractive to the alcoholic, whose middle name is "rebel," but is also in keeping with the inclusive and pragmatic attitude of AA. They are suggested because they *work.* They are the means whereby those who have recovered did so. At every AA meeting these Twelve Steps are prominently displayed visually or read out or both and newcomers and old-timers alike are reminded that these Twelve Steps are the heart and soul of the program. Meetings may follow various formats—a single speaker recounting what his or her past life was like, what happened with drinking and what it is like in recovery. Several such speakers give their personal testimony, or perhaps a small group will share among themselves about their drinking or about their success or difficulties while working one of the Steps, and so on. There are several key formats that all aim at the sharing among alcoholics of their "experience, strength, and hope." This mutual self-help and process of recovery through helping others to recover has remained the core of AA since its inception, and the members constantly remind themselves of the simple program: come to meetings, work the Steps, don't pick up that first drink, and get a sponsor.

In a number of articles now classic in the field of addiction treatment, the psychiatrist Dr. Harry Thiebout attempted to analyze and account for the spectacular success of AA by interpreting in psychiatric terms, still valid today, how and why Alcoholics Anonymous works. Contrasting its success with the historically dismal record of psychiatry, Thiebout asserted that psychiatry's previous failures were the result of faulty theoretical assumptions about alcoholism, particularly those assumptions that led the doctor and patient away from the problem presenting in the here and now (the alcoholic's drinking, ill health, and aberrant behavior). The problem presenting, Thiebout insisted, was the primary issue, and AA was correct in addressing it. Thiebout agreed with his professional colleagues in ascribing to the alcoholic a characteristic kind of personality: egocentric, rebellious against authority and restrictions, pleasure-seeking, insistent on special considerations and entitlement, adept in logic-chopping, markedly irresponsible and along with Freud, latent or overt homosexuality or paranoia about it. Where Thiebout disagreed with his peers was in his seeing the emergence of this type of personality as the consequence rather than the cause of addiction to alcohol. This crucial point, that there is indeed an "alcoholic personality," one shared by alcoholics generally, is attested to daily in thousands upon thousands of stories told about themselves by alcoholics at AA meetings. Where the other point is also vividly evident, that though alcoholics become that way, they start from a myriad of different kinds of personalities ranging from normal to any of the known personality traits to any of the personality disorders. We return below to this discussion about the alcoholic or addictive personality, and for the moment note again that Thiebout's conclusion that such a personality is a consequence rather than a cause of alcoholism is amply supported in the AA experience. In *Slaying the Dragon: The History of Addiction and Recovery*, William L. White (p. 142) summarizes Thiebout's view of alcoholic characteristics:

...not as enduring traits of personality that had caused alcoholism, but as shared adaptations to the progression of alcoholism. In Thiebout's view treatment of alcoholics involved softening the infantile, egocentric shell of the alcoholic so that they could become amendable to influences outside themselves. As he noted, "The fundamental problem of any therapy of alcoholism, whatever its guise, is to help the individual mature." Thiebout believed that AA provided four elements in the transformation of alcoholics that traditional psychotherapy had failed to provide: "hitting bottom, surrender, ego reduction, and maintenance of humility." He viewed the transformation of the alcoholic within AA as a "rapid psychological reorientation"—a conversion process—and believed it was the spiritual force within AA that had the power to break through the alcoholic's narcissistic egocentric core.

Many of the experts in AA refer to this as a *spiritual conversion*. Myself, as a psychiatrist who sees in a healthy personality the existence of a moral personality of moral coping skills, I prefer to view this a *personality conversion* through the use of the six to ten healthy defense mechanisms available by example in AA and also recommended and taught by any good psychiatrist in psychotherapy.

Some years before, psychiatrist Carl Young had concluded an unsuccessful attempt to cure a patient of his alcoholism by giving as his opinion that nothing but a profound and total spiritual experience (spiritual conversion) could help the patient. Dr. Thiebout asserted that AA provided just such a spiritual experience or personality conversion not for one patient but for thousands and potentially millions of suffering alcoholics. For those readers who may, like this author, find the word *spiritual* too abstract to comprehend except in religious terms and who desire a more concrete and non-religious definition of the word *spiritual*, I have a suggestion. The concept akin to "spiritual experience" (spiritual conversion) in psychiatry is to *self-develop or allow oneself to change to a mature personality (personality conversion)*. Both terms have a moral implication. A person with a mature personality is an individual that uses *mature defense mechanisms* (mature coping skills) to resolve stress and produce harmony (homeostasis) in their life. Space does not allow me to go into detail about this. However, the information about defense mechanisms can be found in the *Diagnostic and Statistical Manual (DSM-IV)* of the American Psychiatric Association. Briefly, the Mature Defense Mechanisms in the *DSM-IV* are anticipation, affiliation, altruism, humor, self-assertion, self-observation, sublimation, and suppression. Two other healthy defense mechanisms in the psychiatric literature are asceticism (discipline) and positive identification (moral hero ego ideal). All of these mature defense mechanisms (mature coping skills) are available by example and teaching through the Twelve Steps to the attendees at Alcoholics Anonymous meetings.

I have taken the pains to suggest that in my opinion the best single way to address alcoholism (addiction) itself *without its medical and psychiatric complications* be in AA. That is because its program contains elements that speak to the physical, mental or behavioral, spiritual or personality, and social dimensions. Since the only requirement for membership in AA is the desire to stop drinking, and since AA meetings have no dues or fees, it is the most comprehensive, readily available, and certainly the least expensive resource the alcoholic could possibly have.

Two anecdotes might be instructive. One of the contributors to this book some years before he found AA, on two occasions sought and found psychiatric assistance. On the first occasion he was, with the best intention in the world, admitted to a very pleasant and agreeable private psychiatric hospital, with a diagnosis of acute anxiety and clinical depression. In retrospect, this admission under a wrong diagnosis was either because this patient concealed the fact that he constantly drank a lot or because his physician had not noticed that such was the case. In a half-dozen weeks of treatment in the hospital, he received (for the first time in years) nourishing and regular meals, without cocktails preceding, or wine accompanying, or brandy after, or whiskey or beer between, as well as long and welcome daily naps and nightly sleeping, again for the first time in years. He also received pleasant occupational and recreational therapies, wherein he learned to weave on a small loom and to throw (usually vainly) at basketball hoops, and many agreeable hours of sociable chatting often with other male inmates, occasionally dancing with female ones. Then there were the sedating effects of large quantities of what at the time were called major and minor tranquilizers. At the end of his stay (that is when the time came that insurance coverage expired), he felt wonderful and ready to return home, definitely cured of his anxiety and depression. In the days following he faithfully took his prescribed medication, reduced dosages of his tranquilizers, and returned to his routine work and home life. He had even, somehow, got the notion that he ought to cut down on his drinking, and did so with only an occasional beer or martini.

Within a few weeks he had lost his glow of well-nourished, well-rested, relaxed good physical health and began to feel sluggish, moody, and irritable. Not feeling any better as the days passed, he decided his medication wasn't helping and abruptly discontinued it, not realizing, of course, that he was now addicted to the so-called minor tranquilizers (benzodiazapines). After ten nights without sleep and ten dreadful days he was at his wits' end and began having suicidal ideation. What could he do? He had already had a lengthy and expensive hospital stay with the best medical and psychiatric care (though he couldn't for the life of him remember a single word said to him by the resident psychiatrist, or even having seen such a person). But now he was again very anxious, very depressed (more so than before, it seemed), and not even drinking very much! On the whole, he felt he'd rather be dead. He took extended sick leave from work. On the rare day when he merely got out of bed it was a major achievement.

Somehow, and this is the second anecdote, he began making weekly visits to another psychiatrist. These visits continued for a year and a half, and of these he had a clear and vivid recollection of the weekly dialogue:

DOCTOR: You have to stop drinking; you can't drink at all.

PATIENT: Why? Do you think I'm an alcoholic?

DOCTOR: Yes, I do.

PATIENT: Perhaps you're right. But the question is, why? What makes me an alcoholic?

DOCTOR: I don't know why you're an alcoholic. You have to stop drinking.

PATIENT: Yes, but I think we ought to find out *why* I drink, don't you?

DOCTOR: Oh, I know why you drink—you're an alcoholic. You have to stop drinking.

PATIENT: Yes, but how will that help? I mean, if we don't find out why I'm an alcoholic and why I drink that way, how can I get better? Isn't that what you're supposed to do, help me find the *reasons* why I'm an alcoholic, why I can't drink like everybody else?

DOCTOR: How will the reason help? You have to stop drinking.

PATIENT: Yes, but if we know the reasons why I can't drink, then I'll understand and get well, and be able to drink like everybody else.

DOCTOR: You have to stop drinking.

PATIENT: Yes, but...

DOCTOR: By the way, have you tried AA, as I've suggested before?

PATIENT: No, but...

DOCTOR: Well, you have to stop drinking. See you next week, same time.

Needless to say, after a year and a half of this unvarying, frustrating scenario the doctor absolutely refusing to tell his patient why he couldn't drink and why he was an alcoholic, the patient concluded that he ought to stop seeing this unimaginative, unyielding, and unhelpful psychiatrist. Eventually he did stop seeing him, and sometime later even found a way to stop drinking. Today, this individual remains deeply grateful to this skillful and enlightened psychiatrist, and for his patient wisdom and refusal to put anything else above or before his absolutely accurate and dedicated diagnosis and care of his patient.

There are certain questions about the nature of the disease of alcoholism and certain considerations about the proper place, treatment, theory, and research of those questions. If one is reluctant to accept the American Medical Association's position that alcoholism is indeed a disease, it might be helpful to point out that the great weight of contemporary experience testifies that the best results are obtained if it is at least viewed as if it were a disease. Like other legitimate diagnoses, alcoholism has observable markers, a predictable epidemiological course including classical progression, certain prognosis, and readily available and successful treatment. Although experts from the first half of the twentieth century may still influence some professionals and their unfortunate patients to believe alcoholism is a symptom of some underlying disorder and not a primary disease, a fact that may be true for up to 25 percent of addiction cases, that does not contradict the theory that alcoholism is every much a disease with all of the above described features. To deny alcoholism as a disease would be tantamount to saying that a myocardial infarction (heart attack) is not a disease because it was preceded by a high cholesterol diet and cigarettes. As we have seen, even Dr. Harry Thiebout was close to the mark when he spoke of alcoholism as a "symptom," although one that had "assumed disease proportions."

In the earlier and middle part of the twentieth century the consensus of experts like Robert Night, E.M. Jellinek, Melvin Selzer, and many others was that alcoholism was a symptom rather than a primary disease and their opinion of alcoholics in general was not flattering and, in a few cases, was openly prejudicial. Knight held that alcoholism was always preceded by a personality disorder, as evidenced by the obvious maladjustment in the alcoholic such as neurotic character traits, emotional immaturity, infantilism, and latent or overt homosexuality (1937). He gave no thought that these symptoms could be due to what today is called a substance-induced personality change. Two decades later, Jellinek wrote: "In spite of a great deal of diversity in personality structure among alcoholics, there appears, in a large portion of them, a low tolerance to tension coupled with an inability to cope with psychological stress" (1950). Two decades later, in discussing the etiology of alcoholism in the then latest textbook of psychiatry, Selzer wrote, "Alcoholic populations display significantly more depression, dependency, paranoid thinking trends, aggressive feelings and acts, and significantly lower self-esteem, responsibility, and self-control than non-alcoholic populations." Apparently in these and like pronouncements, little thought was given to the possibility that these were symptoms secondary to alcoholism. Dr. Richard

Bates wrote with a tongue firmly in his cheek when he said, "All alcoholics smoke cigarettes, have cigarette burns on their bodies and clothing, and usually have multiple tattoos,"(1985). He might well have added that at least some of them drink enormous quantities of coffee and frequent church basements at night, while others are to be found disproportionately in the nation's jails and prisons and, until the last quarter of the twentieth century, in the back wards of chronic mental hospitals.

In his book, *The Natural History of Alcoholism Revisited* (1983, 1995), Dr. George Valliant stressed the importance of prospective design in research and writing on alcoholism because, "just as light passing through water confounds the perspective, the illness of alcoholism profoundly distorts the individual's personality, his social stability, and his own recollection of relevant childhood variables." In an earlier work (1960), Valliant reported on a landmark study by McCord and McCord. They were able to refute several hoary hypotheses regarding the etiology of alcoholism, refutations that have held up in subsequent prospective studies. The McCords found that men "with nutritional disorders, glandular disorders, strong inferiority feelings, phobias, and more feminine feelings" were *not* more likely to develop alcoholism as had previous been hypothesized. Further, and more important, they found that men who had "strong encouragement of dependency" from their mothers and who manifested "oral tendencies" such as thumb sucking, playing with their mouths, early heavy smoking, and compulsive eating, were actually *less* likely to develop alcoholism. They found that contrary to longstanding beliefs, pre-alcoholics were outwardly more self-confident, less disturbed by normal fears, more hyperactive, and more heterosexual.

In one stroke, the McCords brought into question many of the leading features of the hypothetical pre-alcoholic personality. Then in 1973, Loped Kammeier, and Hoffman (1974), compared the Minnesota Multiphasic Personality Inventory (MMPI) of thirty-eight male college classmates who had later developed alcoholism with those of 148 matched male classmates. They observed that the pre-alcoholic had been more nonconforming and gregarious, and more likely to answer "true" to items like: "In school I was sometimes sent to the principal for cutting up," and, "I like dramatics." Such observations are in keeping with those of other investigators who have noted that extroverted adolescents tend to engage in smoking, drug experimentation, and sexual behavior earlier than their introverted peers. In the same prospective study of

MMPIs, the authors noted that in college the original composite profile of their thirty-eight alcoholic men had been within normal limits on the traits noted above. However, when the men were eventually hospitalized for alcoholism, their MMPIs were significantly elevated on the depression, psychopathic deviancy, and paranoia scales—elevated to pathologic levels. Once alcoholic, the men's composite profile revealed "the neurotic pattern (anxious personality) consistent with self-centered, immature, dependent, resentful, irresponsible people who are unable to face reality." They were also far more likely to answer "false" to "I am happy almost all of the time," and "true" to "I shrink from facing a crisis," "I am high strung," and "I am certainly lacking in self confidence." What this all means, of course, is that first they develop alcoholism and *then* they conformed to the hypothetical "alcoholic personality."

Another study by Jones at the Institute of Human Behavior at Berkeley (1968-1971), investigating a very small but repeatedly interviewed sample of middle-class youths, made similar observations. Jones used the Oakland Growth Study sample to compare heavy problem drinkers with moderate and light drinkers. She compared the high school evaluations of the six men who became "problem drinkers" with those seventeen who remained moderate drinkers. In high school the six were characterized as "out of control, rebellious, pushing limits, self-indulgent, and assertive." During the same period of time these same six were characterized as "expressive, attractive, poised, and buoyant when among girls."

In passing, it is worth noting that the Jones' study, and in fact all those cited above, conform to the hypothesis that in childhood future alcohol abusers who progress to dependence on alcohol have much in common with hyperactive children (Tarter, et. al. 1977). Could they, as youths, have been insidiously and clandestinely self-medicating their hyperactivity with the depressant alcohol? This would be an instance of what I have been calling the *masquerades* in psychiatry.

George Vaillant (1980) reports an important longitudinal investigation of the mental health and alcohol use of 184 men first studied in their college years. When the men were fifty years old, a rater, blind to childhood data and to other adult ratings, classified the subjects' present alcohol use as (n=49), social (n=110), or abusive (n=36). Other raters, blind to these and other data on the subjects' lives, assessed the warmth of the men's childhoods, familial and social environments, and their personality stability in college and after college. Vignettes identifying "oral" adult behavior (pessimism, self-doubt, passivity, and dependence) were collected for each man by a rater blind to the subjects' alcohol rating and blind to his childhood and to his college rating. A bleak childhood, personality instability in college, and adult evidence of pre-morbid personality disorder were all positive and highly correlated with oral-dependency behavior ratings, but *not* with alcohol abuse. Furthermore, in the college sample reported by Vaillant in 1974, an unhappy childhood led to mental illness in adult life, with lack of friends and low self-esteem but *not* to alcoholism. Many of the twenty-six problem drinkers seem to have become depressed and unable to cope as a *consequence* of their inability to control their alcohol consumption.

In summary then, while historical data used in the first three-quarters of the twentieth century attempting to formulate the cause of alcoholism would suggest that personality and environment play a crucial role, the burden of research in the last quarter of the century tells us that, in fact, such is *not* the case. The most logical conclusion is that the best current medical and psychiatric opinion points to the answer to two of our questions: First, that alcoholism (addiction, chemical dependence) is a primary disease in the majority of cases, especially when there is not another diagnosable aberration of mental thought occurring as a result of a co-existing or pre-existing psychiatric, medical or surgical illness, e.g., increased brain sensitivity to alcohol due to traumatic brain injury. However, there are pre-existing psychiatric, medical, and surgical diseases that could cause alcoholism or addiction to develop when the patient is self-medicating their mental symptoms, medical symptoms, or surgical symptoms with alcohol or addicting drugs or medication. This duality of illnesses is what I refer to as *Dual Diagnosis*. The second answer is that the recognizable and indeed well-known theory of the "alcoholic personality" is a *product* rather than the *cause* of the majority of cases of alcoholism.

Dr. Vernon Johnson who wrote the classic book on alcoholism, *I'll Quit Tomorrow*, says that everyone who originally uses alcohol or addictive drugs does so to make themselves feel better or happier. I agree with him completely. It was a common belief that alcoholics drank because they were depressed or sad or moody and they wanted to do something to make themselves feel better. In that regard alcoholics are not unique. Most anyone who uses alcohol in his or her life does so for the exact same reason. Someone may drink a beer on a hot summer day to cool himself off, but that is exactly the same motivation. That person wants to feel better. It might make him feel better, but not because it lowers body temperature—it doesn't—it usually raises it, but the goal of feeling better is accomplished regardless. That is unless he is already an alcoholic. Once an individual becomes an alcoholic or an addict, if he persists in using, the very substance that used to make him feel better will start causing the same symptom it used to cure. However, having glimpsed something of that happiness and fulfillment in early drinking, he infers that drinking even more and longer—dedicated drinking, as it were—will yield yet more happiness and fulfillment. Even though continued drinking and drug use produces less and less happiness and the goal of spiritual fulfillment becomes more and more elusive for alcoholics or addicts, they (quite admirably like the poet Wordsworth Singer) remember the light and whence it came and continue to seek it. They persevere in regarding happiness and spiritual fulfillment as man's proper estate, and they will attain it along the only path they know, deeper into the dark wood. Here in the mid-point of their journey, they hit bottom, and here in the moment of an extreme crisis they will find both danger and opportunity. Some will plunge further and further on to despair, madness, or death. Others, the fortunate ones, will by some unaccountable good, be called to turn again and go out of the dark wood, to experience a spiritual or personality conversion and find in sobriety the serenity, the happiness, and the spiritual or personality fulfillment they were always seeking, even when in their ignorance they took the wrong path.

This paradoxical reaction leaves them with only two choices: either stop drinking and stop any other addicting drugs, or use more and more of it until they pass into a state of complete oblivion. They don't experience any emotion in the oblivion stage, so that is not satisfactory either, except to escape social and legal problems that the alcohol or drug use caused in the first place. This is the reason why alcoholics or addicts who stop using while in the fellowship of AA refer to their recovery as now feeling "weller" than well.

From a strictly clinical point of view, as a psychiatrist who has treated upwards of 20,000 alcoholics and addicts in private practice and in residential treatment settings, I have found that alcoholics and addicts subjectively feel that they do not drink and use drugs to make themselves happy, but rather to make themselves feel far less miserable. Most of them cannot really remember the happy days but wish that the alcohol would make them "invisible" or at least put them into a state of oblivion, which to them, means absence from misery, or maybe even a way for them to bide their time until they find the courage to commit suicide. They do not believe there is anybody who cares or that there is anything that can be done. In reality, they are wrong on both counts.

Anyone can become an alcoholic if there are sufficient risk factors present in the individual—alcoholism is truly an "equal opportunity" disease. Alcoholics come in all shapes and sizes and genders and races and nationalities and eye color and haircolor and quirks and quiddities. However, once one becomes an alcoholic, there are an enormous amount of similarities, and occasions for mutual identification. Before they became alcoholic it's the diversity of experience, not the similarity, that is remarkable. But *personality traits* and *personality disorders* are *not* among the risk factors. Of course, people with personality disorders are not immune to becoming alcoholics, and many of them do. The same can be said for people who have mental illnesses and many of them become alcoholics too, right along with a lot of people who do not have a mental illness. Clearly, no matter what the pre-morbid state was, and no matter what pathology the alcohol or drugs caused in the brain, proper treatment can be had by most. Proper treatment includes Alcoholics Anonymous meetings with a sponsor, and in severe cases a physician, psychiatrist, or therapist. Why? Because AA contains a two-part program. The first part is directed toward developing a consciousness that consists of attending AA meetings and getting support from a sponsor so that one can begin to break out of the pattern of self-centeredness and begin to socialize again, to receive informal social skills training, obtain some practical advice about employment, family, the law, and gain some raw knowledge about one's addictions or any of the other problems that stunted or regressed personal growth and social development.

Secondly, the program enlightens one on an unconscious level and supplants the *immature defense mechanisms,* or unsuccessful coping skills, characteristic of the practicing alcoholic that will give one serenity, hope, trust, intimacy, spirituality, honesty, and restore a sense of humor. This *unconscious* aspect of the program will free the recovering alcoholic from any personality disorder one may have developed from drinking or drugging (*DSM-IV*, Axis II), or any secondary organic personality (substance-induced) change caused by the drinking or other addictions or even medical or surgical complications from addictions (*DSM-IV*, Axis I).

What this means is that someone who enters recovery with no pre-existing personality disorder or mental illness will receive all the treatment he needs from attending Alcoholics Anonymous meetings and having an AA sponsor. Both of these are readily available at all hours, and at no expense. People who did have a pre-morbid personality disorder can get all the treatment they need from Alcoholics Anonymous meetings and their sponsor if they can make the unconscious part of the program work for their personality disorder. It may take a lot of meetings and total surrender, along with a spiritual or personality conversion, and a growing knowledge and acceptance of the high adaptive level of the mature defense mechanisms that all exist at AA meetings and from an AA sponsor (anticipation, affiliation, altruism, humor, self-assertion, self-observation, sublimation, suppression, discipline, and positive identification).

If AA proves unsuccessful for any given patient, then it is necessary to add a physician, psychiatrist, or therapist who understands the mature defense mechanisms (mature coping skills). Many people with grave emotional and mental problems do recover in AA if they develop the capacity to be honest with themselves (self-observation) and seek professional help from a mental health professional in addition to AA.

Physicians, psychiatrists, and other health professionals may be exclaiming, "What? Is there nothing for us to do? It seems you've left very little, except perhaps to point the way to AA. But that's hardly all we've been training for!" My response is: Don't worry—there is plenty to be done with your expertise and you have a very important role to play in response to alcoholism and other chemical dependencies. For the physician there is the myriad of health needs to correct the multiple side effects that alcohol and drugs cause the body. For the psychiatrist there are an equal number of mental aberrations that alcohol and drugs cause the mind. For social workers and certified alcohol counselors there are the multitude of adjustment disorders and other stress related disabilities resulting from the social breakdowns as a result of addiction.

For example, marital problems, legal problems, and occupational problems may all require crisis intervention in order for the patient to cope with the resulting mental stress. The physician or psychiatrist may diagnose emotional problems that require psychotherapy in addition to any non-addicting medications that may be prescribed. In particular, there is still a tremendous void that needs to be filled to educate the patient who is deficient in social skills and has residual personality disorders. These patients need to be taught how to utilize their mature defense mechanisms. Although the AA program with its Twelve Steps teaches all of the mature defense mechanisms (mature coping skills), professional help is frequently necessary to help the addicts sift out and begin to utilize these skills.

Patients with a personality disorder of any type can and do become alcoholic or have other addictions. Conversely, people with no personality disorders, "normal" people, can and do become alcoholics, and when they do they may well develop a secondary substance-induced personality change that manifests itself, or mimics or masquerades as a personality disorder such as: *paranoid personality disorder or trait, antisocial personality disorder or trait, obsessive-compulsive personality or trait, histrionic personality disorder or trait, or dependent personality disorder or trait.* However, if the symptoms of a personality disorder did not develop until adulthood (i.e., "did not have onset in adolescent or early adulthood"), then it is not considered an Axis II diagnosis and should be considered an Axis I diagnosis like personality changes due to a medical condition or substance-induced changes.

Separating the primary and secondary alcoholism from primary and secondary personality disorders is not easy, but it is important and it may take some time because of the masquerading of symptoms of both categories of the Dual Diagnosis. It is best to start treatment for the chemical dependency problem beginning with detoxification until it is clear whether or not there is a Dual Diagnosis present. Then treatment can become more specific. At this point, the health care professional will use his healing skill, knowledge, and his experiences to treat the patient.

I have already stated that I do not believe that there is such a thing as an addictive personality or alcoholic personality if by that term it is understood that a pre-morbid personality must have pre-existed a person's alcoholism or addiction, and predisposed him to become an alcoholic or drug addict. However, when we look at the personality changes that invariably result from alcoholism or other chemical addictions that cause brain deterioration, then indeed we have a secondary alcoholic personality, to be classified under *DSM-IV* Axis I as Personality Changes Due to a General Medical Condition or Substance-Induced Disorder. The patient with this condition may recover, stay the same, or get worse, but there is no chance whatsoever of improvement in this condition unless and until the patient stops drinking or using other addictive drugs. If the patient had a normal pre-morbid personality, free of any functional or organic brain disease, before the brain deterioration from alcohol or other drugs, he may very well return to a normal state after cessation of drinking or drug taking. However, the patient may have regressed so much during the drinking or drug-taking years and may have developed some immature or even pathological defense mechanisms called "character defects" or "short-comings," in the jargon of AA, and "inadequate coping skills" in the idiom of the general population. These new defects of character may be old immature defense mechanisms from childhood or youth that are now resurfacing after a period of repression, suppression, or sublimation. They may possibly require some professional psychotherapy in addition to the essential elements of recovery (meetings, sponsor, and total abstinence). The same can be said for the difficulties due to a loss of social skills (frequently lost in bars, as well as in the seclusion of home—wherever the dedicated drinking or drugging was done). Finally, the patient may have *anticipatory anxiety* (also called *sentinel anxiety* by Freud) acquired through long years of "bad luck" while drinking, or *free-floating anxiety* secondary to a primary genetic illness that the patient tried to self-medicate for years with alcohol, with predictably decreasing success as he became more and more addicted and experienced the sedative effect less and less. The anxiety becomes worse when the patient undergoes a physiological withdrawal from alcohol or other addicting drugs. The withdrawal syndrome exacerbates the *anticipatory* or *free-floating* anxieties. Skill in diagnosis and careful treatment is certainly required with such cases of Dual Diagnosis.

A second example of a patient with alcoholism who has a distinct need for professional care is the patient with a mental illness, as always is in the case of a Dual Diagnosis. In addition to the addiction disorder he will also be experiencing symptoms related to thought, mood, anxiety, or behavior. These patients probably already have their own psychiatrist unless their mental illness went undiagnosed because it masqueraded as a part of their alcoholism. If that individual doesn't already have a psychiatrist he should have, and treatment should continue. If the patient's mental illness includes a thought disorder (psychosis), he will need treatment for the psychotic illness and simultaneous treatment for his chemical dependency problem in case the substance addiction is the cause of the psychosis, which is a very strong possibility. If the patient exhibits psychotic symptoms it will be too early to attempt to alleviate them through psychotherapy or by teaching him mature defense mechanisms, or even healthy coping skills or social skills except by the therapist establishing a therapeutic alliance. This is because the patient is utilizing mostly the pathological or psychotic defense mechanisms and the psychotic process will be impairing his contact with reality, and he will have to be treated first either through detoxification or by prescribing antipsychotic medications or both started simultaneously.

Medication is the primary treatment for a Dual-Diagnosis patient who has either a psychotic or a mood disorder and may even be needed to treat a severe personality disorder that is interfering with an individual's ability to work, love, and play (disabled).

It is not clear why an individual with a mental illness is attracted to alcohol or other addictive drugs. Bemmy Mayfield has observed that many addicted people with mental illness are attracted to drugs that cause the same subjective symptoms as their mental illness does. For example a schizophrenic may be attracted to marijuana or LSD, while a manic patient may prefer amphetamines or cocaine, and a depressed person may like alcohol or tranquilizers or sedatives. If this is true for some patients, I have deduced that it may be because the use of a drug that gives them the same symptoms as their mental illness produces a feeling of control over their mental illness. (They are causing their own hallucinations with a drug instead of some outside force causing the hallucinations.) Also, it may be true that patients with a mental illness find temporary relief from hallucinations, mania, depression, thought disorders, and anxiety disorders when they first start using addictive drugs or alcohol. However, it is only a short period of time before these "medications" make the psychiatric symptoms worse, and they have two betrothed but separate diseases to cope with.

Personality disorders and mental illness, when coupled with alcohol, produce conditions calling for skilled professional care, although the resultant conditions and type of care needed is probably very different. Remember the psychiatric resident's joke: The personality disorder patient adds two and two, gets four, and just can't stand it. The psychotic patient adds two and two, gets five, and goes happily about his business.

CHAPTER TWO

Red Lights in the Rear-View Mirror

"**O**h, no!" The ominous utterance escaped the lips of the driver. He promptly obeyed the flashing red lights and siren and pulled his car off the main street in the center of Ann Arbor, Michigan. Within seconds he had lowered his window and delivered his license to the polite, but stern policeman.

"Are you Richard A. Morin?"

"I am, Officer."

"Please step out of your car, sir."

Shakily, the driver did as he was told.

"Are you ill, sir?"

"Yes and no, Officer. I just had open-heart surgery six months ago, but I am feeling better than I was before surgery."

"Are you inebriated, sir? I ask because I followed you for a mile from the bar you left at approximately 11:20 PM. Your driving has been hazardous—you are way over the speed limit and in and out of your lane."

The driver answered with slurred speech, "I don't think so, Officer. I have never had a drunk driving violation before or any other type of s-s-s-serious driving violation in my life, and I'm forty-four years old." As the driver was answering the question he fell drunkenly against the officer.

"May I have your keys, sir."

"The keys are in the car, Officer," slurred the drunken driver.

"Sir, you are under arrest. Please lock your car and I will have it impounded."

The driver, suddenly sobered, pleaded for leniency. "I'm a medical doctor, Officer. If you will just take me home, I will be most grateful. I will explain everything to you."

"I can't do that. I am putting you under arrest and taking you to jail. *Now.*"

"Please, Officer. I am not well. Just take me home—it's less than a mile from here. My wife expects me. I have six children. I will be ever so grateful."

"Sir, you are under arrest and you are going to jail. *Period.*"

• • • • •

Dr. Richard A. Morin speaks today of this incident as the most devastating in his life. He lived it on October 9, 1972, and was feeling more shame, desperation, and despair than he ever thought possible. He had hit absolute bottom. He could no longer live with himself. He wanted to die. He was a medical doctor, sworn to cure, relieve, and comfort others, and yet he willfully put others in harm's way by driving while inebriated. His self-disgust had become unbearable.

Dr. Morin totally failed the sobriety test with a reading of 1.9. (The legal threshold at the time was 1.0. It is now only .8.) The test had been administered immediately at the police station. It reflected his consumption of six dry martinis during his one-and-a-half hours at the bar near his medical office, which he had left at 9 PM after a long, hard day at the clinic seeing patients. He was still recovering from the physically and psychologically traumatic experience of his recent open-heart surgery for a dissecting aortic aneurysm.

It had been a long night in the cell for Dr. Morin. He awakened after four hours of troubled sleep; he sat on the edge of his bunk, struggling to recall his late-night drama.

The previous day had been a long one. He was exhausted and depressed about his post-surgical prognosis. As a physician he was aware that this diagnosis was usually made on the autopsy table—he was considered lucky, but nobody was able to estimate how long he might live. He had just read an article in the *Journal of the American Medical Association* that predicted a five-year survival for those who survived the surgery. There were then only thirteen such survivors in the country at that time, but he was the youngest one of the group.

He knew—he just knew—he could not make it home without stopping at his favorite bar near the parking garage. Joe, the bartender, always served him as many dry martinis as he wanted. This time he knew that he was in no condition to drive the mile to his home—but he decided to risk it anyway. After six drinks he felt invulnerable. He was reaching oblivion, a state of mind where he no longer worried about the reality of his serious health problems: *invulnerable* and *oblivious*. After his series of Martinis, he was ready to take on the world and not care about anything. Now, dizzy and nauseous, he just wanted to sleep it off. He would sleep if off that night and for several nights— behind bars.

Mrs. Morin would be relieved—indeed overjoyed—to see him after her sleepless night. She always fell for his promise to "give up the booze for good." She was his sweetheart. She had said yes to his marriage proposal when his becoming a medical doctor was still fourteen years in the future, and she bore him six children as they moved from the poverty line to a lucrative family practice. She never stopped loving him and believing in him. She was aware that he had been experiencing some memory problems after his prolonged period on the heart-lung machine during his heart surgery. The thoracic surgeons and his psychiatrist had recommended not drinking alcohol because it could compound the memory problems caused by the cardiac surgery.

Anne had spent a frantic night searching for her husband on her home phone and in her car. Finally reached by the police she, weary and forgiving, would meet him in court in the morning.

He sat on his bunk, hung over from yet one more drinking binge, and in a state of shame and remorse. He was dreading the future. How was he to go on? The promises he had made to himself to stop drinking were worthless. He was a walking zombie, unable and unwilling, for the last five years, to resist the siren-call of alcohol. Why was he that way? He had gone through under-graduate college and medical schools at the University of Michigan sober except for a few lapses between semesters. Why couldn't he stop now once he took his first drink? Others could—why couldn't he? Why couldn't he just be a social drinker? Could it be because he was—unthinkably—an alcoholic? No, he could stop after one or two drinks if he wanted to. He was free to stop—he just didn't want to do so now that he had funds with which to indulge himself. Hadn't he earned the right to relax and enjoy life as a successful physician? Alcoholics, of course, could not stop—but *he* could. He was indulging in rationalization and denial. His medical practice was not as lucrative as it once was, but he believed that this was because he had moved his practice three times, once in Michigan, then to California, and then back to Michigan. He honestly believed that these moves were because of his depression and his heart surgery; the last move from California and back to Michigan was because he felt he was going to die from the heart surgery. Never mind that his thoracic surgeon and his psychiatrist had ordered him not to drink because of his memory problems from the prolonged time on the heart-lung machine

Dr. Morin had a happy childhood raised by good, religious parents that held and taught a strong work ethic. They had provided a stable home, and his father was a successful contractor who owned a hardware store. His mother never had to work outside the home after she married his father except for a year or two during the Great Depression of 1929 when he was a toddler. He had everything he asked for, but still never felt content. There was this "black hole," as his own mother still alive at seventy-five had called it much later, referring to herself, her two siblings, and two uncles who had committed suicide as middle-aged adults (dynamite, carbolic acid, and two with carbon monoxide). Dr. Morin had known that hole from early adolescence, that dreadful pit of darkness and despair seemingly precipitated by a sense of inadequacy, however ill-defined it was. He had tried to master it by staying busy and became an overachiever.

When he was fourteen or fifteen years old he was nearly expelled from his Catholic high school for hypnotizing his classmates for fun and entertainment until a hypnotist-magician priest came to his rescue. The priest informed the school pastor that it was not immoral and he, a priest, did hypnotizing and magic, likewise for fun and entertainment.

He excelled in grade school and high school, and became a semiprofessional magician with many public performances to his credit, including the county fair. Morin worked as a clerk in his father's hardware store, and in the evenings, sold popcorn in front of his father's store making and saving enough money to purchase a small restaurant and a candy and ice cream shop on Main

Street in Alpena, Michigan when he was sixteen years old.

During his junior year at St. Anne High School he lost his lease on the small restaurant and started the Penguin Steak and Chop House in Alpena. It had a seating capacity of 100 and he had thirteen employees. Anne, his wife to be, was one of his employees. It was love at first sight—he had found the girl of his dreams and married her before he was twenty, and she even younger. They married after a year of courting and quickly had two children.

A third child was on the way when the restaurant business and the country went into a recession (1950). Restaurateur Morin began to feel the onset of a mood disorder, seemingly because of the many problems he was having with his employees and a recent slump in business. He had a long, heart-felt talk over a cup of coffee in his restaurant with a local physician, Dr. Edward Hier, and a local Ford Agency dealer, Frank Doane. Morin was trying to decide where he could best find happiness in his future. The three-way *tete-a-tete* revolved around the discussion that Dr. Hier was the luckiest because he had only one employee, his nurse, and was an essentially self-contained business, while Doane had 100 employees and he felt he was dependent on all 100 employees. Never mind that Dr. Hier's income stopped when he went on vacation and Doane's employees continued the income without him. The young Morin, sitting and drinking coffee with both successful men, quickly concluded that Dr. Hier had the best route to happiness.

The next day the counselor from the public high school came in for lunch and Morin asked him how he could go to medical school. The high school counselor brought him an application for pre-medical school and told him to fill it out and mail it to the University of Michigan in Ann Arbor. He closed his restaurant, sold the equipment, and he and his family left for Ann Arbor, Michigan. Morin started pre-medical school in September 1950 with a wife and two and one-half children and *no* money. Ahead lay pre-medical studies, medical school, internship, residency, and medical practice. Nothing could stop him! He was able to get a job as a cook in the Granada Restaurant full-time.

After the third baby was born, Anne also worked in a restaurant, depending on babysitters to help with the couple's three children. They had made their plans, and a career as a physician awaited Richard. They were ignoring the fact that this would take twelve years and they had no cash and no scholarships. This was just after the end of WWII and the GI-bill had not yet become effective, and there were no GIs or other married students on campus, and married housing was unavailable. Rent controls were in place and it was nearly impossible to rent with three children. They did not have the money with which to buy a home. Student loans were unheard of during their entire educational career. Living below the poverty level was something they would need to become accustomed to.

Generally speaking, both Richard and Anne describe the eight years of pre-medical and medical school plus a year of rotating internship as happy years. Every year brought an improvement and there was always the hope for a better future, especially with the progress in Richard's medical education. Eventually, they were both able to get full-time jobs at the University of Michigan with good benefits. The three oldest children were in St. Thomas Grade School, and twin girls, Patricia and Pamela, were a ton of fun, having arrived New Year's Eve 1957, just before Richard's graduation from medical school. In retrospect, it seems that hope springs eternal with young, healthy children around the house. The couple was excited about Dr. Morin beginning his general practice with his medical school classmate and soon-to-be partner, Walter Bjarnesen, M.D.

But, he had blown it all! His stupidity and recklessness overwhelmed him. He looked about him in the darkened cell for a way out. *Suicide! He could hang his belt over an overhead pipe. It would be over quickly! A moment's pain and he would be out of his misery forever! He would spare his wife and children all the heartache and the pain he was causing them! Yes!*

He lay back on his bunk, pondering his escape. To be or not to be? That was his question, not just that of the fictional Hamlet.

No. He knew he couldn't do it.

Was it cowardice or something else?

Hope. Yes. It was hope.

In all the heartache and pain, he could still hope.

"Rise and shine, Doctor!" said the deputy who came to get him the next morning, adding a mock salutation, "The judge awaits you, and he is one mean mother on drunk drivers!"

He was fed a cold, greasy, unpalatable breakfast, laced with cruel teasing. He bore it because he deserved it. Then he was allowed a trip to the filthy latrine and was rudely shoved into a patrol car for the short trip to the courthouse.

The sun was shining and his darling wife was waiting for him. Her embrace was ambrosia! After an hour's wait in the courtroom, he was standing before the judge with the arresting officer beside him.

"Dr. Morin, you have been charged with driving a car while intoxicated. How do you plead?"

"Guilty, Your Honor."

"This is your first arrest for driving while intoxicated, a very serious crime. As a licensed medical doctor, sir, you should know better. Do you agree?"

"I do, Your Honor. I am addicted to alcohol such that I cannot predict its effect on me after a single drink. This has been a tragedy for me, as well as for my wife and family. Since boyhood, I have also been subject to bouts of depression. It runs in my family. I do not want to go on this way. Frankly, Your Honor, I would rather be dead."

"You were born in 1928. Is that correct?"

"Yes."

"So, you are forty-five years of age?"

"Yes."

"Still a young man...," the judge trailed off.

"Often, I feel very old and weary. Or maybe I wish I was very old and had a right to feel weary. I have fought and lost too many battles with my urge to drink. I am disgusted with myself. I am deeply ashamed. I don't know how I can continue. Lately, I have begun to think that I would be better off dead."

"I know the feeling, Dr. Morin, at least vicariously. I have listened to many sad stories of people—men and women, young and old—who have come before me as you do now to be judged. I have the authority to send you to prison for this serious crime. Mercifully, you did not injure someone. Is this correct, Officer?"

"Yes, Your Honor. Dr. Morin narrowly missed entering the oncoming lane and causing a head-on collision. Had I not arrested him, it was a fatality waiting to happen. I risked my own life overtaking him. He begged me to escort him home to his wife and six kids. I refused, ordered him into my patrol car, and took him to the station house. He cooperated fully and gave me no resistance. I then had his car impounded."

"I commend you for your part in preventing a possible tragedy, Officer. Dr. Morin, You will remain in jail, awaiting your trial."

Dr. Morin spent seventeen days in that jail. He was kept separate from other prisoners for a week, then assigned to live with eight of them. During that time, he was allowed periodic, half-hour visits with his wife. He had a full measure of jail life, its shame and humiliation, seasoned with mockery and topped off with the open contempt of his keepers. He bore it all with no protest, cooperating with the daily routines and rules with growing appreciation for what he had enjoyed as a free man.

One day, blessedly, an officer came to deliver him from the jail to the courthouse. Judge Elden was now ready to decide his case. Morin's mouth was dry, and his heart raced.

Elden managed a faint smile. "Dr. Morin, I am releasing you now for two weeks. Your fine is $200.00. At the end of this probationary period, I will decide the final disposition of your case."

Dr. Morin thanked the judge, shook the police officer's hand, and, happy beyond telling, walked out of the court hand-in-hand with his wife.

It was to be a "short happy life," to borrow the title from one of the famous stories of Ernest Hemingway, a man whose alcoholism, manic-depressive disorder, and traumatic brain injuries Dr. Morin was later to study and write about at considerable length.

When Dr. Morin saw Judge Elden again, the judge threw the book at him. In that two-week period, Morin indulged in more dry Martinis, and was arrested for public intoxication twice, and once more for driving intoxicated.

Gazing down at him from his bench, Judge Elden offered him a choice: three months in jail or three months in any rehabilitation center in the state of Michigan. The doctor chose one in Brighton, twenty miles from Ann Arbor, with the unhurried help of a local psychiatrist who did not hide his disdain for his fellow medical doctor's "weakness." Sheriff Postil was waiting for him outside of the jail when he was released and offered to give him a ride to Brighton Hospital. Morin suggested he could walk home, get his car, and drive himself to the hospital. Apparently, the sheriff did not trust Dr. Morin to get himself to the hospital. Morin reassured him that his driver's license was not suspended yet. This discussion seemed to anger the sheriff, and Morin wisely but not happily accepted the ride. His plans had been thwarted by the wise officer. He knew Brighton Hospital and the Canopy Restaurant were both on Grand River Boulevard. He also knew the Canopy served excellent double Martinis and he wanted three of them before entering the hospital. He had a back-up plan that was just as ridiculous. He planned on asking the sheriff to drop him off outside the hospital and Morin would go in and tell the hospital staff that he was a physician and wanted to study the program because he was writing a book about alcoholism. The sheriff apparently was able to read his mind on both counts because he stopped his car and personally escorted the doctor into the hospital to tell the whole staff about Morin. He thanks his higher power for Sheriff Postill's insight. Dr. Morin has never had any other alcohol since that day, and he was able to fit in and be a patient instead of a physician and participate in the treatment he needed. And, he is finally writing that book about alcoholism.

After three days in the hospital, Dr. Morin also realized he belonged there and that he needed rehabilitation. He agreed in writing to attend three AA meetings a week for at least one year. The judge warned him that if he came before him in the next ten years for inebriety that he would sentence him to serve some serious time behind bars. Morin believed him.

Finally Richard had gotten the message. His romance with alcohol was truly a fatal delusion. He had been attributing to alcohol a magical power that it did not possess. He knew that he would always, from this point forward, be a recovering alcoholic and would never again be able to drink or use mind-altering medication. He had been arrested for driving while intoxicated (DWI), and would now choose to "arrest" his alcoholism, probably just in time to save himself. It was his redemption. About that "gift" of a very wise judge, he would write in his diary, "I thought I had died and gone to heaven!"

He completed his sentence at Brighton Hospital and was invited to earn a salary there as a medical doctor, where he remained for ten years, ending up as co-medical director.

While serving at Brighton Hospital he observed that there were at least two kinds of alcoholics. There were those who came, then came to believe, and then accepted the tenets of AA that they could never drink any alcohol again, or use any mind altering-medication, and they needed an AA sponsor and AA meetings. They more or less stayed sober and lived happily ever after.

The other type of alcoholic came to Brighton Hospital and tried hard to believe what they were being taught but "something was different with *them*." They seemed to have a mental block and could not understand the simple concept that they could never drink or use a mind-altering medication again. Frequently, they are referred to as the "revolving-door type," and they make up about 50 percent of the admissions. They were different all right, but Morin could not determine what that difference was. Clearly, it was very serious and most all of them eventually either died from alcoholism or other addictions or ended up in prisons or mental hospitals.

Morin decided that it was most likely some coexisting mental disorder that was obscured by the alcoholism or some other addiction that he did not understand. With his present medical training he was unable to help them.

In 1980, at the age of fifty-two, Richard Morin resigned his position at Brighton Hospital and enrolled as a resident in psychiatry and did a three-year formal residency that was completed at Wayne State University in 1983. A few years later, he became board certified by the American Boards of Psychiatry and Neurology.

As a result of this additional training in psychiatry and neurology he was able to formulate the concept of *Dually Diagnosed*. Briefly stated, they were patients who had two different but similar illnesses that eventually coexisted with each other, but needed a separate diagnosis and definitive treatment for each illness, administered simultaneously and preferably at the same treatment facility. This meant that each patient's psychiatrist needed training in addiction-ology, and the addictionologist needed training in psychiatry. In 1983, after completing the residency in psychiatry, he was hired by the Sisters of Mercy Hospital known then as Samaritan Health Center to set up in-patient and out-patient units to provide just that service. This two-unit treatment of mental illness and alcoholism and other addictions was a one-of-a-kind facility in the United States. Not only that, but the Dual Diagnosis unit had a recovery rate equal to those units treating just addiction (50–75 percent), which was the national average for rehabilitation centers just treating addiction around the United States. Samaritan Hospital's Dual Diagnosis unit succeeded for the next ten years until the early 1990s and enjoyed the same 50–75 percent success rate that facilities treating addiction alone were getting. Revolving-door patients began to be a minority.

Then came the political and financial problems for all psychiatric and chemical dependency hospitals and units, including the many state psychiatric hospitals, in all fifty states. Less than half of all these facilities survived the slaughter. This threw the bulk of the Dual-Diagnosis patients into private and community mental health clinics that were overworked and understaffed.

Now, at the age of seventy-four, his wife of fifty-five years still by his side, his children fledged, he can look back on those years and be thankful for what his experiences have taught him.

• • • • •

SELF-ANALYSIS AND PSYCHIATRIC FORMULATION
RICHARD A. MORIN, M.D., ABPN

GENETIC HISTORY

What appears to be a strong family history of depression and chemical addiction plagued my mother's (Leona Duby) side of the family. One uncle committed suicide by lying face down on a stick of dynamite; another uncle likewise committed suicide by drinking carbolic acid in his beer in a bar; a third uncle and an aunt killed themselves by inhaling carbon monoxide from their cars. My mother was the second oldest of fifteen children. Three siblings died in 1918 of the influenza epidemic. My mother also had influenza but recovered after a week in a coma. Likewise, her mother had influenza and lived after a week in a coma. One sister burned to death accidentally at five years of age, leaving a twin brother. My maternal grandmother died at age fifty of either asthma or congestive heart failure. She was fondly thought of by her children as a living saint who "loved the smell of chloroform so much" that she would sit by the fire in the evening inhaling the chloroform until she fell asleep. My maternal grandfather made and drank moonshine and was a wealthy farmer who exploited his many children on his huge farm and rewarded the males by buying them all farms when they married. The female children did not fair as well and received only $300 when they married. Most of the surviving twelve children were suspected of having depression and alcoholism, but only my mother and one sister were actually diagnosed with depression by a psychiatrist. My mother went into a psychotic depression when my father died at sixty-five years of age from a myocardial infarction. She received seven electroshock therapy treatments and did well afterwards on Tofranil (imipramine) until she was about ninety years of age. She then had a catatonic depression that lasted until she died at ninety-five years of age.

My mother could never be diagnosed as an alcoholic, although she did like its effect, but her ethics and morals limited her use. However, like her mother, she liked medication and in particular the taste and effect of paregoric (tincture of opium) and looked for excuses to buy her limit at the pharmacy. (I will add that my grandmother and mother both worked like horses, and their homes were always starched and spotless. Literally, you could "eat off of her floor.") My father, on the other hand, never knew what a psychiatric depression was

like, and he never had a drinking problem or an addiction problem of any
kind. When the economic depression ended in the 1930s he would drink his
"tonic" that consisted of $^3/_4$ oz. bourbon with $^1/_4$ oz. of lemon extract before
every meal and at bedtime. He never had two drinks and never got drunk. He,
like my mother, had a strong moral and work ethic. He was the oldest of eight
siblings. His parents both died very young, and he was left to work the farm
and support his brothers and sisters until their maturity. He never could read
or write because he had to quit school in the fourth grade to support his
siblings. But he had a large contracting business and a hardware store—all
successful. He died with his boots on at sixty-five years of age.

CHILDHOOD HISTORY

My childhood was uneventful and the worst thing that happened to me was
that I fell and cut the palm of my hand and had to have staples. At the age of
five, I had a tonsillectomy and an andenoidectomy that were also uneventful. I
experienced no other trauma of a physical, sexual, or emotional nature, and I can
remember my childhood very well. I had lots of friends, and had protective,
loving parents and a sister who was four years my senior. I remember having
a lot of gratitude for the few special gifts my parents gave me, like a new bicycle
and new ice skates. My parents were never demonstrative with their affection,
but I know without a doubt I was loved. Starting when I was about eight years
old I vividly remember my mother being very depressed during the Christmas
holidays every year, and this would depress me some because I did not like to see
her complain about Christmas, which I associated with prospective happiness. I
never felt deprived, depressed, or inadequate until I started my adolescence.

During those years I began feeling inadequate and I felt that my friends
and classmates did not like me as much as others. Perhaps this was because I
really enjoyed working in my father's hardware store, selling popcorn at
night, practicing magic tricks, and hypnotizing my classmates and customers.
I started Dick's Sweet Shop and then expanded it to the Penguin Steak and
Chop House Restaurant—all by the time I was a junior in high school.

What I wasn't interested in was basketball, football, or any other varsity
sports. They were sparse anyway in my very small Catholic school during the
war when many of the male students were enlisting in the military service. I
was asked many times to participate, but I always said I had to work. I don't

know if this was true or not because I never asked my father if I could play basketball. It was sometime during these extracurricular activities and business ventures that I began to feel like an adult. I was the only student in high school that had a car and gasoline ration stamps. I dated upper-class students by preference until I met my future wife who was employed in the sweet shop I purchased at the age of sixteen. Then I always dated her until we married, when I was nineteen and she was eighteen years old. I was always feeling inadequate, and I think I was trying to make up for this by achieving respectable positions, gathering material possessions, keeping up my grades, and protecting my reputation. I did not start to recognize any depression until my business started to fail. My feelings of inadequacy were stronger than ever, and I made the decision to go to college. I had started the restaurants in order to become more independent and pay my own way. My discussion with Dr. Hier and Mr. Doane solidified my resolve. I had to go to college—funds or not.

EDUCATIONAL HISTORY

Grade school and high school were always easy for me, but I attended a small Catholic parochial school in Alpena, Michigan during WWII. Males were scarce in high school because of the draft and the high number of young men who had enlisted. Even in that advantageous position and even though I owned my own business, I still felt somewhat inadequate. It was nothing like I felt when my business failed and I had to dismantle it.

This was during an era when married people with families did not think of a college education, and my parent's attitude was no different. My wife and I were guilty of living in a fantasy about the process and were anxious to get started. I worried about the fact that I had to work full time to support my family and I had not been in high school for a couple of years. I knew that the class size and competition at the University of Michigan would be decidedly different from my high school class of thirty in Alpena.

However, we were still hopeful and off we went to Ann Arbor, Michigan with our two children. Anne was pregnant with our third child, and due in two months. (Anne likes to say nobody told us this was crazy and couldn't be done, and so we did it.) It wasn't easy, but we managed to complete four years of undergraduate school with a Bachelor of Science and four years of medical school with a Doctor of Medicine and one year of a rotating internship at

Toledo Hospital in Toledo, Ohio without interruption and very little debt. During my last year in medical school Anne delivered twin girls, Patricia and Pamela, and off we went to start my internship.

MARITAL HISTORY

The marriage held and I wouldn't say that there were not some rough periods but miraculously, everybody stayed healthy and last year we celebrated out fifty-fifth wedding anniversary.

OCCUPATIONAL HISTORY

During my eight years at the University of Michigan, my wife and I both obtained good jobs working for the University of Michigan. My stipend for the internship at Toledo Hospital plus a few moonlighting jobs at a few clinics allowed my wife to quit working and enjoy raising the twins. A classmate in medical school and I became friends and decided to open a partnership in Durand, Michigan in general practice in 1959. The practice flourished, but the local physicians did not welcome us and in fact were very hostile towards us. We stayed eight years, but that was when my consumption of alcohol became worrisome to my wife. I started using amphetamines again. (I had used modestly in undergraduate and graduate school to study all night after getting home from work at 1:00 AM. Insomnia became a problem and I began to mix and match sleeping pills, tranquilizers, and narcotics in order to get sleep.)

The partnership split up and we moved to Lancaster, California for—what I learned later—was referred to by AA as an attempt at a geographic cure for my addictions and personal problems. Anne was not happy about any of these moves and the changes were hard on her, but she reluctantly came along. I had stopped using narcotics in Michigan and was able to stop alcohol and tranquilizers. But, in 1968 amphetamines were not considered addicting by the medical profession. I continued to take them in large quantities and ended the day by taking barbiturates. This led to a life-threatening medical/surgical crisis (see Medical History below). Within a year the family returned to Michigan. I was in poor physical health and was very depressed. I wanted to return to Michigan to die, and I honestly thought that was what was going to happen.

Back in Michigan I kept the wolf away from the door with a job at a University Student Health Service (1972). It was while I was working there that I got the drunk driving violations. I lost my job at the university because of these charges, went to jail, and then finally to Brighton Hospital for treatment of my addictions.

MEDICAL HISTORY

My medical history is truly traumatic. My family teases me that I must have the nine lives of a cat, but they have lost track of which life I am on now. It is difficult to say why I have had so many life-threatening medical problems, but this I do know, I lived forty-three years with no health problems whatsoever. My first one can be blamed on the fact that I was in private practice in Lancaster, California covering two emergency rooms and abusing Dexadrine (amphetamines) and Ritalin (methylphenidate), both commonly known as *speed*. The California hippies knew more about the dangers of these drugs than the medical profession at the time, which was evident in the popular graffiti seen everywhere during the late 1960s, saying "speed kills." I thought it was referring to speeding automobiles and not to Dexadrine and Ritalin. It was not a legally controlled substance and most physicians were prescribing it for diets and treatment of attention deficit disorder—of course not in the high doses I was prescribing for myself. On May 30, 1971, my blood pressure suddenly rose to 280/160 mg/ Hg and I collapsed on the steps of the post office in Lancaster with chest pain and partial paralysis of both lower extremities. Extensive tests at UCLA Hospital in Los Angeles revealed that I had a dissecting aortic aneurysm of the arch of the aorta, complicated by high blood pressure. The thoracic surgeons could not operate until my blood pressure was under control. I had been taught in medical school that this diagnosis was usually made on the autopsy table and survival was between 5 and 10 percent with surgery, but I was not physically stable enough for the surgical procedure. Eventually they sent me home with multiple blood pressure medications in hand. On July 8, 1971, while walking with Anne at the fairgrounds, the aneurysm ruptured again and I was rushed to UCLA. This time blood dissected all the way down the aorta to both femoral arteries, miraculously sparing both renal arteries. My blood pressure was down, and they were expecting me at the hospital and had the Dacron prosthesis ready. They placed me on the heart-lung machine for eight hours of the thirteen-hour operation. I received fifteen pints of blood during the surgery. I had a cardiac arrest and was resuscitated. I left the hospital ten days later and returned to work in my office thirty days after the surgery. I was so exhausted and depressed I had to rest between patients. During the thirty days off work I attempted suicide once with chloral hydrate (Noctec) and had to be taken back to UCLA to have my stomach pumped. The depression and incapacitating fatigue continued. I wanted to return to Michigan to die, if that was what I was going to do. That is what I wanted to happen.

I had stopped using all addicting drugs but I was so despondent that I started using alcohol again. Within a few weeks I had accumulated four violations related to alcohol and was sentenced by Judge Elden to Brighton Hospital for three months. At the completion of this treatment I was feeling great, and the staff at Brighton hospital thought I was doing so well that they hired me as a staff physician. I stayed there almost ten years and eventually became co-medical director along with Russell Smith, M.D., and he became my AA sponsor.

I never had any health problems or depression during the ten years I worked at Brighton Hospital. My subjective feelings of inadequacy were because I did not understand one aspect of alcoholism and addiction—there were *two types* of alcoholics.

Generally speaking, half of the patients got well and stayed sober after one treatment and the other half were involved in the revolving door phenomenon whereby they were readmitted to various institutions many, many times. While I was doing my three-year residency at Wayne State University, I had a myocardial infarction and was treated at the University of Michigan Hospital with angioplasty and Streptokinase with good results. I returned to Wayne State and completed the residency in 1983.

While I was working as the chairman of the Department of Psychiatry and Chemical Dependency at the Sisters of Mercy Samaritan Health Center, I had a cardiac arrest (sudden death syndrome) at my home. I was resuscitated and shocked on our kitchen floor and admitted to the University of Michigan Hospital. I was in a coma for two days, or at least I had two days of total amnesia. They placed a defibrillator and pacemaker in my abdomen for prophylaxis and treatment of any future cardiac arrests or arrhythmias. The defibrillator and pacemaker were replaced in the sternochleidomastoid region in 1996.

In 1991, while on a cruise in to the Scandinavian countries I had an embolism to my left femoral artery with severe intermittent claudication. After returning home it was successfully dissolved at St. Joseph's Hospital in Ann Arbor with Urokinase. I have been on Coumadin, a blood thinner, since then.

In 1988 I had a TURP for Benign Prostatic Hypertrophy by Dr. Richard Dorr at St. Joseph's Mercy Hospital in Ann Arbor. Then, in 2000 I had a prostate biopsy because of a PSA of 6.5 and a diagnosis of a Gleason 7 Carcinoma. I received thirty-nine radiation treatments at the University of Michigan in August 2000 by Dr. Sandler. The cancer was presumed to be confined to the capsule.

In 1993, I had a flesh-eating bacteria in my left calf with ulceration and unbelievable pain. I recovered completely with IV antibiotics. I was diagnosed with diabetes mellitus and was started on insulin injections.

In 1994, I had a laminectomy at L-4 by Dr. William Chandler at the University of Michigan with good results. On August 23, 2000, I had a successful angioplasty with two stents inserted at the University of Michigan done by Dr. Bates for mild angina and shortness of breath. One month later, on September 24, 2000, I was admitted to University of Michigan for a GI bleed from a gastric ulcer that was no doubt caused by Vioxx, Coumadin, and Plavix that I had been prescribed that could cause bleeding problems. The ulcer healed well in a few months.

One year later I had a recurrence of back pain that was nearly disabling. I got by working for a year with trials of physical therapy and pain clinic injections in my back that improved the condition, but in May of 2000 I again had pain that was not responding to the treatment. Finally, Dr. Swanson at St. Joseph's Mercy Hospital agreed to re-operate my laminectormy at a higher level for stenosis of the distal spine. This was done on August 12, 2002, but by then my luck had run out. The surgical wound developed a nosocomial infection and had to be opened and receive surgical debridement. Many complications set in, including congestive heart failure and pneumonia. Today, I am still recovering but I believe the surgery was successful in spite of the infection.

PSYCHIATRIC HISTORY

I never sought psychiatric help before the post-operative period of my dissecting aortic aneurysm in 1971. It was not because I was always feeling good, but because I was feeling inadequate and I thought the only way to feel good was to do something on my own to alleviate that feeling. I had tried many things, like burying myself in schoolwork, magic, the popcorn and sweet shop business, etc., but nothing seemed to work for very long.

Getting married, having children, going to college and medical school gave me hope, but not the improved self-esteem I craved. After my dissecting aortic aneurysm I wondered if there was something physically or mentally wrong with me. I felt that if I could just take some amphetamines I would feel better, but I knew that would be lethal. I went to a psychiatrist in 1971 or 1972 for the first time, but what I was really looking for was a substitute medication that would make me feel better and maybe help me sleep and not cause lethal medical and mental problems. The first psychiatrist prescribed Tofranil, the same anti-depressant that had helped my mother so much after her electro-convulsant treatments. Tofranil did not work, and I asked about electro-convulsant treatments, but my psychiatrist did not think that was a good idea because of the possible brain damage from prolonged time on the heart-lung machine and the cardiac arrest that I had had in the Intensive Care Unit.

After I returned to Michigan and saw Judge Elden, I went to Brighton Hospital. I was insulted because I knew that was for "alcoholics." I informed the psychiatrist of my opinion that I was *not* an alcoholic. He answered, "Well, I think you are, and you either go there or stay in jail." I accepted his kind offer.

I never had further contact with a psychiatrist for myself until a few years after starting my psychiatric residency in 1980. There I learned about mood disorders and realized it was usually a hereditary illness. It was then that I recognized the severity of my mother's unipolar depression. I saw a psychiatrist who diagnosed me as having a unipolar depression and prescribed fluoxetine (Prozac) for me. After the dosage of Prozac reached 40 mg and the feelings of inadequacy were alleviated, my low self-esteem improved, and the black hole that had surrounded me so often never has returned. I still take Prozac 40 mg daily, but no alcohol or addicting drugs were ever used again. I regularly go to AA meetings. I also learned about manic and hypomanic episodes during my psychiatric residency. It has occurred to me that when I was taking Dexadrine and Ritalin during my college years in normal dosages, it gave me a feeling of euphoria not unlike hypomanic patients describe. Of course, when I increased the dosage to try and maintain the euphoria and became addicted it stopped working like all addictive drugs do when addiction occurs. I am grateful that I have been able to maintain my sobriety continuously since September 5, 1973, through the resources of AA.

ALCOHOL AND ADDICTION HISTORY

During the hot summer months in Alpena, Michigan when I was thirteen to sixteen years of age, I was operating the popcorn machine in front of my father's hardware store until midnight every night, except Sundays. The salty popcorn and the sultry summer heat made my father feel sorry for me. He would leave one bottle of cold beer in the refrigerator for me for when I returned home at midnight warm and perspiring. He never left two, but always one. Later, after I owned the restaurants, I would sometimes have one, two, three, or four beers. Often I wouldn't have any unless there was a group party, and then alcohol was always a sign of fun and relaxation. Because I was well known around our small town and owned a business, most people assumed that I was twenty-one years old, and therefore I could maintain my own supply. It never caused me any trouble and always made me feel happy and adequate—if only temporarily.

After we married and had children, especially after I started college, drinking was only for "party time." Since we were busy with school and working, party time was only a rare occasion between semesters. It caused me no problems that I am aware of; however, the Dexadrine problem started in college. I had a "need" to use Dexadrine every other night to study because I was taking full credits in college and working a full-time job. The University of Michigan Health Service prescribed Dexadrine 5mg twice a day as needed. In 1950, Dexadrine was not a controlled substance and was not considered addicting or dangerous. Of course, the authorities were proven wrong, but not until several years after I had graduated from college and medical school. My problem with Dexadrine and Ritalin started in California in 1968 when I decided to stop using alcohol and sleeping pills because they were interfering with my practice. My problems from alcohol started immediately when I returned to Michigan from California and stopped Dexadrine and Ritalin.

I recall thinking as I was stopped at that red light in Ann Arbor that alcohol had never caused me any health problems, so I decided I should just start drinking again—a mistaken and near fatal decision. Within weeks I had all the alcohol-related violations mentioned above.

In retrospect, if there were any early problems from alcohol it was because it alleviated my feelings of inadequacy and replaced them with a sense of power and omnipotence. Whenever I was under the influence of alcohol I would become very argumentative with friends, competitors, hospital admin-istrators, board members, and even my fellow physicians—to my own detriment. I became an easy scapegoat when there was a really important issue to discuss or decide, or a situation for which someone needed to be blamed.

SOCIAL HISTORY

I have never smoked cigarettes or used any other inhalant, not even once in my life. Don't ask me how or why because I don't know, but it's true. The closest thing to a reason is that neither of my parents ever smoked. I have also never been a gambler.

MENTAL STATUS EXAMINATION

To report on my own mental status is difficult. I have two choices: one is to report my answers on a standard brief mental status exam—but that would be biased because, due to my training, I know all the answers to my own questions. The second would be to summarize the key findings of a few of the many mental status exams that other facilities have done on me plus note observations that others have made about me, personally and professionally. I will do the latter.

Relative to my personality, I like Freud's assessment of a normal personality. He said a person is normal if he can work, love, and play in proper proportions. My assessment of my abilities in these three assets is as follows: I am excellent at work; I am fair at love; I am very poor at play, but I have changed some over the years. This statement gives testimony to the definition given in the *DSM-IV* that a personality disorder is "an enduring pattern of inner experience and behavior that deviates markedly from the expectations of the individual's culture, is pervasive and inflexible, has an onset in adolescence or early adult-hood, is stable over time, and leads to distress and impairment."

Through the program of Alcoholics Anonymous I have gained insight into my defects of character through the healthy defense mechanisms that I have learned through AA and my psychiatric treatment and training. The healthy defense mechanisms are anticipation, affiliation, altruism, discipline, self-assertion, self-observation, positive identification, sublimation, and suppression. If I use the positive defense mechanisms when I'm sober I get along much better in all my relationships. I have not tested if this is true when

I am drinking because I have been sober twenty-nine years.

Another diagnosis that can be determined by the mental status examination is if there is any brain damage such as memory, mathematics, instant recall, or remote recall. When the psychiatrist reported the results of my testing he advised me that alcohol and drugs had impaired my performance somewhat, and he gave me evidence. He said, "I know you are right-handed and you are supposed to do better with your right hand than your left hand, but you should have done better with your left hand than you did. This suggests some minimal brain damage." He further assured me that with prolonged abstinence it could get better, and I believe that it has.

There are various key questions to identify mood disorders in a Mental Status Examination. While it is work, love, and play for personality, it is sleep, appetite, sexual function, feelings of helplessness, hopelessness or worthlessness, sadness, crying, chronic fatigue, suicidality, or mania, hypomania, pressured speech, paranoia, excess energy, hypersexuality, lack of need for sleep, gambling, shopping sprees, and grandiosity are the most common symptoms for depression and mania. I had most of the symptoms of depression for most of my adult life and some of the symptoms of hypomania when I was taking Dexadrine and Ritalin. Perhaps it was the hypomania that heightened my interest in the manic-depressive authors, Edgar Allan Poe, F. Scott Fitzgerald, John Berryman, and Kay Redfield Jamison, described in this book. I am pleased to say that the depression and anxiety has been eliminated with the "new generation" antidepressant, Prozac. There have been no symptoms of hypomania since being off Dexadrine and Ritalin. There are many "new generation" antidepressant/antianxiety medications on the market now in addition to Prozac. Others, to mention a few, are Zoloft, Paxil, Effexer, Celexia, and Lexapro.

The only symptom of a thought disorder I have had has been mental confusion that plagues me still after a general anesthetic. This is a symptom that is getting worse as I age, but only affects me if and when I require general anesthetic for major surgery.

PSYCHIATRIC FORMULATION

While I had a happy and non-traumatic childhood, I was negatively influenced at times by my mother's depression, and I believe, as I matured, I showed definite symptoms of inheriting her depression and also adverse sensitivity to alcohol and sedatives from her side of the family. Both of my parents impressed on me that *laziness* and *slothfulness* were equal or worse than murder and stealing. Consequently, I found that hard work relieved my feelings of inadequacy and the rewards gave me hope that soothed my mood disorder. Later I found that chemicals allowed me to "play" and I associated the mind-altering effects of alcohol, barbiturates, and amphetamines with recreation. This association with play and recreation prevented me from using chemicals at work. On the rare occasions when I used chemicals during working hours I would have to excuse myself and leave work to "play."

The hardest thing for me to evaluate is the adverse effect on my mental functioning that resulted from the use and abuse of alcohol and amphetamines and how much this improved with twenty-nine years of sobriety. Equally difficult to evaluate is the effect on my thinking that resulted from the anoxia of being many hours on a heart-lung machine for the dissecting aortic aneurysm, two cardiac arrests, and multiple general anesthetics. My opinion is that these were all negative experiences, but my family is correct— I am lucky enough to be granted the nine lives of the cat.

FINAL DIAGNOSIS

AXIS I:
1. Major Depressive Disorder, Recurrent, *DSM-IV* (296.3)
2. Alcohol Dependence in Sustained Full Remission, *DSM-IV* (303.90)
3. Amphetamine Dependence with Sustained Full Remission, *DSM-IV* (304.40)
4. Personality Change Due to Multiple Cardiac Illnesses (Heart-Lung Machine, Cardiac Arrest, etc.)

AXIS II:
1. Personality Disorder Not Otherwise Specified in Partial Remission, *DSM-IV* (301.9)

AXIS III:
1. Status Post-Op Thoracic Dissecting Aortic Aneurysm
2. Remote Myocardial Infarction

3. Remote Cardiac Arrest (Sudden Death Syndrome) with surgical implant of Prophylactic Defibrillator and Pacemaker
4. Embolism to Left Femoral Artery with intermittent claudication dissolved with Urokinase and placed on prophylactic Coumadin
5. Prostate Carcinoma treated with thirty-nine radiation treatments
6. Diabetes Mellitus
7. Laminectomy X2 for ruptured disc and stenosis of distal spine

AXIS IV:
1. Problems with Occupation, Social Environment, Legal System in Remission.

AXIS V:
1. Global Assessment of Functioning (GAF): 90

CHAPTER THREE

Unmasking Dual Diagnosis

The Middle Ages (476 to 1453 AD) was characterized for the low value given to life, especially the lives of underprivileged peasants, proletariats, serfs, and the common laborers. Generally speaking, any hope for happiness that they might have earned would be awarded to them after their death, and even then only if they had faithfully served the "lord" during their life on earth. Suffering on earth was expected and would be justified by the reward of paradise or heaven because it would help erase or atone the future eternal punishment in hell by substituting a limited time in purgatory for "original" and subsequent, accumulated worldly sins.

There were relatively few "lords" in comparison to the masses of the common man whose labor was almost worthless in a monetary sense. If, for any reason, they could not perform physical labor, they were considered less than worthless—a burden to the few, but all-powerful landlords and royalty.

The disabled, infirm, insane, and the criminal were put "out of sight and out of mind" by the various devised methods referred to as The Great Confinement. This usually meant that they were institutionalized in various asylums, hospitals, prisons, and "poor houses" for the insane, the criminal, or the disabled. The Crown of England tried many methods of segregation including deportation to the criminal colonies in Australia and Tasmania. Their motivation was to devise cheaper and cheaper methods of imprisonment—of course this was "for their own good." By convincing themselves that they were doing the "right" thing for these people, they were able to rationalize the segregation, isolation, and cruel treatment of this large group of disturbed and troubled individuals that existed in all of civilization, particularly in the growing urban areas.

There was no attempt to separate them into classifications according to their suspected diagnosis or even according to their mental or moral symptoms or behavior, as was being done during that same period for the more objective and scientific medical or surgical illnesses. There was no need to, they reasoned, because the cause of their wayward behavior was suspected to be possession by some evil force or spirit—most likely the devil, a witch, a drug, or a poison. The most likely drug or poison was alcohol, although there were others. The usual treatment of that time was to isolate them and cause their bodies pain or severe discomfort so the evil spirits would leave their bodies and thereby "cure" them. This would be attempted with such things as ice packs, loud noises, and torture of all kinds or attempts to "exorcise" the evil spirit out of these individuals by various religious rituals or "physical" treatments. These methods of untoward and unsuccessful "treatments" were used throughout the Dark Ages (476–1000 AD) and the Middle Ages (476–1453). This system was devised by the popes for punishing the "heretics" or non-believers of the Catholic faith for their failure to believe and comply with the teachings of the Church. The Catholic kings and rulers usually enforced the Church's judicial sentences of fines, torture, or death.

Two monumental revolutions took place in the sixteenth, seventeenth, and eighteenth centuries that slowly began making it possible for citizens with a mental illness, alcohol and drug dependent people, and others with atypical behaviors to start to be recognized as individuals of some possible value—for their labor. This began by creating a system to diagnose these individuals into different classifications, now known as *differential diagnosis*, with specific psychiatric, medical, surgical, and traumatic illnesses. Eventually they began to receive somewhat more appropriate and corrective treatment.

The first revolution we are referring to is the Protestant Reformation started by Martin Luther in the sixteenth-century. Luther's Reformation was a movement for the reform of abuses in the doctrines and practices of the Roman Catholic Church that ended in the establishment of the Reformed and Protestant Churches. This brought about the recognition of the individual's rights over the next two hundred years, and evolved into a system of governments by the citizens of new nations through elected representatives that we now call Democracy.

The second revolution that actually enhanced the progress of the Reformation had its origin in the late eighteenth century in England. It brought about a complex set of radical socioeconomic changes that started an extensive mechanization of the production systems that resulted in a shift from home-based handcrafted products created in the countryside to large-scale factory manufacturing in the cities. It was called the Industrial Revolution. This, in turn, led to mass production and a market economy. The market economy enhanced the value of each individual worker that led to a shortage of skilled and unskilled labor. The employers and the politicians started looking askance at the thousands of unemployed people in the various "institutions" scattered around all of the Western countries, and the concept of rehabilitation rather than storage or confinement began to look attractive to many, if for no other reason than for economics.

But the concept of rehabilitation took a long time to materialize. Philippe Pinel in France introduced what he and others called the *moral treatment*. Through his influence, the patients in "lunatic asylums" were unchained and their tortures ceased and they began to be treated with humane and more rational methods. In England William Tuke insisted that the mentally ill should be treated with kindness and dignity. Benjamin Rush, an American psychiatrist, who signed the Declaration of Independence in 1776, said alcoholism, which he called *inebriety*, was a medical and a mental disease. Emil Kraepelin (1856–1926) in Munich developed a classification of mental diseases that included manic depression and schizophrenia among them. Dorothea Lynde Dix (1802–1887) an American philanthropist, reformer, and educator was a pioneer in the movement for the specialized treatment of the mentally ill. Sigmund Freud (1856–1939) in Vienna worked extensively on the concept of *neurosis*. He used hypnosis in its diagnosis and treatment and pioneered psychoanalysis to uncover the hidden causes of the unconscious mind in this and other psychiatric disorders such as anxiety disorders and personality disorders.

In spite of the many advances in the diagnoses and treatments described above, it did not change the therapeutic outcome for most of the patients with mental illness, alcoholism, or drug abuse except for a very few of the rich and famous. The vast majority of the mentally ill and alcoholics were in the chronic wards of state mental hospitals—most of them stayed there for decades until death finally ended their bleak existence.

It was not until the multitude of the many unnamed psychiatrists and scientists working in research hospitals, pharmaceutical laboratories, and university medical school departments in the middle of the twentieth century that there were some true breakthroughs. I am referring to the discovery of *psychotropic* medications (antidepressants and antipsychotics) that have an uncanny ability to normalize the imbalances of the brain's neurohormones and stabilize patients' thoughts, feelings, and sometimes their behavior. The changes in thoughts, feelings, and behaviors that these newer medications were able to evoke made it possible for the majority of mental patients to leave the crowded asylums and be mainstreamed into their communities. Instead of institutionalization, they could be treated in their own homes, psychiatric outpatient clinics, psychiatric day-hospitals, psychiatric foster-care homes, and acute psychiatric hospital units. Only a few were required to be institutionalized in long-term state mental hospitals for the chronically mentally ill.

Things began to look very hopeful for the mentally ill, the alcoholic and drug addicted, the traumatic brain injured, and even the demented for a short while. The new scientific discoveries plus the *moral treatment* already in vogue for these patients were producing real, objective therapeutic results. These previously debilitated patients were becoming happy, useful, and productive citizens. What a miracle! Alcoholics and drug addicts were recovering in droves in specialized rehabilitation treatment centers like the Betty Ford Center, Hazelton Rehabilitation Center, Brighton Hospital, and/or at Alcoholics Anonymous meetings. Community mental health clinics would replace long-term legal commitments to institutions for the chronically insane and the demented that were long-term residents of the many state mental hospitals. Hundreds of state mental hospitals would be closed. However, most of the state mental hospitals were closed so quickly that there was not sufficient time for the health departments to mature enough to be a viable substitute for the old, outdated mental asylums and institutions for the care and treatment of chronic mental patients. The result has placed the mental health care community into a state of persistent chaos in many clinical arenas and many geographical areas that persists to this day.

We say *chaos* because, as the inadequately diagnosed and inadequately treated patient masses were discharged from the chronic care mental hospitals and those hospitals closed, many patients with multiple, inadequately diagnosed and treated mental illnesses continued to cause problems in their communities. These under-diagnosed and under-treated individuals with mental illness, alcohol and drug problems, personality disorders, traumatic head injuries, mental illnesses due to medical and surgical illnesses, and substance-induced mental disorders were still largely ignored. Their care went under-funded by the same state and local governments that were responsible for their premature eviction from the chronic mental hospitals in the first place. When these former mental and addicted patients had conflicts with the law, in most cases because of their mental illnesses or their addictions or other illnesses that affected their behavior, they were arrested and imprisoned. Hundreds of new jails and prisons were constructed to accommodate them.

Now, once again, many of them reside in institutions where there have been many improvements in their psychiatric care. However, there is often still limited opportunity for them to receive a proper diagnosis and appropriate treatment because correctional staff's authority supersedes medical treatment. Therefore, these regressive changes are like giant steps back to the period of The Great Confinement of the Middle Ages. Just like during the Middle Ages, if an individual causes society significant problems and he is not productive he is put away in an institution. Although the lunatic asylums are now replaced by newer and better prisons, only a very few of them are appropriately staffed to treat these "criminals," whose only crime may be to have an illness with psychiatric symptoms that brought them to the attention of law enforcement. Another all too common scenario is the inadequate treatment they received for their psychiatric disorder from the new, ill-equipped, and inadequately staffed community mental health clinics. When they were between institutions and trying to be "mainstreamed," their mental illnesses had become so neglected that many of them did, in fact, commit a serious crime that might not have happened if their mental disorder had been appropriately diagnosed and treated. Proper treatment could have prevented the crime from occurring and reoccurring.

The period of The Great Confinement has been replaced by a period that I call the Great Masquerades. During the period of The Great Confinement there was not the scientific, medical, or psychiatric knowledge available to separate individuals between psychiatric illness, medical illness, alcoholism and substance-abuse disease, toxins and poisons, traumatic brain injury, and seizures. They were mistakenly intermingled with the many bizarre afflictions that charlatans, witch doctors, crooks, and other types of swindlers usually managed to label them with—the purpose being to frighten them and the public and then sell them or their families various snake oils, patent medicines, and magic or religious rituals to exorcise the evil spirits from their bodies. Although there will probably always be quackery around to harass the gullible, there are now also well-trained physicians, psychiatrists, neurologists, psychologists, and addiction-ologists, as well as the necessary CT scans, MRIs, x-rays, and laboratory tests of all kinds that permit an accurate diagnosis and treatment. However, the shortage of funds caused by the new managed care medical and hospitalization insurance companies and the closing of the many kinds of multidisciplinary and specialized clinics, hospitals, and institutions have forced many but the very rich to try to survive without a proper diagnosis and treatment. In many ways we are back in the Middle Ages, but this time patients are being forced to accept an inadequate diagnosis and therefore improper treatment because of the economics of the insurance industry and federal, state, and local governments rather than the inadequacy of scientific knowledge.

This tragedy brings us to what this book is all about—*masquerades*. Once we understand how and why the mentally ill, the alcoholic, and the drug addict, as well as the disabled and infirm, were mistreated during the Middle Ages, it begins to make more sense and become almost forgivable. Indeed, there was inadequate medical knowledge to diagnose or to treat the many ailments that masqueraded as the unproductive, ill-behaved, generally unkempt, and usually homeless individuals. They were unfairly and unscien-tifically classified as "lunatics" or "crazies" who frequently ended their lives prematurely or were institutionalized for storage during the time of The Great Confinement. But that was then, and this is now.

We have learned, during the fifteen years of insight brought about by the "revolution," of the treatment for alcoholism and drug dependence by pioneers like Betty Ford, Wilbur Mills, Harold Hughes, and the program of Alcoholics Anonymous that precipitated the dramatic recoveries for so many in the 1970s and 1980s. We likewise must give credit to the research teams in university medical schools and pharmaceutical research laboratories for the dramatic discoveries made in the psychiatric treatment of anxiety, depression, mania, and psychoses that proved just as miraculous. We now know how well the proper classification of mental illness and addictions and specific treatments for all of them can result in the "miracles" of recovery and rehabilitation of these previous "dregs" of humanity.

This author knows from firsthand experience the before and after of both of these types of illnesses. I personally have experienced the refractoriness of having two separate illnesses—psychiatric and addictive—that I could not conquer when they were treated one at a time. I have chosen to document how I could not recover until I was correctly diagnosed, and only when I received specific treatment for both of my diagnoses did satisfactory recovery follow. It is for this same reason that I have included in this volume the psychiatric biographies of Edgar Allan Poe, F. Scott Fitzgerald, and John Berryman, all three geniuses of exceptional magnitude who struggled throughout their lives over the past two hundred years with similar Dual Diagnoses. All of them died prematurely, some of them at their own hand because they did not recover and for the same reasons as discussed earlier—inadequate diagnosis and inadequate treatment. A fourth famous author, Kay Redfield Jamison, a very gifted individual born in the last half of the twentieth century and still alive and thriving today, was fortunate enough to have the correct diagnosis (manic-depressive disorder) and modern treatment (lithium).

Today many new mood stabilizers, like Depakote and Tegretol, are being added to the list almost monthly. The antipsychotic agents like haloperidol and chlorpromazine and many others are also available for crisis management. These life-saving medications and treatments were available to Jamison and many others, and she and many others did and continue to make remarkable recoveries. Jamison, a clinical psychologist and author, relates her story in her book, *An Unquiet Mind.*

I have given the reader a focused satellite view through Alley Oop's time machine, a perspective of 500 years of the treatment of mental disorders without any attempt at a diagnosis and certainly without a scientific treatment. (My apologies to those readers too young to remember this humorous and intellectually stimulating comic strip.) Also, I presented similar perspectives, over approximately the same number of years, of the slow but steady improvement in the diagnosis and treatment of alcoholism and other chemical addictions.

In the last twenty-five years we have reached the epitome of progress in the addiction field and significant progress in the diagnosis and treatment of the mental illness arena, but now we are on the edge of a precipice. If we are not careful, we can lose all the gains we have enjoyed over the last twenty-five years. Progress has allowed us a glimpse over the mountains to the discovery that has allowed recognition of Dual Diagnosis and its appropriate treatment, but that is not enough. The obstacles that are before us are of a political and economic nature that could force us back toward the Dark Ages, back in time to where the individuals with mental disorders and addictions became scapegoats for the rest of society.

We have seen it before and we are seeing it again. Simply put, when services need to be cut for economic reasons, mental illness and addiction treatment is the first to be considered unnecessary by the politicians and bean counters. This is because citizens who have alcoholism, drug addiction, any type of mental illness, dementia, and disabilities in general are always the groups easiest to be downtrodden simply because they are the groups with the least support representatives to rally behind them. The glaring exception to that statement is the tremendous support given to alcoholics by Betty Ford and other celebrities since the mid-seventies to the present.

Let me present to the reader an outline, whereby each group frequently masquerades as each other and can present as an individual disease or diagnosis that can constitute a Dual Diagnosis.

I. PSYCHIATRIC DISORDERS WITH A KNOWN CAUSE OR ETIOLOGY
    A. Psychiatric Disorders Due to a Medical or Surgical Condition:
        1. Mood Disorder Due to...[Indicate the General Medical or Surgical Condition]
        2. Psychotic Disorder Due to...[Indicate the General Medical or Surgical Condition]
        3. Anxiety Disorder Due to...[Indicate the General Medical or Surgical Condition]
        4. Dementia Due to...[Indicate the General Medical or Surgical Condition]

5. Personality Change Due to...[Indicate the General Medical or Surgical Condition]

B. Substance-Induced Psychiatric Disorders:
   1. Substance-Induced Intoxication Disorder
   2. Substance-Induced Withdrawal Disorder
   3. Substance-Induced Mood Disorder
   4. Substance-Induced Delirium
   5. Substance-Induced Hallucinatory Persisting Perception Disorder
   6. Substance-Induced Anxiety Disorder
   7. Substance-Induced Persisting Amnesic Disorder
   8. Substance-Induced Persisting Dementia
   9. Substance-Induced Sexual Dysfunction
   10. Substance-Induced Sleep Disorders

C. Substance-Induced Disorders:
   1. Substance Dependence
   2. Substance Abuse

All of the combined illnesses listed under A, B, and C above appear in the American Psychiatric Association's *Manual of Mental Disorders, Fourth Edition (DSM-IV)*. They are *not* classified as examples of a Dual Diagnosis, but they do differ from most psychiatric diagnoses in the *DSM-IV* by the fact that they are determined to have a known or at least a probably known cause or etiology. Technically, they do not fulfill our criteria for examples of a Dual Diagnosis because the paired diagnoses are causally related and cannot be separated into two separate illnesses with distinctly different causes or etiologies.

There are some technical and semantic differences between what we are referring to as a Dual Diagnosis and the *masquerades* of psychiatry and medicine. When we complete this section detailing some of these semantic and technical differences, we will not try to keep these small differences separated.

Remember that the *DSM-IV* does not use the term Dual Diagnosis as a classification category. Instead, they make use of a broad category that they call *Differential Diagnosis* (or most recently co-morbid or co-occurring illnesses.

II. Psychiatric Disorders With an Unknown Cause or Etiology:

To avoid classifying individuals with a Dual Diagnosis, the *DSM-IV* uses a common medical term, *Differential Diagnosis*. The purpose of this term is to determine which diagnosis an individual might have amongst a group of diagnoses that presents with the same or similar symptoms. No consideration is given to the possibility that the individual could have two or even three of the ailments from the list of Differential Diagnoses (Dual or Triple Diagnosis). When we are talking about a Differential Diagnosis between psychiatric disorders with *unknown* cause or etiology it seems unreasonable to assume that there is only one possible diagnosis when one cannot be certain of any of the causes of the multiple diagnoses. The famous German psychiatrist, Emil Kraeplin (1856–1926) published his psychiatric nosology and systematization to classify the difference between manic-depressive psychosis and dementia praecox (schizophrenia) in an attempt to sort out these and other psychiatric illnesses (endogenous and exogenous depression). His work went underutilized for almost 100 years. However, only when successful treatment for manic-depressive psychosis (lithium) and schizophrenia (chlorpromazine) became available and gave indirect evidence of the neurohormone hypotheses for these diseases were psychiatrists able to differentiate between the two psychotic illnesses in a meaningful way.

When a psychiatrist is trying to determine the different diagnoses of a Dual or Triple Diagnosis he must choose between three possible groups or classification systems:

(A) Psychiatric Disorders Due to a Known Medical or Surgical Condition;

(B) Known Substance-Induced Psychiatric Disorders;

(C) Psychiatric Disorders With Unknown Cause of Etiology.

The actual Dual or Triple Diagnosis could consist of one or more from any of these three categories.

One of the advantages of the *DSM-IV* and its predecessors has been the Axis I, II, III, IV, and V classification system because it gives the clinician a mental review of many of the diagnostic possibilities for any given psychiatric case. This has proven to be especially pertinent for Axis II, the personality disorders. We have found our system of using the concept of Dual and Triple Diagnosis equally efficient to use in conjunction with the five Axis system because it makes us do a similar mental review of the diagnostic possibilities, especially for Axis I, Axis II, and Axis III.

Examples of the five classifications of general medical and surgical conditions that might cause one or more of the five psychiatric symptoms or disorders listed in section I of the outline are as follows: HIV disease, head trauma, Parkinson's disease, Huntington's disease, Pick's disease, and Creutzfeldt-Jacobs disease as well as normal pressure hydrocephalus, hypothyroidism, brain tumor, brain stroke, vitamin B-12 deficiency, intracranial radiation, plus many other medical or surgical conditions. The following discharge summary of an actual patient, we will call Annie Kojak, illustrates how the classification system is used in reaching a diagnosis. This patient had severe mood disorder with psychotic symptoms due to a medical or surgical condition (hypothyroidism from a total thyroidectomy for carcinoma of the thyroid and post-operative hyperthyroidism from excessive exogenous thyroid medication).

DISCHARGE SUMMARY

Name: Annie Kojack   *Date of Birth: 02/04/45*
Date of Admission: May 11, 2001

IDENTIFYING DATA:

Ms. Kojack is a fifty-six-year-old white female, who was transferred to this acute psychiatric prison hospital because of being uncooperative and having hallucinations and delusions and denying her crime and being hostile. She was responding to both external and internal stimuli. She entered the regular prison population after having spent six months' time in the county jail. She was received at the prison 5/11/01 and transferred to the acute psychiatric prison hospital on 05/17/01. She was married, divorced prior to the murder of her ex-husband, and she has three grown children. She states she is not guilty of the crime. She made many irrational statements at the time of admission such as, "Yes, voices throw dustballs at me. The voices are outside of me, voices are detoxifying me from flashing lights." She is a white female appearing approximately her stated age of fifty-six years. She has blackish/white straight hair and her affect is flat. She has a slight bend of her neck from multiple previous surgeries to her cervical vertebra for congenital torticollis. She readily admits that she became addicted to several narcotic and tranquilizing pain medications that she used prior to, during, and following these multiple surgeries. These medications included Percodan, Demerol, Vicodin, Darvon and Valium and Klonopin as well as liberal use of alcohol.

REASON FOR ADMISSION AND CLINICAL CONDITION AT ADMISSION:

The patient was first admitted to a correctional facility for females, as stated, on 5/11/01, and because of her bizarre behavior, she was almost immediately transferred over to the Acute Psychiatric Unit. The reason for admission was because she was inappropriate in her behavior with some crying, some pacing, and some inappropriate manipulation for analgesic drugs that she has taken for years for her torticollis and the multiple surgeries following this diagnosis for relief of pain from the surgical defect to her cervical spine. There is little doubt that this patient was addicted to the narcotics from either an iatrogenic response to her legitimate torticollis pain or an opportunistic addiction because she had a medical excuse or reason, if you will, to obtain and abuse the narcotics. Her family agrees that she was abusing the narcotics. There is, of course, some possibility that the narcotics and the hypothyroidism played some role in either a medical or substance abuse etiology for her depression, in other words, a substance-induced mood disorder with a psychotic depression.

PROVISIONAL DIAGNOSES:
(At the time of admission to the psychiatric unit in prison.)

AXIS I:
   Rule out Psychotic Disorder, Not Otherwise Specified
   Rule out Dysthymia
   Rule out Depressive Disorder, Not Otherwise Specified

AXIS II:
   Personality Disorder, Mixed, Passive Aggressive, and Narcissistic

Axis III:
  Post-op thyroidectomy for Carcinoma of Thyroid
  Hypothyroidism secondary to the above surgery
  Cervical Laminectomy and other cervical surgeries (eight) for torticollis

Axis IV :
  Recent incarceration

Axis V:
  Admission GAF: 20

PHYSICAL, LABORATORY, AND HYPERSENSITIVITY FINDINGS ON ADMISSION:

The patient's physical exam was within normal limits except for the residual torticollis of her neck, which leaves her neck twisted slightly but apparently does not give her any pain any longer. Her white blood count was somewhat depressed and her last white count was 3.4 with normal ranges of 3.8 to 11. This leukopenia was felt to possibly be due either to Loxitane or the Klonopin bone marrow depression. The Klonopin has been discontinued at patient's request so that she will be eligible for a transfer to a less restricted facility. This abnormality will have to be followed and resolved before discharge back to the open population in the prison, but it is not deemed life threatening at this point in time. Her white blood count on admission was within normal range of 6500 to 7500. As stated, her TSH was elevated, which is to be expected with her having had a recent total thyroidectomy for carcinoma of the thyroid gland and before taking exogenous thyroid medication. Her EKG was normal except for a few ventricular premature complexes. There was also a ventricular premature beat abnormality in the anterior leads with her long QT interval and a T wave abnormality. The date on this abnormal EKG was 8/24/01. There had been a previous EKG on 8/29/01, which was normal. The Internist did not feel any intervention needed to be done regarding this finding at that time. The rest of the laboratory work during her stay here was within normal limits. She is allergic to Demerol. It gives her a rash. She has no food allergies. Physical examination was within normal limits except for the torticollis described above. She did have the abnormal EKG, but this resolved itself.

COURSE OF TREATMENT:

The patient, although she has never had any psychiatric history prior to admission, became seriously mentally ill almost immediately after being placed in the prison for the first-degree murder of her ex-husband and given a life sentence without the possibility of parole. She seems to be playing the role of the victim in that she was not responsible for the murder and that it was really her brother who killed her husband and was also in prison for the same crime. As a patient, she paced the floor a lot, and was placed in seclusion frequently for hallucinations and uncooperative passive-aggressive types of behavior.

She was reported to have been unclean in her hygiene and the sheets of her bed were said to be black because she would not bathe and did not change the sheets of her bed.

This situation cleared while she was a patient in the Acute Psychiatric Unit and her hygiene became adequate. She was treated with Loxitane 15 mg at 9:00 AM and 9:00 PM for her psychotic depression and she received two different types of antidepressants including Paxil 30 mg 9:00 AM and 20 mg at 9:00 PM also for a total of 50 mg. She also received Desyrel 100 mg at 9:00 PM. For her extrapyramidal symptoms, she was put on Artane 2 mg twice a day. Prior to admission to prison she had had a thyroidectomy for cancer of the thyroid. Her thyroid studies on admission to the Acute Psychiatric Unit revealed that she had an underactive thyroid with a TSH at 35.180, but subsequently the exogenous thyroid increased to .175 produced a depression of her TSH to .304 with normal of .270–420 and she was taking Synthroid 0.125 mg in AM along with a .05 mg tablet—total 0.175 mg/day. Her thyroid studies early on during her stay in the Acute Psychiatric Unit were in normal range except the TSH was elevated which was consistent with her diagnosis and her therapy. Then suddenly the patient developed symptoms of anticipatory anxiety with tremor, heat intolerance, and sweats that were to her very reminiscent of the same symptoms she used to have with alcohol and tranquilizer withdrawal and that she had had recently in association to the discontinuation of her Klonopin. She was treated with moderate relief with propranalol (Inderal) 20 mg four times a day for what was believed to be anticipatory anxiety. Because of her surgical history of a thyroidectomy for cancer of the thyroid a few years earlier and her relatively large dose of exogenous thyroid, repeat thyroid studies were obtained. These repeat thyroid studies revealed that she now had thyrotoxicosis from her Synthroid (thyroid) medication. Her TSH was very low (.02) and her T-3, T-4, and T-7 were all markedly elevated. She now had hyperthyroidism from too high a dose of Synthroid (.175 mg) and she was now hyperthyroid instead of hypothyroid as she was at the time of her imprisonment. She now had symptoms of generalized anxiety disorder and panic attacks instead of psychotic depression with delusions that she had at the time of her admission to the Acute Psychiatric Unit.

The patient had been on a lot of analgesics and tranquilizers prior to committing this murder. She was no doubt addicted to the medications. Her medicines of choice were Vicodin, Valium, and Klonopin, and she was demanding in her use of analgesics, saying that she was allergic to Demerol, and her life more or less revolved around the tranquilizers and the analgesics for a period of time. Her goal is to go back to the Women's Correctional Facility because there are more educational programs that she could use for her edification and, she stated, for her future employment although she is on a life sentence without parole. When she was informed that she would have to get off of the Klonopin in order to be eligible for a transfer back, she willingly accepted a detoxification regime and was taken off of Klonopin with surprisingly little withdrawal symptoms. She participated in the program and essentially did it quite well and was a cooperative patient after the first couple of months.

CONDITION AT DISCHARGE:

The patient's psychiatric condition at discharge can be described by saying that the patient is somewhat passive-aggressive. She is also detached from the group as a rule and keeps to herself most of the time. The hallucinations and passive-aggressive behavior that were prevalent at the time of admission have disappeared. Her massive denial of being guilty of the crime for which she was sent to prison seems to have resolved. Her hygiene is improved. Her affect is still flat and she is oriented as to person, time, and place. She participates in all of the group activities. Her appetite has been good and she has educational goals and is interested in returning to the main prison. There has been no disruptive behavior for several months now.

MEDICATION, DIET, AND ACTIVITY INSTRUCTIONS AT DISCHARGE:

Medication is Loxitane 15 mg twice a day, the Artane 2 mg twice a day, the Desyrel 100 mg at bedtime and Paxil 50 mg daily in the morning. She also uses aspirin on an as necessary basis. As stated, she is totally detoxified from the Klonopin. She will be discharged with seven days' supply of Hydrodiuril 25 mg every morning, Synthroid at .1 mg daily, Loxitane 15 mg twice a day, Artane 2 mg twice day, Desyrel 100 mg at bedtime for sleep and depression, and Paxil 50 mg in the morning for depression.

AFTERCARE ARRANGEMENTS:

Aftercare plan includes returning to the general population of the main prison with follow up by outpatient mental health team.

This patient was on a regular diet during her entire hospitalization at the Acute Psychiatric Hospital and on admission her lipids were elevated with her cholesterol profile Cholesterol/HDL ration showing high risk of 6.12 (females high risk is 5.7-10). This was resolved with increasing her Synthroid gradually to .175 mg. There are no restrictions on her diet and any cardiac problems were removed also by treating her hypothyroidism secondary to thyroidectomy. However, when she developed Thyrotoxicosis from exogenous Synthroid, her Synthroid dosage had to be reduced to .1 mg and eventually she was treated for her hyperlipidemia with Mevachor and a low-cholesterol diet.

DISCHARGE (OR FINAL) DIAGNOSES:

AXIS I:
1. Mood Disorder (Psychotic Depression) Due to Hypothyroidism caused by surgical removal of thyroid for carcinoma of her

thyroid gland and subsequent hyperthyroidism from excessive replacement thyroid (Synthroid), *DSM-IV* (293.83)
2. Substance-Induced (Exogenous Synthroid) Anxiety Disorder, *DSM-IV* (292.89)
3. Polysubstance Dependence (Iatrogenic?) in Remission, *DSM-IV* (304.80)
4. Alcohol Dependence in Remission, *DSM-IV* (303.90)
5. Factitious Disorder with Combined Psychological and Physical Signs and Symptoms, *DSM-IV* (300.19)

AXIS II:
1. Passive Aggressive Personality Disorder, *DSM-IV* (301.90)

AXIS III:
1. Post-op thyroidectomy for carcinoma of the thyroid, ICD-10-193
2. Multiple (eight) surgeries to cervical vertebrae for correction of congenital torticollis, ICD-10-722.91

AXIX IV:
1. Incarceration.

AXIS V:
GAF: 55

DISCHARGE LEVEL OF CARE RECOMMENDATIONS:

She is recommended for discharge to the prison general population with follow up by the outpatient mental health team.

PROGNOSIS:

Prognosis is fair to good with continued treatment

Richard Morin, M.D.

ACCESSING PROPER TREATMENT

Researchers at the University of California at Los Angeles (UCLA) studied a group of Americans with probable depression or anxiety symptoms and found that only 30 percent received proper treatment, such as medication or counseling.

Proper treatment was even more unlikely among Blacks and Hispanics than Whites and less likely still among men than women. Furthermore, proper treatment was less likely among adults under thirty years and over sixty years of age. The study revealed that the people who had severe enough depression and/or anxiety to interfere with their enjoyment of life and the ability to function in work, love, or play did not usually receive it, although they would have benefited from appropriate treatment of these symptoms. The statistics of the study revealed that 83 percent of the people with probable depressive illness did see a health care provider, but only 30 percent received what the report called "proper" treatment.

Why are such poor results tolerated for a *treatable* mental illness? Could it be that health care professionals do not recognize the symptoms of depression? Or, could it be that the symptoms were acknowledged by the health care professional but the diagnosis used for treatment was incorrect? Perhaps both the clinician and the patient believed that the symptoms were due to a "normal" reaction to sad or tragic life experiences? The fact is that all three of these explanations are correct in many cases.

To put things into perspective, I would like to pose an analogy to a patient of a family practitioner, internist, or general surgeon. Can you imagine any one of these specialists accepting a 30 percent recovery rate for any of his patients with acute appendicitis or pneumonia? This would mean that 70 percent of his patients would have either a poor outcome or even death. This would be totally unacceptable to the patient with pneumonia or appendicitis, his family, and his physician. Why should these statistics be any more acceptable for a depressed patient or a patient with anxiety or an addiction that could present with depression or anxiety? Should it be acceptable for individuals struggling with alcoholism or chemical addiction that both have correlation with primary or secondary depression and anxiety?

The simple answer is that it isn't any more acceptable for a depressed patient or a person with anxiety or a substance-abuse problem with those symptoms to receive the wrong diagnosis or the wrong treatment. There is no acceptable excuse, but I will offer a few possible explanations.

First, there is an enormous difference between the diagnostic techniques used by the physicians practicing medical and surgical specialties, and physicians practicing psychiatry or a psychologist practicing behavior modification, cognitive-insight therapy, or doing psychological testing. The medical and surgical physicians make a diagnosis based on information gathered from a history of the patient's physical symptoms. Then he does a physical examination, laboratory tests, x-rays, EKGs, ultrasound, or even exploratory surgery and other invasive tests until there is a diagnosis based on objective physical findings. The psychiatrist and psychologist make a diagnosis entirely on the patient's subjective symptoms and objective behavior.

In the past there were no physical or laboratory tests of any kind, with the possible exception of psychological testing, which is also based on the patient's symptoms and behavior. A psychiatric or psychological diagnosis is a symptom-driven diagnosis with no objective physical or laboratory findings. Medical and surgical physicians prove their preliminary diagnosis after physical examinations, laboratory tests, and other objective testings single out a final diagnosis from what was originally a Differential Diagnosis. In the past, if a psychiatrist or a psychologist was treating a mental patient for psychiatric or psychological symptoms and abnormal behavior and it was discovered that there was an organic cause or etiology for his symptoms (brain tumor or brain stroke), or a behavior that was treatable (psychomotor seizures or normal pressure hydrocephalus), he would have ethically discharged that patient to a medical or surgical physician for a definitive physical treatment.

Another example in this category would be Syphilis. In the early half of the twentieth century Syphilis was diagnosed by its symptoms and characteristic behavior (in tertiary phase there were physical symptoms like tabes dorsalis, dementia, or aortic aneurysm). Later it was discovered that the spirochete bacteria was the unequivocal cause of Syphilis and the spirochete could be found in the blood stream or spinal fluid and that penicillin was an effective cure for the disease. The psychiatrist or psychologist would feel obliged to transfer that patient to a medical physician for treatment. Today, the psychiatrist might be requested to continue treating the patient for his psychiatric symptoms because, even if cured, the psychiatric symptoms caused by having had Syphilis may persist (delusions or paranoid hallucinations).

Second, in the historical past, and even now, the negative and condescending attitudes of medical and surgical physicians toward psychiatric physicians and psychologists and their patients interfered with their ability to correctly diagnose these individuals. At that time there wasn't any definitive diagnosis or treatment, or medications for psychiatric patients, and they were warehoused in insane asylums, lunatic houses, or prisons without much hope of ever being cured or released. Even today, patients with depression and/or anxiety symptoms are frequently unwilling to see a psychiatrist or a psychologist because they feel it will stigmatize them. Never mind that they are frequently suffering from a debilitating, miserable disease and are even suicidal and that their suffering can be relieved. Perhaps this fear of being labeled as depressed or anxious by a psychiatric physician or a psychologist is what made them prefer to see a medical or surgical physician hoping against hope that they had a physical illness causing their psychiatric or psychological symptoms. It may even be that their reluctance to seek psychiatric treatment may be the cause of the unacceptably low 30 percent recovery rate. The fault is not always the patient's. Their medical or surgical physician should know that there are marked changes in the fields of psychiatry and psychology and the dismal outcomes of yesterday are no longer the rule today.

Third, the fate of the Dual-Diagnosis or Triple-Diagnosis patient is no doubt the most ominous of all unless there is psychiatric or psychological input into their diagnosis and treatment. Without a mental health professional's expertise in diagnosing and treating a Dual- or Triple Diagnosed patient, his illness is like a millstone around his neck.

Many medical and surgical illnesses including alcoholism and other addictions masquerade or mimic psychiatric and psychological illness. The reverse is also true. Many psychiatric and psychological illnesses also masquerade or mimic medical or surgical illnesses (physical factitious disorders and conversion disorders to mention two of many), alcoholism, and other addictions. In the Dual- or Triple-Diagnosis patients there often must be medical and surgical physicians on the treatment team along with psychiatrists and psychologists. It is necessary that they work together or, tragically, some or all of a Dual- or Triple Diagnoses may be missed.

Fourth, alcohol and drug dependence also frequently mimic or masquerade as a psychiatric or psychological illness. The reverse is also frequently true. Therefore, the alcoholics and drug addicts usually start their life without mental illness, but their drinking or drug use frequently leads to symptoms of mental illness. On the other hand, many people with mental disorders or personality disorders try to self-medicate a preexisting anxiety or depressive symptoms of their mental illness or personality disorder with alcohol or addicting drugs. They then develop a coexisting alcohol or drug problem along with their mental illness or personality disorder. For instance, people with manic-depressive disorder use alcohol or drugs to bring themselves down from a manic high and many use addictive stimulants like amphetamines or cocaine to try to relieve their depression. It may even work for a while until they become addicted to the alcohol and/or drugs. Other patients with panic disorder or generalized anxiety disordered discovered that while they were experimenting with alcohol during their youth it miraculously relieved their symptoms of panic or anxiety. They happily continued to self-medicate to relieve their anxiety symptoms but soon discovered they needed to increase their daily dosage of alcohol or drugs to obtain the same effect. The result was inevitable addiction. Now when they try to stop drinking they discover that the withdrawal symptoms from alcohol include anxiety with tremor, sweats, and chills and, in some cases, even panic attacks. Now, instead of the alcohol or drug relieving their anxiety, it produces even more anxiety symptoms than they had before they started to drink or use—especially during the alcohol or drug withdrawal. There may also be a deterioration of personality as a result of alcoholism or drug addiction. They may have started out life with normal personalities, but because of damage to their brains from the chronic effects of alcohol or drugs there has been a personality change. These changes may be reversible or irreversible. These diagnoses should be recorded, according to *DSM-IV* guidelines, as Personality Change Due to Alcohol (or drug) Dependence *DSM-IV* (310.1) under Axis I, or as Alcohol or Drug Related Disorder not otherwise specified *DSM-IV* (291.9), also under Axis I.

Fifth, the older concept of having a reactive depression gave many individuals who were suffering from a severe depression a false hope of having a spontaneous recovery over time. The theory was that a reactive depression was "normal" and that it was the result of a personal loss either through death, financial problems, personal tragedy, family problem, or other similar situation causing substantial grief. It was believed that these "griefs," like bereavement, would clear slowly but spontaneously resolve themselves over a two- to six-month period of time and usually without psychotherapy or medication. The primary care physician would usually treat this type of patient with reassurance and a tranquilizer, usually a benzodiazepine. If the traumatic experience occurred in childhood, it is believed to result in a personality disorder such as a depressive personality disorder, dysthymia, or obsessive-compulsive disorder. If the traumatic experience occurred in adulthood it could cause a mental illness such as postraumatic stress disorder or acute stress disorder with depression as one of its many symptoms. In the past, a depression caused by a traumatic event was usually diagnosed as a reactive depression. It is because of this implication, that recovery is more or less spontaneous without specific diagnosis or treatment, that the term reactive depression is no longer in vogue. Likewise, the term endogenous depression is no longer used because it was too limiting, although it was a beneficial term because it implied that the depression was an inherited or genetic illness. Today, the preferred term for a severe depression is mood disorder or major affective disorder and includes major depression, manic-depressive disorder, dysthymic disorder, cyclothymic disorder, and similar mood disturbances. Many of the mood disturbances have been proven to be on a genetic basis, but the primary change in thinking is that prolonged stress caused by any stressful situations can evolve into a major affective disorder, especially in genetically vulnerable people. Therefore, an individual with a traumatic memory from childhood, such as rape or incest, can, in time, develop major depression. Likewise, an adult constantly exposed to stress from physical and/or mental trauma can develop major depression. The theory behind this phenomenon is that prolonged stress and sadness exhausts the individual's brain neuro-hormones (serotonin and norepienephrine) and produces a major depression. Some genetic or familial predisposition to depression is also considered a factor. This secondary depression can evolve into depressive symptoms that often are considered clinically indistinguishable from major affective disorder.

Of the five theories given above to explain the resistance of the patient and the psychiatrically untrained physician from embracing any psychiatric diagnosis is the basic difference between the mental process that each specialty goes through to make his or her diagnosis. Since the time of Hypocrites, medical or surgical physicians depended on the history of the illness, the patient's symptoms, the findings from the physical examination, and laboratory and x-ray findings to come up with a final diagnosis. The psychiatrist and the psychologist do not have these objective findings and laboratory tests to help them with their diagnosis. Instead, they must depend on the subjective symptoms of the patient and the psychologist's or psychiatrist's own objective evaluation of the patient's behavior. This means that for the psychiatrist and the psychologist their diagnosis is primarily symptom-driven, while for the medical and surgical physicians their diagnosis is primarily physical-driven. A psychiatric or psychological treatment plan is based primarily on the patient's symptoms, and the medical and surgical physician's treatment plan is based primarily on physical findings and a conclusion about the underlying cause or etiology of that illness. This makes a tremendous difference. The medical and surgical physician's treatment is directed primarily toward one physical finding and the underlying cause of the illness. The psychiatric and psychological diagnosis and treatment is based primarily on the patient's symptoms and his behavior. This is a necessary but tremendously different approach. If a psychiatrist treats the subjective symptom of hallucinations he will use an antipsychotic medication like haloperidol (Haldol) to relieve the distortions of reality symptoms, regardless if it is being caused by a brain tumor, schizophrenia, alcohol withdrawal, psychic trauma, medication reaction, mania, or psychotic depression. Of course, the psychiatrist will need a neurosurgeon to treat the brain tumor, detoxification medication to treat the alcohol withdrawal, knowledge of the side effects of the different medications that might be causing the hallucinations, psychotherapy for the psychic trauma, lithium for the mania, and antidepressants as well as antipsychotic medication to treat the psychotic aspect of the depression.

There are two exceptions in the above list of examples. The brain tumor will be diagnosed with an x-ray and removed by a neurosurgeon, the alcoholism will be diagnosed by a variety of laboratory tests, including a blood alcohol test, as well as the patient's subjective and objective symptoms. In other words, the psychiatrist and the psychologist treat the symptoms, and a medical physician and the surgeon treats the underlying cause or etiology. Of course, all physicians will treat the pain with analgesics while they are also treating the underlying cause of the pain. This is also true of psychiatrists, but they will not usually use analgesics because a psychiatric patient's pain is not usually physical, although the discomfort and suffering may be just as severe.

Finally, I would like to say that there are changes being made in this system. Many psychiatric diagnoses are being found to have a physical cause or etiology, and therefore diagnosis and treatment are slowly becoming more objectively based. However, the laboratory tests to prove neurohormonal imbalances are still in the research stage and many are based on laboratory animal experimentation. But progress is being made, and it is only a matter of time before objective laboratory tests will be available to prove the cause or etiology of a psychiatric diagnosis.

Now we will turn to the next and last four chapters to illustrate the practical application of these theories using the biographies and autobiography of four famous authors. The reader will see the failures in the brilliant lives of Edgar Allan Poe, F. Scott Fitzgerald, and John Berryman, and be able to compare them with the autobiography of Kay Redfield Jamison. The reader will observe a dramatic difference. Jamison's life would almost certainly have had the same tragic outcome if it weren't for the medications that were made available to her. She had the insight and the determination to follow her psychiatrist's modern treatment recommendations.

Mania, Melancholia, Morphine, and Mayhem: A Psychiatric Biography of Edgar Allan Poe

BIOGRAPHY

Edgar Allan Poe was born on January 19, 1809, in Boston, Massachusetts. He grew up in Richmond, Virginia and lived out a tremendously creative, but short and troubled life in half a dozen eastern cities, moving restlessly from place to place. He called himself a "Virginian," but his true home was always in the "misty mid region of Weir" of his own fertile and troubled imagination.

By profession and occupation, Poe was a magazine and newspaper editor for many different publications. He is best known as a brilliant, sensitive poet and writer of short fiction. Often referred to as the father of the detective story, he virtually created that form of writing and preferred the psychological thriller. He deserves more credit than any author for the transformation of the short story from anecdotal tale to work of masterful art. He also produced some of the most literary criticism of his time and important theoretical statements of poetry and the short story—and his critical, as well as creative work, has had a worldwide influence on literature. He was indeed a literary genius.

But Edgar Allan Poe had a dark side that is still shrouded in mystery. His unfortunate choice of the talented writer, Rufus Griswold, whom he thought a friend, as literary executor resulted in a distortion of the record that has clouded Poe's posthumous reputation. Proving himself a traitor to Poe, Griswold wrote a scathing obituary depicting him as a sadistic drug addict and alcoholic. This has led many to falsely consider Poe's personal life to be the origin of many of his own dark characters and has caused much to be written about Poe that is untrue. Diligent research has made available to us a body of accurate information about Poe's life and times, information about his developmental history and adult behavior sufficient to the task of psychiatric evaluation. Although such an evaluation is of necessity posthumous and couched in current psychiatric terminology, the data available are sufficiently extensive and substantial to permit a fair and accurate psychiatric and substance-abuse diagnosis, certainly one better informed and more accurate than that of anecdote and legend.

We will start with the history of his occupational and social life after completion of his formal education of one year of college at the University of Virginia, and less than one year at the United States Military Academy at West Point, which was preceded by slightly less than two years in the U.S. Army.

Poe's foster parents, Mr. and Mrs. John Allan of Richmond, who had originally planned formally to adopt Edgar—though they later declined to do so—had given the boy a first class education in private schools both in the United States and abroad in England and Scotland. But Mr. Allan, a wealthy, though not extravagant businessman in Richmond, definitely did not approve of the drinking and gambling way of life that marked Poe's first year of college at the University of Virginia. Never too generous with spending money for Edgar, Allan forced his withdrawal from the university, though the boy's grades had been very good, by refusing to pay his debts and living expenses. Allan tried to get Poe to work in his business, but Poe rejected employment as a "bean counter." As a consequence he was forced to leave the Allan home without money or prospects. He tried to support himself by enlisting in the U.S. Army but disliked army life and at length prevailed upon Allan to buy out his discharge. He next secured an appointment to West Point but disliked military life there as well and managed to get himself court-martialed and dismissed by cutting classes and military exercises after Allan absolutely declined to assist him any further.

Poe moved to Baltimore to live with a paternal aunt, Mrs. Maria Poe Clemm, without money or job. There he began his career as a writer and editor and was—more or less—regularly paid. He had earlier published two little volumes of poetry and would come out with a third.

At age eighteen he published *Tamerlane and Other Poems*, at twenty, a second book, *Al Aaraaf, Tamerlane and Minor Poems*, and a third, *Poems by Edgar Allan Poe, Second Edition*.

While living with his aunt in Baltimore, Poe also began writing prose tales, five of which appeared in 1832 in the *Philadelphia Saturday Courier*. Continuing his writing career, Poe's fearless literary reviews and sensational tales made him widely known as an author. He failed to find a publisher for a volume of burlesques, *Tales of the Folio Club*, but in July 1838, Harpers Publishing Company printed his book-length narrative, *Arthur Gordon Pym*.

Meanwhile, Poe had taken his first job as an editor, working for Thomas W. White of the *Saturday Literary Messenger*, beginning with the December issue of 1835 and holding the position until January 1837. He was editor of Burton's *Gentleman's Magazine* from July 1839 to June 1840, and *Graham's Magazine* from April 1841 to May 1842. In 1840, Poe's *Tales of the Grotesque and Arabesque* was published in two volumes in Philadelphia.

Poe married his young thirteen-year-old cousin, Virginia Clemm, in Richmond on May 16, 1836, to whom he had been betrothed since she was eight years old. In April 1844 with barely the means to move his family of three—himself, his wife, (Poe's first cousin) Virginia, and Virginia's mother (Poe's aunt), who lived with them, Poe went to New York, where he found work on the *Evening Mirror*.

The next year was a memorable one in Poe's life. He published, to spectacular success, his most famous poem, "The Raven," four of his most celebrated short stories, a volume of his tales and the first collected edition of his poetry in book form since 1831. In March of that year, he joined C. F. Briggs in an effort to publish *The Broadway Journal*, and finally became editor, and eventually a major contributor, and ultimately proprietor of that publication. Poe was enjoying a growing recognition of his literary work at home and abroad. The revision of his stories alone called for unremitting care, and for a time he carried on the *Broadway Journal* virtually alone. His recorded estimate that his working day lasted fifteen hours seems not exaggerated. Though in 1845, Wiley and Putnam issued *Tales by Edgar A. Poe* and *The Raven and Other Poems*,

Poe ended the year defeated and with no reward other than the consciousness of his widening fame. But that would not provide support for the little family group, and the worry about his wife's illness and decline faced him every day.

The next years were tragic ones for Poe. He rented a little cottage at Fordham, about fourteen miles from New York City, where he lived the last three years of his life in his very impoverished state. The *Broadway Journal* failed, his wife, Virginia, became ill and finally succumbed to tuberculosis on January 30, 1847.

After his wife's death, Poe seems to have yielded more often to a weakness for alcohol, one that had beset him at intervals since early manhood. His history indicates some relationship between alcohol and periods of incapacitating madness and marvelous creativity and longer periods of nonproductive melancholia—what would be called *major depression* in today's usage. Many have said that he was unable to take even a little alcohol without a change in personality, and any excess was accompanied by physical prostration. My interpretation of this recurrent and problematic illness of Poe's was that he was suffering from cyclic manic-depressive disorder and intermittent acute alcoholism. When his manic phase would first start, he would become magnificently creative; as the mania worsened, he would try to control it with alcohol. The combination could make it appear that he got disgustingly drunk on a drink or two, when in fact it was the combination of alcohol and mania that caused his disability. Throughout his life those illnesses combined to interfere with his success as an editor. They also earned him a reputation for intemperateness that he scarcely deserved.

Later, we will study a similar case in the poet John Berryman. Born a century later, when he went "crazy" from mania or became drunk from alcohol, Berryman wound up in a hospital, where he was "detoxified" with Sparine, a neuroleptic drug, meant to target his presumed alcoholism, which inadvertently treated his manic-depressive disorder, of which neither his doctor nor he was aware. Berryman would end up in a hospital for treatment of what was presumed to be acute alcoholism. Berryman would get well (or, at least improve), and would continue to take Sparine and Vivactil (an antidepressant) after discharge from the hospital, but, unfortunately, he did this irregularly. Thus, unknowingly he would "treat" his undiagnosed manic-depressive disorder.

Edgar Allan Poe was not so lucky. Drugs for his manic-depressive disorder had not yet been invented, and his manic-depressive disease was not even recognized or diagnosable as distinct from his supposed alcoholism, schizo-phrenia, or dementia.

Still, Poe grew better, revived his plan for a magazine, and began new projects. His energy was probably coming from a recurrence of the manic phase of his disorder. He was full of ambition, and he was becoming more and more grandiose.

In 1847, Poe began steady work on his "Eureka," a prose poem dealing with the universe. This work that was, to a certain extent, the climax of his creative life, to which he had devoted so much time and effort, is of great importance in his biography. An analysis of it will decide whether Poe's mind was weakening during his last years or whether it was clear, active, and still creative. For the true life of Poe lay in the mind of Poe. The "Eureka" work provides convincing evidence that Poe's mind was clear, his creative powers undiminished during his last years, unless his errors in theory of the creation suggest that Poe's mind was weakening during those last years. In the Preface to "Eureka," Poe said:

> To the few who love me and whom I love—to those who feel rather than to those who think—to the dreamers and those who put faith in dreams as in the only realities—I offer this Book of Truths, not in its char-acter of Truth-teller, but for the Beauty that abounds in its Truth, consti-tuting it true. To these I present the composition as an Art-Product alone:—let us say as a Romance; or, if I be not urging too lofty a claim, as a Poem.
>
> What I here propound is true:—therefore it cannot die:—or if by any means it is now trodden down so that it die, it will "rise again in the Life Everlasting." Nevertheless, it is a Poem only that I wish this work to be judged after I am dead.

Many of Poe's modern critics and commentators insist, despite Poe's explicit statement of intent, that "Eureka" be regarded and evaluated as a scientific treatise. The scientific ideas in "Eureka" are not the ravings of a maniac—though he suffered from a manic-depressive disease. Poe asked that the work be considered a poem. If the scientific ideas in "Eureka" are wild and incoherent, or were written without knowledge of what had been discovered in Poe's own day, the essay may be dismissed as unimportant so far as its thinking is concerned. If, on the other hand, it is based on accurate knowledge of the latest scientific discoveries of its *own time* then it is entitled, from that point of view, to respect. I do not believe that anyone would claim that Poe has solved the riddle of the creation and the destiny of the universe. From my perspective, I think his presentation confirms not that he was becoming demented, but that his grandiosity was getting out of control and this project was so grand that he was silencing the critics at the gate. He was saying it was a *prose poem* but was offering information that was scientific and he did not have the training to promote concepts for which there has never been proof. I can remember a few patients like this I had in my private psychiatric practice. One was a manic depressive who came to see me about hallucinations and started out saying he hated his teachers and previous psychiatrists because they did not understand that he had discovered the secret of quantum mechanics. There was no way that I could have or should have tried to prove him right or wrong. It would have only proven to him that I, too, did not understand quantum mechanics, and he would have been absolutely correct. The young man was a junior in undergraduate school at the University of Michigan majoring in mathematics.

It should be fair to say that to regard "Eureka" as an attempt to put forward a new physical theory, would be, by most if not all scientists, regarded as a crank-theory. (The trouble with cranks is not that they are not far-seeing, but that they have no appreciation of the immediate obstacles in the road.) Poe's more definite suggestions (in the contemporary state of science) were not unintelligent, but amateurish. But, as a *poem* on the significance of things, partially revealed in the state of science of the time, it showed a fine comprehension.

In 1848, Poe was not, as has been frequently suggested, entering into a period of mental decline. His mind was clear and his imaginative power was still capable of dealing with scientific problems that tax the best of modern thinkers. Just how far he might have developed his theories had he possessed adequate technical training in science we can only surmise. That "Eureka" produced little effect upon the science of its own day is not surprising. Its concepts were in most cases unusual, and the hospitality of science to unusual theories, especially those originating from men of letters, is not large.

And yet, ironically, for the ideas to be readily grasped, the general reader must have the help of a scientist in understanding the essay. Even when they are, the mysticism of the essay is forbidding to those who are realistically inclined. Poe's message is not to these, and yet, as A.S. Eddington says, "It is reasonable to inquire whether in the mystical illusions of man there is not a reflection of an underlying reality," may not be a commonplace sentiment among scientists.

Certainly, as a prose poem, "Eureka" rises to lofty heights. Poe's conception of the relations of God to man, of the Creator for the created, is one of the important steps taken during the nineteenth and twentieth centuries in that spiritual succession in which William Vaugn Moody and Eugene O'Neil and other artistic observers and writers were involved. When that spirituality is fully understood, then perhaps at last "Eureka" will come to be widely appreciated.

The whole project of "Eureka" makes it appear to me that Edgar Poe's manic-depressive disorder was getting worse as he got older, and this would be anticipated during this era of no diagnosis and no treatment. It may also explain why some individuals believed that he was becoming demented.

In his later years, Poe was interested in several women. They included the poet, Mrs. Sarah Helen Whitman and the widow, Mrs. Sarah Elmira Shelton, whom he had known in his boyhood and to whom he had been engaged to marry at one time in his youth. Just before he died of *delirium tremens* in a Baltimore Hospital after a head injury from a fall, he resumed an engagement with Mrs. Shelton. One of the unproven theories about Poe's death involves the three brothers of his fiancée, who feared that he was marrying their sister for her money. In his book, *Midnight Dreary,* an intriguing story about the mysterious death of Poe, John Evangelist Walsh concludes that the three brothers conspired to get Poe drunk and thus break his commitment to his fiancée that he would remain sober—a commitment he had sealed by joining the Men of Temperance Movement.

There is another unproven scenario that has Poe overhearing two men plotting to murder him while they were all on a train to Baltimore. In this account, Poe is said to have claimed that a normal person would not have heard the men whisper but that his hearing was abnormally acute. This claim, if truly made, suggests grandiosity and paranoia and also suggests the hyper-acoustica often noted in alcohol or sedative withdrawal (but this is more to noise than the spoken word). We are told that Poe exited the train in Baltimore to escape the men and exchanged his fashionable clothing for cheap workman's garb in an attempt to disguise himself. He then proceeded to visit a Baltimore friend, Mr. John Sartain. To complete his disguise he asked Sartain to shave off his mustache. Mr. Sartain also said that Mr. Poe was somewhat suicidal that night, but in the morning he left his friend's house in a good mood. This scenario ends with the three Roysters, brothers to Mrs. Shelton, discovering Mr. Poe despite his disguise and forcing him to drink a large quantity of alcohol. Their plan was to cause a rift between their sister and Poe, ending the engagement. They had not anticipated Poe's developing DTs as a result of the forced drinking and the exacerbated pain from the head injury that caused his death in the hospital. Many of the facts of Poe's fateful last night are unknown.

DEVELOPMENTAL AND EDUCATIONAL HISTORY

Though Edgar Allan Poe proved to be a genius, he still suffered from the absence of adequate parental figures and from not achieving the necessary resolution of normal developmental learning experiences. He had a difficult start in life: his mother died before he was three years old and by that time his father had either died or "disappeared." Little Edgar did not have an opportunity to resolve basic issues of trust and mistrust, nor to develop a sense of control over his life. His basic personality therefore was rife with anxiety, shame, guilt, and fear. Throughout his life he would also have problems with interpersonal relationships and intimacy. During the crucial first five years of life, he lacked a healthy father figure or a figure of authority to help him develop a sense of competition with important people in his life including viable intimate relationships. His foster father, Mr. John Allan, who didn't have children of his own, tried mightily to correct and control what he saw as little Edgar's disobedient behavior. Poe needed affection and understanding—perhaps a skilled brand of tough love—instead of warnings and threats. When these failed, he resorted to demeaning Edgar for his Irish ancestry and for the low social status of his birth parents as actors. Edgar had "bad blood" and was inferior by inheritance, an attitude commonly held by the "proper citizens" of that era. John Allan had intended and had promised to adopt Edgar, but he eventually called it off because of the youth's gambling and drinking. He even refused Poe the use of the Allan family name except as a middle name.

His search for a father figure included his school masters in grade school in Scotland and England, his grade school in Richmond, and the English and

Classical School of Joseph H. Clarke, followed by William Burke, also in Richmond, as well as at the University of Richmond, the U. S. Army, and at the West Point Military Academy. He never found the authority figure or role model for whom he was searching.

In all cases, Poe would start by idealizing his superiors and then testing their love for him by involving himself in some overt misbehavior regarding institutional rules and regulations. Allan had good grounds for his considerable financial investment in the youth. One of Edgar's English schoolmasters, the Reverend John Barnsby, praised Edgar highly, stating that when the child left he could speak French fluently and read Latin with ease, and that he was far better acquainted with history and literature than were any of the other boys in his classes. In the United States the boy's education was continued at prestigious establishments and, at the age of seventeen, he was admitted to the University of Virginia, unluckily into a student body far more socially than academically inclined. The young men drank too much, gambled too much, fought for the sheer enjoyment of violence, and rampaged over the campus at all hours. In this worst of all possible environments for a young man with Poe's unstable temperament and his predisposition to family inebriety and genetic manic-depressive disorder, he immediately began to get involved in spending money extravagantly and gambling recklessly, incurring debts worthy of any potential manic that he could not begin to repay. He had to beg John Allan to make good his indebtedness. Allan reluctantly did so, but warned Poe that he would not continue to support him at the university. At this time Poe was reported to be unusually susceptible to alcohol. One mild drink was said to put him into a state of wild excitement. The question is whether this was the beginning of a manic episode precipitated by alcohol, or in association with alcohol, or whether the alcohol was dissolving his conscience (superego) and making him feel invincible. Either is possible. Poe sustained financial humiliation, and the fact that he was a genius who viewed himself as an aristocrat became harder and harder to reconcile with his actual condition as the foster child of an aristocrat, and one not too favorably disposed toward him by this time. Many viewed John Allan as abusive toward Edgar; others saw him as a strong authoritarian. Whatever Allan's personality and conduct, it was extremely detrimental to Poe. He left both the university and family home in Virginia and went to Boston.

Poe did try to overcome his dependence upon his foster father by joining the U. S. Army, but eventually failed and again with financial help from Allan, he bought his way out of the Army and with Allan's help enrolled in the Military Academy at West Point. There he was court-martialed and expelled for failure to be present at classes and on parade.

Edgar Allan Poe never reduced to thinking of himself as anything but an aristocrat when at home or when away at school. John Allan willingly supported him in these schools until Edgar went to the University of Virginia when he was seventeen years old. Mr. Allan would not pay off Edgar's indebtedness until Edgar was forced to beg him to do so. It was unfortunate that the university was only one year old at the time and the student body was more social than academic. This was the worst possible environment for young Poe with his emotionally unstable temperament.

FAMILY HISTORY

Edgar Allan Poe's paternal grandfather was David Poe. He was born in Ireland about 1743 and died on October 17, 1816, in Baltimore, Maryland. He married Elizabeth Cairnes, born in Lancaster County, Pennsylvania somewhere about 1756. Of their seven surviving children, one was David Poe, Jr., Edgar's father. He was born on July 18, 1784. David's six siblings were John Hancock, William, George Washington, Samuel, Maria, and Elizabeth.

Elizabeth Cairnes Poe, like her husband, was energetic and patriotic. David Poe, Jr. married Elizabeth Arnold Hopkins in 1806, and they had three children: William Henry, born January 30, 1807, in Boston; Edgar, born on January 19, 1809; and Rosalie born on December 20, 1810. It is important to note that Maria, daughter of David Poe, Sr., born on March 17, 1790, married William Clemm, Jr. on July 12, 1817. They had three children: Henry, born Sept 10, 1818; Virginia Marie, born August 22, 1820, and buried November 5, 1822; and Virginia Eliza, who was born August 15, 1822, and died on January 30, 1847. It was this last born cousin, Virginia, who was to become Edgar Allan Poe's wife, at the age of thirteen.

There were three hereditary or familial illnesses in the family. David Poe, Jr. (Edgar Poe's father) had severe alcoholism and Elizabeth Poe (his mother) had tuberculosis (consumption) that caused her premature death. Also, Edgar's first cousin and future wife, Virginia Eliza Clemm had tuberculosis. Edgar's older brother and younger sister both had some type of undiagnosed mental illness.

Poe's mother, Elizabeth Arnold Poe, was a precocious actress. She started to take adult roles at the age of nine and could play the roles of the leading lady in three plays running in repertory. This degree of energy and extroversion does suggest a level of brilliance that would be compatible with the possibility of her having a manic-depressive disorder that Edgar Poe might have inherited. We know that on the opening night at the Portland Theatre, November 25, 1797, she played Biddy Bellair in Garrick's farce, *Miss In Her Teens*. To sustain this leading part she had to flirt with three lovers, a role calling for dexterity that seems extraordinary. Of her performance it was written, "Miss Arnold, as Miss Biddy, exceeded all praise. Although Miss Arnold is only nine years old, her powers as an actress would do credit to any of her sex of maturer age." There was evidently a spark of genius in that sprite-like figure and her courage as well as her charm descended to her son Edgar. We do know that her Grandfather Arnold was a Major General in the Revolutionary Army as a patriot and served with recognized distinction. Edgar's father David Poe, Jr. was also an actor, though much less talented than his wife. He was described as being very handsome and charming, as well as an alcoholic. History does not record how he lived or died, which was before Edgar was three. Mrs. John Allan, wife of a wealthy Virginia businessman learned of the boy's condition and persuaded her husband to take Edgar into their care, with the intention of eventual adoption. His older sibling, William Henry, was placed with his paternal grandfather, David. He had some minor success as a writer and is known to have died from some mental disorder. Another acquaintance, Mrs. William MacKenzie, took Rosalie to raise. Rosalie also had some mental disease that inhibited her mental growth after twelve years of age.

Clearly, Edgar was born into a family that displayed strengths and weakness in all its members through several generations. The boy, who won lasting fame as a poet and writer, also continued his family's struggles with illness, both mental and physical. Tuberculosis, a contagious disease, deprived him of his young wife and cousin, and manic-depressive symptoms were not strangers in his ancestry, nor was alcoholism. Genius came to full bloom in him, but hints of it can also be found in his forbears, in his actress mother, for example.

Edgar Allan Poe's destiny was to some extent determined by his genes and his changing environment. For instance, his genius had an influence on his manic-depressive disorder and his manic-depressive disorder fed, distorted, and inhibited his creative genius. His biological father's alcoholism gave him a predisposition to a conduct disorder or at least an unusual sensitivity to alcohol. Having inherited these strengths and weaknesses from his biological parents, their premature deaths before he was three years of age completed the separation from his two biological siblings and threw him totally into the hands of his businessman foster father who was a disciplinarian par excellence. It is hard to imagine a more incompatible father-son relationship—a controlling, authoritarian father and a creative, freethinking son.

MARITAL HISTORY

As noted above, Virginia Eliza Clemm, was a first cousin of Edgar Poe. He was betrothed to Virginia Eliza when she was just eight years old, with full permission of her mother, Poe's aunt. When Virginia was thirteen, Mrs. Clemm signed an affidavit falsifying the girl's age in order to get a marriage license. They were married on May 15, 1836, when Edgar A. Poe and Thomas W. Cleland filed a marriage bond in the office of the Clerk of the Husting Court for the City of Richmond, in connection with the marriage of Edgar Poe and Virginia Clemm. Mr. Cleland also signed an affidavit that Virginia "was the full age of twenty-one years," while, of course, she was not quite fourteen. The Reverend Amasa Converse, a Presbyterian minister who apparently asked no questions, performed the ceremony in the evening of the same day at a Mrs. Yarrington's house. Poe and his bride spent a brief honeymoon at Petersburg, Virginia. This ceremony seems to be the best evidence that no secret marriage took place in 1835 as previously written above and as historically rumored.

The rumor was that these two had previously been married on September 2, 1835, in a secret marriage performed at Old Christ Church in Baltimore by Reverend John Johns, DD, who later became Protestant Episcopal Bishop of Virginia. Eugene L. Didier writes that the very next day after the marriage ceremony, Poe went to Richmond and did not see his darling for a year, when she and her mother joined him in Richmond. Poe's supposed two marriages to Virginia Clemm have generated many questions and speculation. His first rumored marriage to Virginia on September 2, 1835, has never been substantiated by any church marriage records and the affidavit attesting to Virginia's age can substantiate the marriage ceremony performed on May 15, 1836. Perhaps the following letter may be helpful in understanding Poe's motivation in regard to this marriage:

Aug. 29, 1835

My dearest Aunty,

I am blinded with tears while writing this letter—I have no wish to live another hour. Amid sorrow, and the deepest anxiety your letter reached [me]—and you well know how little I am able to bear up under the pressure of grief—My last, my last, my only hold on life is cruelly torn away—I have no desire to live and will not. But let my duty be done. I love, you know I love Virginia passionately, devotedly. I cannot express in words the fervent devotion I feel towards my dear little cousin—my own darling. But what can [I] say. Oh think for me for I am incapable of thinking. All [my] thoughts are occupied with the supposition that both you & she will prefer to go with N. Poe; I do sincerely believe that your comforts will for the present be secured— I cannot speak as regards your peace—your happiness. You have both tender hearts— and you will always have the reflection that my agony is more than I can bear—that you have driven me to the grave—for love like mine can never be gotten over. It is useless to disguise the truth that when Virginia goes with N.P. that I shall never behold her again—that is absolutely sure. Pity me, my dear Aunty, pity me. I have no one now to fly to—I am among strangers, and my wretchedness is more than I can bear. It is useless to expect advice from me—what can I say? Can I, in honour & truth say Virginia! Do not go!—do not go where you can be comfortable & perhaps happy— and on the other hand can I calmly resign my—life itself. If she truly loved me would she not have rejected the offer with scorn? Oh God have mercy on me! If she goes with N.P. what are you to do, my own Aunty?

I had procured a sweet little house in a retired situation on Church hill—newly done up and with a large garden and [ever]ly convenience—at only $5 per month. I have been dreaming every day & night since of the rapture I should feel in [seeing] my only friends—all I love on Earth with me there; the pride I would take in making you both comfor[table] & in calling her my wife. But the dream is over [G]od have mercy on me. What have I to live for? Among strangers with not one soul to love me.

The situation has this morning been conferred upon another, Branch T. Saunders, but White has engaged to make my salary $60 a month, and we could live in comparative comfort & happiness—even the $4 a week I am now paying for board would support us all—but I shall have $15 a week & what need would we have for more? I had thought to send you on a little money every week until you could either hear from Hall or Wm. Poe, and then we could get [a little] furniture for a start—for White will be able [to] [a]dvance any. After that all would go well—or I would make a desperate exertion & try to borrow enough for that purpose. There is little danger of *the house being taken immediately. I would send you $5 now—for White paid me the $8 2 days since—but you appear not to have received my last letter and I am afraid to trust it to the mail, as the letters are continually robbed. I have it for you & will keep it until I hear from you when I will send it & more if I get any in the meantime. I wrote you that Wm. Poe had written to me concerning you which I answered. He will beyond doubt aid you shortly & with an effectual aid. Trust in god.*

The tone of your letter wounds me to the soul—Oh Aunty, Aunty you loved me once—how can you be so cruel now? You speak of Virginia acquiring accomplishments, and entering into society—you speak in so worldly a tone. Are you sure she would be more happy—Do you think any one could love her more dearly than I could? She will have far—very far better opportunity of entering into society here than with N.P. Every one here receives me with open arms.

Adieu my dear Aunty. I cannot advise you. Ask Virginia. Leave it to her. Let me have, under her own hand, a letter, bidding me good bye—forever—and I may die—my heart will break—but I will say no more. Kiss her for me—a million times.
E.A.P.

For Virginia,
My love, my own sweet Sissy, my darling little wifey, think well before you break the heart of your cousin Eddy.

[Illegible. Probably "Dear Aunty,"] *I open this letter to inclose* [sic] *the 5$— I have just received another letter from you announcing the rec't of mine. My heart bleeds for you. Dearest Aunty consider my happiness while you are thinking about your own. I am saving all I can. The only money I have yet spent is 50 cts for washing— I have now 2.25 left. I will shortly send you more. Write immediately. I shall be all anxiety and dread until I hear from you. Try and convince my dear Virg'a. How devotedly I love her. I wish you would get me the Republican wh[ich] noticed the Messenger & send it on immediately by mail. God bless & protect you both.*

These letters from Poe to his aunt and cousin illustrate just how bizarre the relationship among these three people seems to have been. Although females at this time entered marriage in the United States, at least in some regions at relatively young ages, to be betrothed at age eight years and married at thirteen years has to be unusual. Then for Edgar, the very next day after the marriage, to leave the area for a year seems unexplainable even if indeed there was a "secret" marriage. This seems even more bizarre when you consider what amount of begging Edgar did to bring the marriage off in the first place. I suppose alcohol could have played a role in this unusual arrangement but their separation for a year does not seem to make any sense for either party. Certainly Edgar's pleading letter on August 29, 1835, just four days before the "secret" marriage when he was in such a state of poverty makes it even harder to understand. I can understand Mrs. Clemm's motivation, to some extent, because Virginia had "consumption" and needed someone to care for her. With a marriage, Poe's responsibility for Virginia (and her mother) would pass from voluntary assistance to an obligation. And Edgar was an interesting, handsome, and educated man and known to be a genius in his work as a poet, fictionist, editor, and literary critic, so it was also understandable that an alliance would be favored. But how Edgar could put the pressure on these two people to bring about this marriage can only be understood if you consider a *personality disorder* or *personality disorders* in Edgar. This topic will be discussed in the Psychiatric Formulation that follows. Here, I will suggest that his behavior is explainable on the basis of what today would be called a mixed personality disorder consisting of a *narcissistic, dependent,* and *obsessive-compulsive personality.* Edgar's needs came first because of his grandiose sense of self-importance and his need to have total control in his interpersonal relationships and his inability to compete in intimate relationships. These were caused by the developmental interference occurring during the first five years of his life when he was living through the Freudian Oral Stage, Anal Stage, and Oedipal Stage. The "normal" child being raised by adequate parents learns basic trust, control, and competition during these first five years. Instead, Poe learned mistrust, doubt about his ability to control, and fear of competition during his first five years of life.

Poe's first engagement to be married, one that occurred when he was seventeen years old and before he went to the University of Virginia, was to a woman named Elmira Royster. Elmira's family objected to the engagement and blocked letters and any communication between the two while Poe was at the University of Virginia. Each of them thought the other had lost interest and this ended in Elmira eventually marrying a man named Shelton. After Poe's young wife had died and after Shelton died, leaving Elmira a wealthy woman, Poe began courting her again and not long before his death in 1849, they were again engaged to be married. One scenario about the cause of Edgar's death that holds some measure of credibility, has Elmira's three brothers bringing about Edgar's death inadvertently, as a result of their determination to prevent the marriage.

Mrs. Sarah Helen Whitman, a widow living in Providence, Rhode Island, knew him in both his loftiest and weakest moods. They became engaged, and their love story was broken in a manner painful to both. Poe's distress, according to his own account, led him to attempt suicide. Yet, although Mrs. Whitman broke the engagement, she defended him at all times, and, in 1860, she wrote the first book in his defense that still remains not only a convincing personal tribute but also one of the most sympathetic and brilliant interpretations of his poetry and fiction.

Apparently, he ended his life having been married only once, but had at least three, if not four, other engagements that were all broken off. Was it his *alcoholism* or his *personality disorder* that caused these broken engagements? Or, could it have been his presumed manic-depressive disorder that went untreated and left him with mood swings that are as hard to live with as alcoholism and personality disorders?

Edgar Allan Poe never had any children.

MEDICAL HISTORY

Poe's biography indicates that, from the physical point of view, he enjoyed good health all of his short life; his illnesses were from alcoholism and a psychiatric disorder that will be covered in the next two sections of this account. In personal appearance he was slightly built, five feet, eight inches tall, and was a quiet, timid-looking, handsome man. His mouth was considered beautiful. His eyes, with long dark lashes, were hazel gray. He had no difficulty doing the training and maneuvers in the U.S. Army and as a cadet at West Point. He did have a chronic ear infection at one time but this was not known to have resulted in a hearing problem. There was one episode of hyper-accoustica whereby his hearing was unusually acute and allowed him to hear other passengers' conversation on the train. Was this from alcohol withdrawal and/or hallucinations, from *delirium tremens*, or from hallucinations resulting from a manic psychosis from manic-depressive disorder?

ALCOHOL AND DRUG ABUSE HISTORY

That Poe had a weakness and a low tolerance for alcohol has been established beyond a shadow of a doubt. In the nineteenth century it was called "dissipation" or "inebriety," but it was exactly the same illness that is today called alcoholism. Not only did he have alcoholism but he suffered intermittently with the most lethal complication of alcoholism—*delirium tremens*, or DTs, and indeed it was in one such episode that Poe died, at the age of forty. This too, was reported but unproven. It could have been the result of a traumatic brain injury that was said to have occurred about the same time in his life and could have been mistaken for DTs. During his era, mortality from *delirium tremens* was 20 percent because there was no effective treatment. Today, it is still very serious but the mortality rate is much lower because of the availability of sedatives, minor tranquilizers, and anticonvulsants for use in detoxification and neuroleptic (antipsychotic) medication for the symptoms of psychosis.

Poe himself observed in a letter that he had inherited dissipation from his father, David Poe, who had a tendency toward instability due to liquor, which was a family failing. Exactly how much alcohol Poe drank is really not the issue. What is known is that when he drank alcohol he lost control of his behavior on some occasions. There is ample evidence that drunkenness in Poe sometimes occurred with bouts of very heavy drinking. At least sometimes, however, according to several sources, Poe was highly sensitive to alcohol and would "get drunk and go into a frenzy" with one or two drinks. There are just a few illnesses that can cause such a low tolerance for alcohol in humans such as Hodgkin's disease, dementia, and traumatic brain injury.

There is no history indicating that Poe had any of these illnesses (except a questionable head injury just before he died of DTs). Nor did he have any other chronic illness except the three I will be discussing below in my psychiatric formulation: personality disorders, alcoholism with complications of *delirium tremens*, and manic-depressive disorder. In my opinion, it was Poe's manic-depressive illness that accounts for the observation that he would sometimes seem to get drunk on very little alcohol during unsuccessful attempts to arrest the mania.

I believe Poe would start drinking when his mind would begin racing in the manic phase of the illness. His purpose in drinking was to try to abort the racing mind and the impending hallucinations he had learned to associate and expect at such moments. Many patients with manic-depressive disorder have tried this "treatment" with similar unsatisfactory results. So Poe's "frenzy" was a manifestation of mania in mental illness, and alcohol played very little part in those aberrations of thought (psychosis). This explanation does not mean that Poe was not also an alcoholic nor that he would not have developed alcoholism absent his manic depression. He was showing signs of alcoholism in his early school days and certainly when he was at the University of Virginia, in the U. S. Army, and while at West Point. What it does mean is that Poe had already experienced the "medicinal power" of alcohol so that when he began having mental problems as a result of manic-depressive disorder it was more or less natural for him to try to control the mania and the depression by self-medicating with alcohol.

Certainly, there was no way for him to understand the disease he was insidiously nurturing and inadvertently treating because it was not yet known or named. All mental illnesses at that time were grouped together under the term *insanity*, for which there was no hope of effective treatment or recovery. Today, we know that there is a relationship between the body's biochemistry and mental illness, and that proper medication can change the biochemistry and remove the symptoms of insanity.

For some, particularly those unfamiliar with the role of biochemistry in the cause and treatment of mania, depression, alcoholic hallucinations, secondary depression from alcoholism, insomnia, nightmares, and all of these same symptoms that can occur with traumatic brain injury, may find this explanation too much of a stretch to believe. However, those of us who have witnessed all of these clinical phenomena and have learned that the same neurohormones (mainly dopamine, norepinephrine, and serotonin), play a role in the manifestation of all of them, feel strongly that the relationship is demonstrably established and that the theory is correct.

Hallucinations and delusions are figments of the imagination caused by too much or too little of the three neurohormones. Therefore, since alcoholism, mental illness, and traumatic brain injury can all involve an imbalance of the same three neurohormones, the symptoms of hallucinations and delusions of all three groups of illnesses can be "cured" if these neurohormones of the brain can be adjusted. Fortunately, today that is possible, as it was not before.

There were a few occasions when Poe tried *laudanum* (an opium narcotic) in an effort to treat his psychotic symptoms. He had a low tolerance for it, but there is no evidence that he was, at any time, addicted to the drug.

The reader will have a better understanding of the discussion above when we give an account of the Psychiatric History of Dr. Kay Redfield Jamison, who has written about her manic-depressive disorder and the treatment of it that has enabled her to lead a normal and productive life. She has had the advantage of modern medicine and an opportunity for the correct diagnosis of and treatment for her mental illness. The result has been that she has had a much better outcome than Poe and others had in previous times. She is leading a very successful life because of her treatment and her compliance with it.

PSYCHIATRIC HISTORY

A closer examination of Poe's psychiatric history from available documents explains behavior that frequently (and wrongly) was said to be due to alcohol. It is important to remember two facts about Poe: First, he was a literary critic and editor and in these two roles frequently made enemies of other poets and writers, some of whom resented adverse criticism and rejection of their work.

Secondly, Poe appointed Rufus W. Griswold to be his literary executor, believing him to be a trusted friend. Griswold did everything in his power to paint Poe as an insane drunk and a drug addict. At the same time, Griswold stole from and capitalized on Poe's literary creations, published and unpublished. I have therefore diligently pursued several biographies in an attempt to sort out the falsehoods from the truths as far as I possibly could. The evidence, only a fraction of which can be detailed here, persuades me that Poe did indeed have an undiagnosed manic-depressive disorder.

Mr. Miles George, Poe's classmate at the University of Virginia, wrote a letter on May 18, 1880, to E. V. Valentine that deals directly and clearly with a number of points about which there have been disputes in accounts of Poe's life:

Poe, as has been said, was fond of quoting poetic authors and reading poetic productions of his own, with which his friends were delighted & entertained, then suddenly change would come over him & he would, with a piece of charcoal, evince his versatile genius by sketching upon the walls of his dormitory, whimsical, fanciful, & grotesque figures, with such artistic skill, as to leave us in doubt whether Poe in future life would be a Painter or Poet. He was very excitable & restless, at times wayward, melancholic & morose, but again—in his better moods—frolicsome, full of fun & a most attractive & agreeable companion. To calm and quiet the excessive nervous excitability under which he labored, he would often put himself under the influence of that "Invisible Spirit of Wine" which the great Dramatist has said "If known by no other name should be called Devil."

Other symptoms of manic-depressive disorder include decreased need for sleep, continuous activity through the night and the preference for elegant or gaudy clothing, and these traits were certainly true of Edgar Allan Poe. Two newspapermen, Lambert Witmer and John H. Hewitt, categorically deny the stories concerning Poe's drinking. Since Witmer spoke of Poe's temperance later in Philadelphia, his testimony as to his friend's sobriety has some credibility. And his tribute to Poe's industry rings true: "He appeared to me to be one of the most hardworking men in the world. I call to see him at all hours, and always found him employed." His description of Poe's appearance at this time too helps in its implications: "I never saw him in any dress, which was not fashionably neat, with some approximation of elegance. Indeed I often wondered how he could contrive to equip himself so handsomely, considering that his pecuniary resources were generally scanty and precarious enough."

People with manic-depressive disorder usually have cyclic periods of mania, euphoria, and depression. This was certainly true of Edgar Poe. The following is an excerpt from a letter written to John P. Kennedy, a good friend, by Edgar Poe on September 11, 1835:

Excuse me, my dear Sir, if in this letter you find much incoherency. My feelings at this moment are pitiable indeed. I am suffering under a depression of spirits, such as I have never felt before. I have struggled in vain against the influence of this melancholy—You will believe me, when I say that I am still miserable in spite of a great improvement in my circumstances. I say you will believe me and for this simple reason, that a man writing for effect does not write thus. My heart is open before you—if it is worth reading, read it. I am wretched and know not why. Console me, —for you can. But let it be quickly—or it will be too late. Write me immediately. Convince me that it is worth one's while—that it is at all necessary to live, and you will prove yourself indeed my friend. Persuade me to do what is right. I do not mean this. I do not mean that you should consider what I write you a jest—oh, pity me! For I feel that my words are incoherent—but I will recover myself. You will not fail to see that I am suffering a depression of spirits which will (not fail to) ruin me should it be long continued. Write me then, and quickly. Urge me to do what is right. Your words will have more weight with me than words of others—for you were my friend when no else was. Fail not— as you value your peace of mind hereafter.

This letter to Kennedy is followed by one dated eight days later, in which Poe set forth rather composedly details about the publication of some of his stories. This understanding of Poe must take into account his duality. With the surface of his mind (neo-brain) he writes calmly about publication of his stories. Within his inner and deeper consciousness arising from the limbic system of the hypothalamus (old brain), he was fighting the most desperate conflict any man can face, the struggle for sanity. That this is so is even more evident when the reader observes that the letter above was written nine days after his rumored first marriage to Virginia, and thirteen days after the August 29, 1835, letter to Mrs. Clemm quoted above. He tells Kennedy that he does not know the cause of his wretchedness. The facts of his recent desperate plea, the attainment of his marriage if there was one, his immediate removal and departure—these can hardly have slipped his mind at this juncture, not to be assigned or denied as the cause of his depression.

Highly nervous natures like Poe need no cause for their unhappiness and he had reason enough for his. His brother's recent death through mental and physical exhaustion, and the reminder through his sister Rosalie's lack of mental growth of the heritage that was his, must have brought up over and over again the fear that one day he himself would pass over that line that divides the sane from the insane. Only those who have known such a fear, or who have been closely associated with those who have been subject to such terror, can appreciate the very real suffering Poe was experiencing in the drab surroundings of a cheap boarding house in Richmond. If at times he drank to relieve his cares, he did not do so from the love of liquor. He drank in order to reach a state of oblivion, to forget—for a short time—who and where he was. His physical condition had been weakened by privation and anxiety as well, and he could not throw off the dread that he might have been able to dismiss in earlier times. It must be remembered that in those days, sanity and insanity were final terms and the possibility of returning back across the line into mental health had hardly begun to be entertained. Furthermore, mental illness was viewed by many as either punishment for your sins, or the work of the devil, or the outcome of some inexplicable evil agency in which one bore some measure of guilty responsibility.

In a letter dated April 1, 1841, Poe gives to his friend, Dr. J. E. Snodgrass, what appears to be an honest, accurate description of his use of alcohol during his lifetime. It is especially noteworthy that he mentions his occasional use of alcohol for medicinal purpose:

It is, however, due to candor that I inform you upon what foundation Mr. Burton has erected his slanders. At no period of my life was I ever what men call intemperate. I never was in the habit of intoxication. I never drank drams, and so forth. But for a brief period, while I resided in Richmond, and edited *The Messenger* I certainly did give way, at long intervals, to the temptation held out on all sides by the spirit of Southern conviviality. My sensitive temperament could not stand an excitement which was an everyday matter to my companions. In short, it sometimes happened that I was completely intoxicated. For some days after each excess I was invariably confined to bed. But it is now quite four years since I have abandoned every kind of alcoholic drink—four years, with the exception of a single deviation which occurred shortly after my leaving Burton and when I was induced to resort to the occasional use of cider, with the hope of relieving a nervous attack.

On July 2, 1844, Poe wrote a letter to James Russell Lowell, a writer who had been assigned the task of producing a biography of Poe for *Graham's Magazine*, and in it Poe was able to identify in himself periods of mania and depression recurring in a cyclic fashion.

My Dear Mr. Lowell,

I can feel for the 'constitutional indolence of which you complain—for it is one of my own besetting sins. I am excessively slothful and wonderfully industrious by fits. There are epochs when any kind of mental exercise is torture, and when nothing yields me pleasure but solitary communion with the 'mountains and the woods'—the altars of Byron. I have thus rambled and dreamed away whole months, scribbled all day, read all night, so long as the disease endures. This is also the temperament of P. P. Cooke, of Virginia, the author of 'Florence Vane,' 'Young Rosalie Lee,' and some other sweet poems—and I should not be surprised if it were one of your own. Cooke writes and thinks as you—and I have been told that you resemble him personally.

These letters describe some symptoms of manic depression in three contemporary poets, well before Emil Kraepelin (1856–1926) attempted to sort out manic-depressive psychosis from schizophrenia and before psychiatry had given it a name.

Nathaniel T. Willis wrote many complimentary defenses of Poe, including one copied (with acknowledgement) from Dr. T. D. English's *Aristidean*, in a column headed "Notes from Men of Note":

> "He [Poe] never rests," the article said. "There is a small steam engine in his brain which not only sets the cerebral mass in motion, but keeps the owner in hot water. His face is a fine one, and well gifted with intellectual beauty."
>
> And Poe's letter to Frederick W. Thomas, dated May 4, 1845, says in part, "The fact is, that being selected, of late, with a fit of industry, I put so many irons in the fire all at once, that I have been quite unable to get them out. For the last three months I have been working fourteen or fifteen hours a day—hard at it all the time—so, whenever I took pen in hand to write, I found that I was neglecting something that *should be attended to*. I never knew what it was like to be a slave before."

Parenthetically, the above letter contains one of Poe's most striking epigrams: *"Man is now only more active—not more happy—not more wise, than he was 6,000 years ago."* Perhaps it is as true today as it was in 1844. That is a good description of a person in a hypomanic state or a fit of mania.

PSYCHIATRIC AND SUBSTANCE ABUSE FORMULATION

We will investigate four areas of aberrations in living—work, love, play, and creativity—that one could possibly expect given that Poe had a genius level intellect. These are: (1) Poe's personality traits and disorders from his traumatic environmental and developmental years; (2) the cause or etiology of any substance-abuse problem he may have had or the effect of the use of such substances on his life and illnesses; (3) the source of his severe mood disorder; (4) the relationship between creativity and intellect of all the three foregoing with his genius.

It is true that I am analyzing Poe's psychic aberrations 150 years after he died, and psychiatry was in its infancy during his lifetime. I believe, however, that with proper caution, we can deduce a Psychiatric Formulation for Poe's personality and his mental disorder, as we can for his genius and brilliant artistic successes, from the available documented facts of his life and works. Sigmund Freud and Erik Erikson, about one hundred years after Poe's death defined the influences of a traumatic childhood development and environment in the formation of an individual's personality. Poe's childhood was traumatic enough to illustrate exactly what Freud's and Erikson's developmental theories are all about.

In 1896, a half-century after Poe's life ended, Emil Kraepelin, building on the knowledge gained by previous French and German psychiatrists, described a concept of manic-depressive psychosis that contained most of the criteria that psychiatrists now use to establish the diagnosis of manic depression, and they are very relevant to Poe's mental disorder. The absence of a dementing and deteriorating course in manic-depressive psychosis, Kraepelin noted, differentiated it from *dementia praecox* (schizophrenia).

The practice of psychiatry has developed after Kraepelin's time, and there has been much impressive scientific research that has focused on the theoretical personality structures advanced by Freud and Erikson regarding the development of an individual's personality traits and disorders as a result of traumatic developmental and environmental experiences, in comparison to the normal personality of unfettered childhood experiences of individuals with good parenting and happy memories. This knowledge about Poe's developmental and environmental experiences has enabled me to come to some reasonable conclusions about how they could and did affect Poe's life and career.

There is much fascinating, well-documented information about Poe that one can, with some confidence, deduce from the formulations indicated above. For instance what type of personality traits and disorders did Poe likely have and why? The only big variable, it seems to me, is the extent to which his genius level of intelligence might have modified the expected outcome.

I would like briefly to repeat, summarize, and interpret the developmental information documented above.

Edgar Allan Poe's mother died when he was less than three years of age, and his father died or disappeared about the same time. John Allan of Richmond, a wealthy businessman without children of his own, took the boy with plans to adopt him. Allan changed his mind about immediate adoption, and never did bring about a formal adoption. Although Allan's initial treatment of young Edgar was, by report, good and the boy enjoyed all the advantages of being raised in a wealthy and aristocratic Southern family, Mr. Allan eventually became disillusioned with him and hostile to the idea of adoption. Some commentators have claimed emotional abuse and physical abuse of his ward, for that was Edgar's status. Others have called Allan a very strict disciplinarian or, more gravely, an "authoritarian personality." One of the things that perturbed Allan was Edgar's ancestry. He shared a common social attitude that held actors to be immoral and Irish-descended persons inclined to be more so. Edgar's heritage, then, was suspect on at least two counts. Allan apparently tried to teach the boy the difference between right and wrong through the usual method of fear and guilt and then, not getting the desired results, he shifted to the technique of trying to induce shame. He taught Edgar that he was inferior because his parents had been inferior. He told Edgar that his biological parents had been Irish and actors and alcoholic—yet a third count against them—and therefore, they had been deficient. He conveyed to the boy that it was his fate to be flawed as well.

The death of his mother at three, coinciding with the death or disappearance of his father, surely weighted heavily on young Edgar. He missed the normal opportunities afforded children for socializing, i.e., learning trust, control, and reaping the rewards of healthy, competitive behavior in the formation of a personality. Looked at in purely Freudian terms, he never had the opportunity to work through his Oedipal Complex with his foster father, during the fourth and fifth years of life. According to both Freud and Erikson, resolution of the issues of right and wrong and their relationship to guilt and shame occurs (or not) during this crucial developmental period (*Oedipal Phase*). Poe was deprived of the ongoing care and affection of his two birth parents, although the record shows that the childless Mrs. Allan embraced the boy with motherly affection and love. It was she who proposed his adoption to her reluctant and judgmental husband.

Poe became very confused in his understanding of right and wrong and their relationship to guilt and shame. This is normally resolved when the little five-year-old boy gives up his incestuous love for his mother for fear of retaliation by the father. (Likewise, a little girl gives up the incestuous love of her father for fear of losing the love of her mother.) Poe, it would seem, got more love and intimacy from his foster mother than from Mr. Allan, and he was exposed to learning atypical reactions to both the guilt and shame promulgated by his foster father.

Gradually Mr. Allan began reducing all of the advantages Poe had been receiving by being raised in the home of a wealthy family. By the time he reached the age of seventeen, he had completed one year at the University of

Virginia. Poe experienced open antagonism and was treated like a pauper. As a result, he developed an obsessive-compulsive personality disorder and tried to relieve his developing anxiety by using the immature defense mechanisms of *repetition compulsion and dependency*. Confused about guilt and shame, he continued repeating the same distasteful behaviors that brought about alienation and rejection in the home. He was thinking that he would know when his foster father learned to accept him without reservation. Proof of Mr. Allan's love would finally come when he would change his response to Edgar's compulsive and dependent behavior and stop punishing him for it. Further alienation, however, increases antagonism, detachment, retaliation, anger, and punishment, and the decline of a parent-child relationship is the more common consequence of such obsessive-compulsive, dependent, and antisocial behavior (pathological defense mechanisms), and so it was in this case. Increasing withdrawal of financial support can also result in a dependent personality because of the feeling of hopelessness it induces.

An objective observer watching all this destructive behavior in an individual like Poe might be at a loss to understand it and would be inclined to ask, "Why does this young man continue to do things against his own best interest and force himself to suffer so much?" Freud's or Erikson's simple answer to this question would be something like this: Because the child had gone through an inadequate development early in life, in his first five years, he experienced traumatic developmental interference. This resulted in his having failed to develop trust, control, and a healthy sense of competition and appropriate respect of authority. Instead, he has learned and acquired unusual levels of anxiety, shame, and resistance to authority. The end result is that he develops the immature defense mechanism (immature coping skill) of *repetition compulsion and dependency* that drives him to perform again and again the same destructive behavior while magically expecting a different and better outcome each time around. Without the theories of Freud and Erikson to guide him, Poe was left to his own introspective devices to ruminate upon and attempt explanation of this mysterious, destructive phenomenon.

Faced with John Allan's opinion and prejudicial and negative attitude toward Poe's ancestors, Poe, with the brilliant and educated mind of a genius, was able to come up with a "logical" explanation for his recurring destructive behavior. In fact, Poe wrote one of his most popular and sophisticated stories, *The Imp of the Perverse* about this very phenomenon. Describing a soul that is driven to do the very thing it knows to be to his disadvantage, Poe writes about this compulsion:

> "Perhaps now my father will yield to respect me for my genius and to love me."
> Such being the thought and motivation of a young man, now keenly aware of high intelligence and literary gift and craving help and understanding from the only "father" he really ever knew?
> "Might he [Allan] then change his response to my misbehaviors (drinking, carousing, gambling into debt) and stop punishing me for them?"

In *The Imp and the Perverse,* Poe described one phase of this attitude that deals with a soul that is driven to do the very thing that he knows is to his disadvantage. John Allan gradually lost interest in adopting Edgar Poe over the years because of his continued refusal to abide by the "rules of the house of John Allan." Neither John Allan nor Edgar Poe could have had any way of knowing about the psychiatric theories that would eventually be discovered by Sigmund Freud explaining the compulsive behavior of the person to win and be accepted regardless of how many times the "repulsive compulsive" behavior needed to be repeated. Nor could he have known about the formation of *repetition compulsion* as an unconscious, immature defense mechanism used in those instances.

Mr. John Allan, on observing the many behavioral compulsions of Edgar such as gambling, drinking, and his failure to follow rules, saw these behaviors as evidence that Edgar had inherited the same traits that his biological father, David Poe, Jr., had demonstrated during his brief life. Mr. Allan, of course, did not see Poe's *repetition compulsion* as a reaction to his failure to compete with his foster father for the love of his foster mother, as frequently occurs during the crucial Oedipal Phase of development. While the socially acceptable, holier-than-thou attitude perhaps embarrassed Allan—Poe's strategy still didn't work. Further alienation, anger, and punishment were Poe's "reward" for his efforts, unconsciously compulsive at one level, and consciously chosen at the other level. Hopelessness and despair surrounded the teenage Poe: a true, nineteenth-century "Catch-22."

Faced with John Allan's negative and unenlightened opinion of him—which Poe could neither refute nor, being more intelligent than his foster

father, accept—Poe eventually took his "revenge." Later in life Edgar began to
see this defense mechanism of *repetition compulsion* in himself and wrote the
short story entitled *The Imp of the Perverse* to explain his self-destructive behavior.
Poe wrote about this compulsion as follows:

> Through its prompting we act without comprehensible object; or if
> that shall be understood as a contradiction in terms, we may so far modify
> the proposition to say, that through its prompting we act for the reason
> we should not. In theory, no theory can be more unreasonable, but in
> fact, there is none more strong. With certain minds, under certain condi-
> tions, it becomes absolutely irresistible. I am no more certain that I
> breathe, than that the assurance of the wrong or error of any action is
> often the one unconquerable force which impels us, and alone impels us
> to its prosecution....
>
> Nor will this overwhelming tendency to do wrong for wrong's sake,
> admit of analysis, or resolution into ulterior element. It is a radical, a
> primitive impulse—elementary. It will be said, I am aware, that when we
> persist in acts because we feel we must persist in acts because we feel we
> should not persist in them, our conduct is but a modification of that
> which ordinarily springs from the combativeness of phrenology.

If the reader will take a moment to view the discarded phenomena of
phrenology as arising from an inherited or traumatic visible defect of the skull,
much as Freud or Erikson viewed childhood developmental interference as an
invisible defect of the brain, then we have very little difference between what
Freud believed and what Poe believed. In other words, Freud saw adverse
emotional and environmental experiences to the brain influencing personality
development and Poe saw phrenology, with pressure exerted by the pressure
points of the skull on the brain as accounting for personality development and,
therefore, Poe saw phrenology as explaining hereditary influences on personality formation.

The emphasis I would like to make here is that personality traits and
personality disorders and/or temperament are ingrained in us from birth, as
Poe would have us believe, or during childhood, as Freud and Erikson suggest.
In both scenarios there is an imprint on our personalities that affects our
behavior and that is difficult to change. It is important to note that modern

usage of the term *temperament* implies that it is more genetic or familial in nature and the term *personality* implies that the etiology or cause is developmental or experiential in nature. In the era of Poe, his reasoning regarding personality formation in *The Imp of the Perverse* we would expect to be focused on familial, hereditary, or ethnic phenomena. Today, personality formation would be more commonly viewed as revolving around development and environmental experience, as conceptualized by Freud and Erikson. This would be especially true in Western cultures.

If we follow the thought of Freud and Erikson, we can see two sorts of developmental problems, both of which are relevant in the case of Edgar Allan Poe.

An individual who has not resolved his Oedipal Complex becomes guilt-ridden, has trouble with competition, and may learn to use the immature defense mechanism of *repetition compulsion, dependency, and antisocial behavior.* Such an individual will try to obtain pity from significant people in his life by playing games with them like drunkenness, excessive gambling, and other high-risk behaviors in order to be rescued by them, especially by those in authority (a father figure) or, in Poe's case, his foster father John Allan. This person will do the same thing over and over again hoping his target will surrender and do what the dependent person wants, believing that if his antagonist truly loves him he will surrender and comply. If the compulsive person wins the game, he is "forgiven" for his offending sin. If he loses, he knows he was "doomed" from the start because nothing he could do would have worked anyway (Catch-22*).*

An individual who has failed to resolve the issue of *control* connected with the "Anal Phase" of development will experience *shame, as opposed to guilt, and may develop behaviors that are self-destructive.* This individual, feeling that he has no control over his life, sees himself as bad, inadequate, and worthless. He may even become suicidal. In *The Imp of the Perverse* Poe describes this type of situation:

> We stand upon the brink of a precipice. We peer into the abyss—we grow sick and dizzy. Our first impulse is to shrink from the danger. Unaccountably we remain. By slow degree our sickness and dizziness and horror become merged in a cloud of unnamable feeling. By gradations still more imperceptible, this cloud assumes shape, as did the vapor from the bottle out of which arose the genie in the Arabian Nights. But out of this our cloud upon the precipice's edge, there grows into palpability, a shape far more terrible than any genie or demon of a tale, and yet it is but a

thought, although a fearful one, and one that chills the very marrow of our bones with the fierceness of the delight of its horror. It is merely the idea of what would be our sensation during the sweeping precipitancy of a fall from such a height. And this fall—this rushing annihilation—for the very reason that it involves that one most ghastly and loathsome of all the most ghastly and loathsome images of death and suffering which have ever presented themselves to our imagination—for this very cause do we now the most vividly desire it. And because our reason, violently deters us from the brink, therefore do we the most impetuously approach it. There is no passion in nature so demonically impatient, as that of him who, shuddering upon the edge of a precipice, thus, meditates a plunge. To indulge, for a moment, in any attempt at thought, is to be inevitably lost; for reflection but urges us to forbear, and therefore it is, I say, that we cannot. If there be no friendly arm to check us, or if we fall in a sudden effort to prostrate ourselves backward from the abyss, we plunge, and are destroyed.

In this accumulation of feelings and impulse, shame, not guilt, is the primary motivating force impelling to self-destruction. Both shame and guilt, arising from unusual childhood traumas and fixations, were vividly operative in Edgar Allan Poe, the diagnosis of whose personality type, following Freud and Erikson, would be *obsessive-compulsive personality disorder, dependent personality disorder* and *antisocial personality disorder*. Only his brilliant and creative intelligence allowed him to achieve some liberation and success out of his confused childhood.

The next category of illness that needs to be formulated for Poe is from his history and symptoms of alcoholism and drug abuse. There is absolutely no doubt that Poe suffered from and struggled with alcohol starting at an early age; there is nothing in his biography to suggest that he suffered from or struggled with abuse of other drugs. As to the latter, although accusations were and have been made that he was a drug addict, there is only evidence that he used *laudanum* on very rare occasions, and only in small amounts as a medication. At this time the narcotic drug was commonly used as a medicine; it was readily available and there were no government controls. Poe was reported to have had a very low tolerance for alcohol, but in my opinion this impression was erroneously formed when he was using alcohol medicinally to control his undiagnosed psychiatric manic symptoms. That is to say as he was becoming manic, and probably psychotic, he would start using alcohol to try to control the extreme mood swings that occur with a manic-depression disorder. His bizarre behavior was misinterpreted as the result of drunkenness after one or two drinks. But in fact, the liquor had not yet started having its effect; the mania was operating. This was not only confusing to people observing Poe when he was afflicted thus, it was equally confusing to Poe himself. Poe was rumored to have a lifetime of drinking (with periods of abstinence) until he had the complications of severe terminal alcoholism, including possibly *delirium tremens* on several different occasions. The reported episodes of DTs could, on the other hand, in fact have been manifestations of the symptoms of manic-depressive psychosis that mimic or masquerade as each other and often become extremely difficult to deal with, especially at that time in history because the diagnosis was unknown and there was no treatment. The episode that occurred on the day of his death, however, could only have been *delirium tremens* even though it may have been in association with a painful traumatic brain injury that was also reported. The DTs followed the classical time sequence for DTs, including the lucid period immediately before death. The fact that he died from the DTs should not be surprising, given the fact that death occurred in 20 percent of the incidences at that time, when there were no medications to prevent it.[1] Poe never had any withdrawal seizures or any other history of seizures. The absence of seizures, however, does not have any diagnostic significance. I diagnose Edgar Poe as having Clonninger Type II Alcoholism in partial remission.

Poe's third psychiatric illness was one that brought him great misery and often something near despair; it was probably the biggest single factor contributing to his early demise because it went undiagnosed and because there was no known treatment for it in his century. I refer now to his presumed diagnosis in today's terminology of *manic-depressive disorder.*

This disorder is proportionately much higher among practicing poets than in the general population. About one in five poets, so diagnosed, have ended their lives by suicide. In the general population the incidence of manic-depressive disorder is about one and one-half percent with the same percentage all over the world and affects males and it affects females equally.

It would not be professional of me to make a diagnosis for any individual on the basis of statistics about a group. And, in any case, I am not doing this for Poe. As a practicing psychiatrist, I have diagnosed him on the basis of his known behavior and on his self-reported thoughts and feelings and on his writings. Poe exhibited almost all of the symptoms of manic depression in a cyclic fashion and seasonal pattern.

Overall, when Ludwig compared individuals in the creative arts with those in other professions (such as businessmen, scientists, and public officials), he found that the artistic group showed two to three times the rate of psychosis, suicides, suicide attempts, mood disorders, and substance abuse.[2] The rate of forced psychiatric hospitalization among artists, writers, and composers was six to seven times that of the nonartistic group. Poe was known to have periods when he was grandiose, unable to sleep, hypersexual, voluble with unceasing speech, paranoid in thought, expansive in ambitious projects, and when he engaged in impulsive behavior such as excessive gambling, increased risk-taking, and financial indiscretions, that, in his mind he experienced as a torrent of ideas and racing thoughts. It was during these periods of expansiveness that he was most creative. He shared with many artists an intuitive knowledge that their creativity was somehow linked to such periods of expansive moods; like others, too, he knew that at times these expansive moods made him lose control of his creativity, and then he would turn to liquor to relax himself and slow his racing mind.

These are the times he would refer to as *mania a potu*. This is a state, characterized by extreme excitement and sometimes homicidal assaults, produced by alcohol. The attack is usually brought on, in susceptible persons, by ingestion of comparatively small amounts of alcohol. In the *DSM-IV* it is referred to as *pathological-intoxication, paradoxical intoxication,* or *idiosyncratic intoxication.* It occurs predominately in persons with a low tolerance to alcohol. The syndrome usually lasts several hours, although it may continue for a whole day. As said, it is characterized by extreme excitement ("alcoholic fury") with aggressive, dangerous, and even homicidal reactions. Persecutory ideas are common. The condition terminates with the patient falling asleep; there is usually a complete amnesia for the episode. Such cases are rare occurrences.

I believe the phenomenon just described is exactly what can occur when an undiagnosed manic depressive who feels himself starting into a manic phase tries to abort the episode by using small quantities of alcohol to relax. The small amounts of alcohol consumed probably have little if anything to do with the intensity of the mania, but the mania continues to escalate until this person is in a fury. The bizarre, frenzied, paranoid, and frightening behavior continues until the person falls into a profound sleep. Because the purpose for drinking a small quantity of liquor in the first place is to induce relaxation and perhaps sleep, and because an observer and even the person drinking is unaware that he has a second illness—manic-depressive disorder—the whole episode is blamed on the small quantity of alcohol consumed. Poe also had periods of creativity during his depressed moods. It was during his depressed moods that he wrote his morbid stories and sad poetry. [3]

The fourth and last consideration relevant to Poe, but not considered a psychiatric diagnosis, is his genius intellect. Certainly not a mental illness itself, nor the cause of any aberrations in thought, feeling, or behavior, his heightened intellectual power did amplify sorrow and happiness, frustration, and euphoria. The psychological trauma of his childhood, for instance, severe in itself, must have been felt more intensely by Poe than another person. Rejection by his foster father, who first promised and then denied Poe adoption, had to have been a tremendous disappointment to him. His foster father's blaming his misbehavior on the "blood" (I would say "genes") of his biological father and mother was very traumatic and gave him little hope of recovering from or even surviving a fate similar to theirs. His genius allowed him to justify his ancestral weakness by writing *The Imp of the Perverse*: there describing his perverse need to do things compulsively against his own best interest which was blamed on his Irish ancestors. That same ancestral line allowed him to blame his love for alcohol on his forbears, too. He also wanted to believe in the way alcohol dissolved his superego and his feelings of guilt, and made him feel "invisible."

Poe's very early commitment to marry his consumptive eight-year-old first cousin could have stemmed from such a low self-esteem that he believed no one outside of a blood relative would take him for a husband and certainly not a healthy, mature woman. (His first broken engagement seems germane at this point.)

Last, but not least, his manic-depressive disorder turned normal sadness and happiness into suicidal depression (melancholia) or ecstatic euphoria (mania) that distorted reality for him.

DIAGNOSTIC IMPRESSIONS ON EDGAR ALLAN POE:

AXIS I:
1. Manic-depressive Disorder Mixed Psychotic Features with Seasonal Pattern, *DSM-IV* (296.64)
2. Alcohol dependence in Early Partial Remission, *DSM-IV* (303.90)
3. Alcohol Induced Intoxication Delirium, *DSM-IV* (291.0)

4. Idiopathic Intoxication, or Paradoxical Intoxication, or Pathological Intoxication or mania a potu, *DSM-IV* (291.40)
5. Alcohol Withdrawal Hyperacoustic
           * Possible Dual or Triple Diagnosis

AXIS II:
1. Dependent Personality Disorder, *DSM-IV* (301.6)
2. Obsessive-Compulsive Personality Disorder, *DSM-IV* (301.4)
3. Antisocial Personality Disorder, *DSM-IV* (301.7)

AXIS III:
1. Chronic Otitis Media

AXIS IV:
1. Psychosocial and Occupational Problems
(Problems related to occupation, social environment, and access to health care)

AXIS V:
1. Global Assessment of Functioning (GAF) Scale = Variable + 75-100

(Because of Poe's genius intellect, the only logical way to apply classical numbers to it would be to divide his functioning into four component parts: Work = 65, Love = 75, Play = 50, and Creativity = 100.)

CHAPTER FIVE

Money, Moonshine, Movies, and Morals: Psychiatric and Substance Abuse Evaluation of F. Scott Fitzgerald

BIOGRAPHY

Fitzgerald's family hailed from the East Coast. His great-great-grandfather was the brother of Fitzgerald's namesake, Francis Scott Key, a Maryland lawyer who wrote the "Star Spangled Banner" during the British naval bombardment of Baltimore in 1814. He was christened Francis Scott Key Fitzgerald following his birth on September 24, 1896. Fitzgerald was acutely aware of the embarrassing comparison between the genteel but impoverished background of his father and the crude but wealthy elements in his mother's background. He felt himself to be a cultural "upstart" at times and perhaps learned the role of *nouveau riche* too quickly during the Roaring Twenties.

Fitzgerald's father, Edwin, was a small, ineffectual man who wore well-cut clothing and had fine Southern manners. He also enjoyed reading the romantic poetry from Byron to Poe and browsing over the miscellaneous knowledge in the *Encyclopedia Britannica*. Although Fitzgerald's parents were registered in the *St. Paul Social Register*, they lived, for the most part, on the inheritance of several hundred thousand dollars that Edwin's wife, Mollie Fitzgerald, received from her father, Phillip McQuillan. He was an Irish immigrant and wholesale grocer and he left Mrs. Fitzgerald this fortune when he died at the age of forty-three in 1877.

As a boy, Scott was troubled by his father's failures in his work and business ventures. Arthur Miller, as a matter of fact, has perceptively observed that most modern American male authors—from Fitzgerald and Hemingway, to Lowell and Berryman, have tried to compensate for their own weak fathers: "One rarely hears of an American writer...whose father was to be regarded as, in any way adequate or successful." Scott was also ashamed of his mother's eccentric dress and peculiar behavior.

Born in St. Paul in 1860, Mollie McQuillan was educated at that city's Visitation Convent and at Manhattanville College in New York. She was a voracious but indiscriminate reader in sentimental poetry and popular fiction. She would carry piles of books from the local library. She toted an umbrella even in fine weather and wore mismatched shoes of different colors as well as other wild clothing and exhibited a lifetime of eccentric behavior. Mollie was accustomed to blurting out embarrassingly frank remarks without realizing their effect on her acquaintances. She once stared at a woman whose husband was dying and said, "I'm trying to decide how you'll look in mourning." (All of her behaviors are consistent with *mania* or with a *hypomanic episode*.) Fitzgerald inherited his elegance and propensity to failure and alcoholism from his father, and his social insecurity and absurd behavior, and *intermittent hypomanic episodes* (probably as a result of an undiagnosed and untreated manic-depressive disorder) from his mother.

Fitzgerald never liked his mother. He said, "Mother and I never had anything in common except a relentless stubborn quality," and added, "but when I saw all this it turned me inside out realizing how unhappy her temperament made her." Fitzgerald once recorded a disturbing dream about his mother in which he was ashamed of her for not being young and elegant, and for offending his sense of propriety by her peculiar behavior. He described her as "a neurotic, half-insane with pathological nervous worry." Mollie remained locked in her own hysterical world. She looked down on her husband, who began to drink too much.

Scott's swashbuckling adolescent roles as "actor, athlete, scholar, philatelist and collector of cigar bands," were undermined by his mother's insistence that he demonstrate his "accomplishments" by singing for company. The attractive, selfish, egoistic, and socially insecure boy now revealed a crucial lifelong flaw in his character, which would hurt him as a writer. He had a weakness for showing off instead of listening and observing and was unaware of the effect he had on others. He is quoted as saying, "I didn't know until I was fifteen that there was anyone in the world except me, and it cost me *plenty*." This quote reveals symptoms of a narcissistic personality.

Two of his closest friends later criticized the narcissistic self-absorption that limited Fitzgerald's knowledge of other men and women. Sara Murphy wrote, with some exaggeration: "I have always told you that you haven't the faintest idea what anybody else but your self is like." And Hemingway, who agreed with her, told their editor Max Perkins: "Scott can't invent true characters because he doesn't know anything about people." One of his fellow students in high school recalled he was "eager to be liked by his companions and almost vain in seeking praise." His roommate remembered him as having "the most impenetrable egotism I've ever seen." Was this mania, hypomania, or narcissism? We will go on to clarify and answer this question when we detail his Developmental History, Family History, Educational History, and Psychiatric and Social History.

Fitzgerald's grandmother, Louise McQuillan, died in the summer of 1913 and left his mother an additional $125,000 of the family fortune. This inheritance rescued Fitzgerald from the anonymity of an education at the University of Minnesota or a parochial education at his father's alma mater at Georgetown University. It allowed him, instead, to become a gentleman scholar at Princeton.

Fitzgerald chose Princeton as much for the ambiance as for the scholastic reputation. It was in the same state (New Jersey) as his prep school and, to a man who identified with his Maryland ancestors, was more social and "Southern" than Harvard or Yale. Fitzgerald imagined the Princeton man to be more like him—lazy, good-looking, and aristocratic. Princeton drew him most, with its atmosphere of bright colors and its alluring reputation as the pleasantest country club in America.

Fitzgerald was grandiose and found it easy to imagine himself a great football player and strongly identified with the heroes of the Princeton team. He was conditionally admitted to the Princeton class of 1917 and after wiring his mother for football pads and shoes, and weighing only 138 pounds, he tried out for the freshman team and was cut from the squad on the first day.

Nevertheless, he found the spire-filled college, surrounded by luxurious estates, and rising out of the flat midlands of New Jersey, to be "the loveliest riot of Gothic architecture in America." Anglophilia prevailed at Princeton, whose fifteen hundred students cultivated a tradition of gentility, charm, and honor that reaffirmed the values of Fitzgerald's father.

After meeting privileged beings like Richard Cleveland, son of former president Grover Cleveland, and David Bruce, son of a United States Senator, who himself became an ambassador, Fitzgerald soon discovered that there was a vast difference between young men from St. Paul's School and a young man from St. Paul, Minnesota, and the student body at Princeton. Surrounded by very rich Eastern, Anglo-Saxon Protestants from the most elite private schools, the poor (i.e., merely well off), provincial Irish Catholic from obscure and undistinguished (i.e. not Episcopalian) Newman felt socially and financially inferior. But neither then nor later, in similar circumstances, did this prevent Fitzgerald and his wife, Zelda, from hobnobbing with the rich and the ultra rich. His married life with Zelda Sayre took them into the East Coast enclaves and resorts of the wealthy, and on the Riviera in Italy, and London, Paris, New York, Monte Carlo, Hollywood and every place with elite apartments and mansions. He always lived beyond his income but managed through his writings or his contacts to bail himself out of debt. Fitzgerald later told a friend that he never had the money to sustain the precarious position he had struggled to achieve: "That was always my experience—a poor boy in a rich town, a poor boy in a rich boy's school; a poor boy in a rich man's club at Princeton." He also became, after his fortune failed in the 1930s, a poor man at a luxurious resort in North Carolina and a poor writer among the fabulously rich film stars in Hollywood. He never accumulated any wealth, property, or even his own private home.

At Princeton he did not excel as a student. Though Fitzgerald's grades were predictably terrible because he did not attend classes on time, his excuse for this wayward behavior was: "Sir—it's absurd to expect me to be on time. I'm a genius." He managed to survive his freshman year but he established the disastrous pattern of trying to make up deficiencies while failing current courses. Christian Gauss, who taught French Romantic Poetry and was one of the few teachers Fitzgerald admired, gave a perceptive analysis of the character, ambitions, and defects of his bright but wayward student: "He was impatient of discipline...and was fascinated by the operatic pageantry of the pre-World War campus.... He yearned rather consistently to dominate the world, become president of the Triangle Club and be a 'big man' on the campus. He possessed far less solid background in reading than his friends but was deeply interested in the problems of art and its techniques.... He pursued his studies only spasmodically."

Fitzgerald studied the "amazing lyrics" of Gilbert and Sullivan's *Iolanthe* and *Patience* when writing his own songs and modeled his witty dialogue on the plays of Oscar Wilde. In 1924 Fitzgerald recalled: "I spent my entire freshman year writing operetta for the Triangle Club. I failed algebra, trigonometry, coordinate geometry and hygiene, but the Triangle Club accepted my show, and by being tutored all through a stuffy August I managed to come back a sophomore and act in it as a chorus girl."

Though Fitzgerald reserved for himself the role of the sexy and seductive showgirl, his poor grades made him ineligible to act in the play. He had to be content with dressing up for the part in a blond wig, glamorous hat, tulle shawl and flowered gown, and having his theatrical photograph published in the newspaper of all the cities in the Christmas tour. Fitzgerald was five feet, eight inches tall, with blond hair and green eyes, perfect features, and a smooth, almost honeyed voice. He was "pretty" without being effeminate (his class poll gave him two votes for handsomest and five for the prettiest man). A St. Paul friend recalled: "He was strikingly good-looking and when his eyes sparkled and his face shone with that powerful interior animation it was truly an exciting experience." And a Princeton contemporary, noting that male students (a Princeton tradition then) played all the female parts in the musicals, agreed that, "Besides being one of the prettiest girls in the shows, he looked exactly like a beautiful lady and acted like one."

While at Princeton Fitzgerald maintained the careless indifference to academic life that had characterized his years at Newman and would continue during his training in the army. He did not even attempt the minimum work required to pass many of his courses and took the maximum of forty-nine absences allowed during his freshman year. He failed three courses in both his freshman and sophomore years, failed his makeup exams in Latin and chemistry at the beginning of his junior year, which again made him ineligible for Triangle Club show, and barely managed to survive without expulsion. He never even learned to spell correctly (he was perhaps dyslexic) and despite his training in Latin and French, was hopeless at foreign languages. He concluded that if he could not achieve great success at Princeton, he did not see any point of struggling through his courses. He managed through some political maneuver to obtain a classification of "withdrawal" rather than "expulsion" from the university.

Fitzgerald dedicated the summer of 1917 to drinking gin and reading Schopenhauer, Bergson, and William James. But the gin had a more powerful effect than the philosophy, and he returned to Princeton to await his commission in the army rather than to get his degree. Fitzgerald was among the most famous alumni Princeton never graduated. Though bitter about his failures, he always remained intensely idealistic about and deeply devoted to Princeton.

In July 1917, after his brief bout with Schopenhauer, Bergson, and William James, Fitzgerald went to Fort Snelling, near St. Paul, and took the exams required for an appointment as a second lieutenant in the regular army. He could not become an officer until he reached the age of twenty-one in September. When, on October 26, he received his commission as second lieutenant, he immediately ordered his smart uniforms from Brooks Brothers—very much as he had ordered his football equipment the day he was admitted to Princeton.

He was sent to training for three months from November 1917 to February 1918, to Fort Leavenworth, Kansas, on the Missouri River northwest of Kansas City. The captain in charge of training professional lieutenants in exercise, calisthenics, and bayonet drill was Dwight Eisenhower. Fitzgerald was not as appreciative of his training under Eisenhower as his fellow trainees were. He did as badly as an army officer as he had as a college student. Just as classes seemed to interfere with his theatrical career at Princeton, so drills and marches became an irritating interruption of the novel he wanted to write. Though he intended to lead an infantry platoon into battle, he never took his training seriously, never realized that it was vitally important to acquire basic military skills.

After his superiors had reluctantly entrusted him with a command, Fitzgerald got involved in many dangerous and absurd misadventures. One example of many was when he was directing a mortar company, he mistakenly ordered his men to fire on another unit. His soldiers, nearly blown up when a shell jammed in a Stokes mortar, were saved at the last moment when Dana Palmer bravely tipped the barrel and spilled out the shell.

Fitzgerald's regiment was about to leave for France when the Armistice ended the war on November 11, 1918. He never even got close to making the fatal sacrifice of the twenty-one Princeton boys (5 percent of his class) who were killed in the war. He wanted to prove his courage, gain some glory, and win the acceptance of his comrades. He always considered his lack of combat experience one of the deepest disappointments in his life.

Responsible as a supply officer for unloading equipment on the docks of Hoboken, New Jersey when his unit was on its way to France, Fitzgerald left the train to visit Princeton and allowed thousands of dollars of materials to be stolen. He falsely claimed to have commandeered a special locomotive to take him to Washington with an urgent message for President Woodrow Wilson. While stationed at Camp Mills on Long Island, Fitzgerald went to New York for a party, borrowed a friend's room at the Hotel Astor, and was caught there by the house detective—naked and in bed with a girl. He tried to bribe the detective with a dollar bill folded to look like a hundred, but he was caught again and was saved from jail only by being put under military arrest in his army camp. This type of recurrent antisocial, narcissistic, and grandiose behavior suggests a significant personality disorder at a minimum, as well as hypomania and alcoholism. His impulse control was clearly inhibited.

Fitzgerald's one redeeming act occurred when a ferry used to get troops across the Tallapoosa River near Montgomery was swamped during maneuvers. Fitzgerald helped save a number of men who had fallen into the water.

Despite his manifest incompetence, Fitzgerald's good looks, well-cut uniforms, Princeton charm, and Irish-Catholic background (for once an advantage) attracted the attention of Brigadier General James Augustine Ryan who, in December 1918, appointed him aide-de-camp. He apparently thought Fitzgerald would be useful—or at least harmlessly decorative—in this quasi-diplomatic role.

Except for a brief period of time at Camp Mills on Long Island, Fitzgerald was stationed from June 1918 until February 1919 in Montgomery, Alabama. In that hot, static little town of forty thousand souls, nothing much had happened since the Civil War. Fitzgerald described Montgomery as a "languid paradise of dreamy skies and firefly evenings and noisy, niggery street fairs—and especially of gracious, soft-voiced girls who were brought up on memories instead of money."

At a country club dance on one of those "firefly evenings" in July 1918, Fitzgerald met a gracious, soft-voiced girl named Zelda Sayre. She let her long hair hang loose and wore a frilly dress that made her look younger than her eighteen years. She came from a prominent, though not wealthy, family and had just graduated from Sidney Lanier High School.

Four years younger than Scott, Zelda was born on July 24, 1900, and named for the romantic gypsy heroine in Robert Edward Francillon's *Zelda's Fortune* (1874). Zelda was known for her striking beauty, her unconventional behavior and her sexual promiscuity. Her powerful father protected her from the usual societal repercussions for her behavior. The family and Zelda also kept their family history of mental illness from Fitzgerald. (This will be covered in detail in the Marital History below.) Her penchant to always do things to shock people and her gorgeous looks kept her surrounded by young males who would line up the whole length of the ballroom to dance with her for one minute.

There was a tremendous difference in their backgrounds—Fitzgerald was from a lower middle-class Irish Catholic family from the upper Midwest, who had lived in five different towns, and had been to college; Zelda was from an upper middle-class Anglo-Protestant family from the Deep South, who had spent her entire life in Montgomery and had completed a patchy high school education. But Scott and Zelda actually had a great deal in common. They were spoiled children of older parents. They had the same blond hair, fair skin, straight nose, and thin lips and looked enough alike to be brother and sister. They even wore matching jackets and knickerbockers on their drive from Connecticut to Montgomery in the summer of 1920. Both liked to exchange sexual roles. Scott dressed up as a showgirl for the Triangle Club. Zelda put on men's clothing and went to the movies with a group of boys. Women always surrounded Scott who had a weak father, strong mother, younger sister, a wife, daughter, and several mistresses. He believed: "I am half-feminine—which is where my mind is," (ego-syntonic homosexual). Zelda told a friend: "I have always been inclined toward masculinity." Both spent extravagantly, drank heavily, behaved irresponsibly, and did not care what people thought of them.

Seven months after meeting Zelda in Montgomery, probably because he was seen by the army as "unusually dispensable," Fitzgerald was one of the first officers to be discharged from his unit in February 1919. That same month he went to New York and renewed acquaintance with a somewhat older college friend, Edmund Wilson. He found Wilson still occupying an apartment on West Eighth Street in Greenwich Village and working for the *Evening Sun*. Bunny Wilson seemed to Fitzgerald to embody the ideal literary life. Fitzgerald found that the "shy little scholar of Holder Court" in Princeton had been transformed into a promising symbol of cosmopolitan sophistication. "That night, in Wilson's apartment," Fitzgerald recalled, "life was mellow and safe, a finer distillation of all that I had come to love at Princeton...and I began wondering about the rent of such apartments."

Fitzgerald now assumed he could easily duplicate Wilson's attractive way of life and earn enough money to marry Zelda. But he lacked his friend's discipline and found it difficult to break into a commercial or a literary life in New York. Instead of a congenial flat in the Village, shortage of money forced him into a remote and depressing room at 200 Claremont Avenue, near Columbia University in uptown Manhattan. He took an unappealing job with the Barron Collier advertising agency at thirty-five dollars a week. He continued to drink when he was not working and acted out with suicidal behavior and indulged in sophomoric pranks that became tediously familiar throughout his life. He decorated his room with a frieze of 122 rejection slips he received for all of the various film scenarios, sketches, jokes, and nineteen stories he submitted for publication.

That spring he made three trips from New York to Montgomery wooing Zelda. In April they became engaged and slept together for the first time. Fitzgerald resented her family's opposition to the marriage. They felt (with good reason) that she needed a strong, stable husband who could control, rather than indulge, her wild behavior. In their view he was an unstable Irish Catholic who had not graduated from college, had no career and little prospects, and drank too much. Zelda claimed that, "Scott was the sweetest person in the world when sober," to which Judge Sayre sternly replied: "He's never sober." When Scott pleaded with the judge to believe in him, the only thing that the judge would say was, "Scott, I think you will always pay your bills." Though often in debt because of an extravagant lifestyle, Scott *did* sooner or later pay his bills.

Fitzgerald tried to persuade Zelda to marry him immediately by threatening, pleading, and overwhelming her with kisses. But in June, impatient with his failures, she broke off their engagement and ended their sexual relations.

Fitzgerald rationalized his deteriorating situation as being the result of his having allowed himself to be dominated by mentally inferior "authorities," first at St. Paul and Newman and Princeton, then in his army regiment and now in advertising. Clearly unsuited to a regular office job, he loathed business as much as he had hated the strictures of academic and army life. He was fearful of losing Zelda forever to a prosperous local rival and determined to win her back by writing a successful novel. Haunted by the drab room and the crowded subway, obsessed by his shabby clothes, his poverty and his hopeless love, he quit his job. "I was a failure—mediocre at advertising work and unable to get started as a writer. I got roaring, weeping drunk on my last penny and went home to St. Paul," he said of himself. There, on the top floor room of the family home at 509 Summit Avenue he began writing his novel *This Side of Paradise*, working away at it through the hot summer and fall and into the cold Minnesota winter.

Upon publication on March 26, 1920, the novel won instant and sensational acclaim and Fitzgerald became famous at once. On April 3, 1920—eight days later—though Scott was no longer a practicing Catholic and Zelda was Protestant, they were married in the rectory of St. Patrick's Cathedral on Fifth Avenue in New York.

George Orwell described *This Side of Paradise* as a "good-bad book—superficial and immature, but still lively and readable, and valuable both as an autobiography and as social history." Fitzgerald had persuaded Scribner's to advertise the book as "A Novel about Flappers Written for Philosophers," and with Zelda in mind, he popularized the term "flapper." Originally denoting a wild duck, the word had evolved in application to meaning a young harlot in the early nineteenth century, to an immoral with her hair not yet put up at the turn of the century, to an unconventional young woman with short hair two decades later. The novel had an immense social as well as literary impact. One of its characters, Amory Blain, and his girlfriends—fired by wealth, alcohol and automobiles—became models for unconstrained behavior. The book threw off pre-World War I respectability and alarmed protective parents. It baptized the Jazz Age and glorified its fashionable hedonism. Criticism of his first novel by his friends in the literary world said that it reflected Fitzgerald's immaturity, vanity, narcissism, shallowness, and undistinguished military career—in all of which they were absolutely right. They probably knew that their remarks would not upset Fitzgerald both because it had been such a fantastic success—a dream come true—and because he himself instinctively perceived that his work evolved from his personal faults and emotional crises. He was also proof against adverse criticism because he knew that with the novel's publication he had made good on his promise and his career was realized: Scott Fitzgerald was a writer.

No longer a poor boy in a rich boy's (and a rich man's) world, Fitzgerald now revealed a vulgar streak that seemed to illustrate Thorstein Veblen's concept of conspicuous consumption. Intoxicated by the excitement of money and eager to advertise his success, he would prepare lavish parties by prominently displaying hundred dollar bills in his vest pockets. His reckless expenditures marked him as *nouveau riche*. Once he developed luxurious tastes, he preferred to sacrifice his independence and go deeper into debt rather than reduce his standard of living to match his diminished income.

As with many artists and writers of this era, he felt he had to live like a gentleman and, even pressed for money, provide his family with maids, governesses, nannies, expensive hotels, leased mansions, luxurious cars, private schools, and the finest hospitals. Forced to borrow from his publisher and agent to get what he needed, he became financially dependent on them. He and Zelda never owned a house of their own and they were often evicted from places they rented or hotels in which they resided, many of which were the world's best and most famous.

Their wild and well-publicized pranks soon became notorious. Watching a comedy in the front row of a theater, they annoyed the actors by laughing loudly in all the wrong places. When they were kicked out of the Biltmore Hotel for disturbing other guests, they celebrated their move to the Commodore by spinning through the revolving entrance door for half an hour. They frequently did exhibitionistic dancing in Metropolitan water fountains together and separately. Zelda paid a surcharge to ride on the hood of a taxi. She more than once summoned the local fire department for a "blaze in [her] breast." Zelda, as daring in her social escapades as Scott and frequently, though not always, as drunk, had few inhibitions and would do almost anything she or anyone else could think of. Both had an urgent need for drama—or farce.

Alcohol fueled most, though not all, of these unconstrained episodes, which changed from high-spirited pranks to maliciousness as the Fitzgeralds' drinking intensified and Zelda's mental illness (schizophrenia) got worse. F. Scott confirmed his diagnosis of alcohol addiction when he said, "I could never get sufficiently sober to endure being sober." As they whirled around from party to party and from country to country their chaotic and alcoholic way of life seemed to sustain them in a cataclysmic sort of way. But it put an enormous strain on their marriage. Zelda's extravagance and flirtatiousness, which at one time seemed so delightful and charming, grew intolerable. Spoiled and acquisitive, having to be courted with feather fans and expensive jewelry, she believed "having things, just things, objects, make a woman happy." Fitzgerald believed that having your name in the public eye helped to sell books. Whether this was a truism or a rationalization, they did not have trouble with the sensation of getting their notoriety printed in the magazines and newspapers.

In 1923 with the failure of his play *The Vegetable* that he was counting on to bring him in a small fortune, Fitzgerald was broke and $4,500 in debt. When the play failed, he was forced to go on the wagon and write himself out of debt. Working in a large, bare, and badly heated room, he took two days to turn out a seven-thousand-word story that paid the rent and the most pressing bills. He then worked "twelve hours a day for five weeks to rise from abject poverty back to the middle class." This type of physical energy in a state of alcohol withdrawal does suggest either mania or hypomania. By March 1924 he had earned enough money from magazine stories to pay off his debt to Harold Ober and finance a trip to Europe. The Riviera would provide a stimulating change, cost less than Great Neck, and be more conducive to work. Though he had told Wilson, "France made me sick," he sailed there in early May with plans to write his third novel, which was to be *The Great Gatsby*.

Constructive and creative periods in Fitzgerald's career like this make me believe that he was not manic depressive (bipolar I) but rather had intermittent *hypomanic episodes* (bipolar II) intermittently with *major depression*. Both Poe and Berryman were creative during the manic phases of their illnesses, and they both used alcohol and sedatives to slow down their racing minds, which enabled them to write productively. Fitzgerald found it necessary to stop drinking to become creative and productive. When he was sober his *hypomania* came forward, and along with its excessive energy and its insomnia, he was able to imagine and produce both voluminously and with growing artistic skill. The price of these hypomanic episodes, together with his *narcissistic personality disorder*, created a grandiosity that demanded self-reward with all types of extravagant luxuries well beyond his income, including the compulsive need to show off his elite lifestyle during their excessive and expensive foreign travel.

Scott and Zelda were on their way to the Riviera when they stopped in Paris in order for Scott to gather the right atmosphere that would enable him to begin to write *The Great Gatsby*. Their bizarre and drunken antics started in Paris and stretched to the Riviera. Scott got drunk and wrote on the breast of a friend's wife in lipstick. Zelda got up from their table at a restaurant, lifted her skirts above the waist, and just as she had done in Montgomery, danced like Salome before startled diners.

Two of Scott and Zelda's best friends in France were Gerald and Sara Murphy, a wealthy couple with literary tastes, talents, and sociability, and who had the means to bring together a wide circle of writers and artists in their home. The Murphys and Fitzgeralds were attracted to each other not only because they shared literary interests but perhaps also because they were directly in contrast when it came to money and conduct. The Fizgeralds were broke and flamboyant and the Murphys were wealthy and conservative. The charming and amusing Scott nevertheless severely tested the Murphys' patience and tolerance. He seemed to have to prove to himself again and again that they would, no matter how badly he behaved, always forgive him and love him. Fitzgerald's compulsive and narcissistic behavior is reminiscent of Poe's compulsive and narcissistic attitude toward his foster father, Mr. Allan. Neither Poe nor Fitzgerald could tame the offensive and self-destructive behavior that so repulsed the Allans and the Murphys. Sara later connected the selfishness and insensitivity of Scott's narcissistic character with a defect in his literary work. She bluntly told him, "Consideration for other people's feelings, opinions or even time is *completely* left out of your make.... Why, for instance, should you trample on other people's feelings continually with things you permit yourself to say and do—owing partly to the self-indulgence of drinking too much." It was also Sarah who made the following criticism about Scott and his work: "I have always told you, you haven't the faintest idea what anybody but yourself is like." Scott was forced to agree: "My characters are all Scott Fitzgerald."

In 1925—the year Dreiser published *An American Tragedy*, Dos Passos' *Manhattan Transfer*, and Hemingway's *In Our Time*—Fitzgerald made an impressive leap from his deeply flawed first two novels to his first masterpiece, *The Great Gatsby*. *This Side of Paradise* and *The Beautiful and the Damned* were sensational and loosely constructed and drew rather too directly upon the author's own life and sentiments. *The Great Gatsby* was imaginative rather than autobiographical, unified rather than episodic, classically balanced and shaped in form, beautifully clear-eyed and lucid in tone—almost epic, Homer-like. In place of the loosely constructed story of a young man's life, Fitzgerald set out to capture a social world. He succeeded in this effort and in this novel in a manner and to a degree equaled by no American novelist other than Henry James and William Faulkner, and in our day approached by John Updike.

Fitzgerald wrote *The Great Gatsby* when the influence of Freud was perhaps at its zenith in artistic and literary circles. To however conscious a degree, Fitzgerald portrays his narrator Nick Carraway as the author's *ego-ideal* (the mature personality Fitzgerald would have liked to be) and the novel's hero Jay Gatsby, a.k.a. James Gatz, as Fitzgerald's *ego-alien* (immature personality that Fitzgerald actually was). In other words, the personality of the character Gatsby is close to what Fitzgerald's personality in real life actually was, while Carraway's personality is what Fitzgerald believed his own personality should have been. To say this another way, Gatsby's uninhibited ego is an immature narcissistic personality functioning at the level of the *id* and using only immature defense mechanisms or the intermediate defense mechanism of *reaction formation* and *denial*. Carraway's *ego* has been able to develop and grow above and beyond Gatsby's. Both Gatsby and Carraway were parts of Scott Fitzgerald's original but changing personality because he was gradually able to form a more mature personality by discarding immature defense mechanisms and using more mature defense mechanisms (humor, anticipation, discipline, positive identification, sublimation, and altruism). Scott Fitzgerald matured not only in his literary work but also in his life, achieving a more ego-syntonic and stable personality, overcoming his earlier immature, narcissistic personality so characteristic of infancy in all humans, but prolonged in some instances, like Fitzgerald.

All the finest authors and critics of that time (and since) admired *The Great Gatsby,* seeing that Fitzgerald had fulfilled his artistic potential and written a great novel. But the sale of the book, about 25,000 copies (far less than his original two novels) did not match his expectations and barely paid off his advance. The dramatic adaptation of the novel by Owen David opened in New York in February 1926, ran for 112 performances and earned Fitzgerald $18,000, with another $17,000 gained through the sale of the film rights. These sums, large for the day, did not come close to supporting the Fitzgeralds' style of life; Scott had to turn to the more lucrative production of magazine stories until he had banked enough to devote himself again to novels.

The writer who had published *The Great Gatsby* at the age of twenty-eight and seven books before he was thirty would seem to have a great career before him. But Fitzgerald succumbed to the temptation of easy money. He scarcely considered trying to live on the modest royalties of a serious novelist. Though he had earned a great deal, he and Zelda spent a great deal more. Trapped in an increasingly, hand-to-mouth existence, he never broke loose from the short story market and brought out only two more novels during the last fourteen years of his life. Admittedly, some of Fitzgerald's short stories have literary merit far above run-of-the-mill fiction, and both the later novels (*Tender Is the*

Night and *The Last Tycoon*) were written and re-written, endlessly revised, perhaps from a literary point of view over-written, but Fitzgerald never again achieved the artistic majesty in the form of his masterpiece, *The Great Gatsby*.

A new type of professional writing opportunity (and source of income) presented itself as soon as he returned to the United States from the French Riviera in January 1927. He received an offer from the United Artists Studio in Hollywood. They wanted a modern flapper story for the popular and vivacious comedy star Constance Talmadge, for an advance $3,500 and an additional $12,500 if his film story was accepted. Scott and Zelda were received enthusiastically by the Hollywood community and were immediately caught up in the swirl of parties. Attempting to live up to their glamorous legend, they got drunk and acted outrageously. They turned up uninvited at Sam Goldwyn's party, got down on their hands and knees outside the front door, and barked until they were reluctantly admitted. They made a late night visit to John Monk Saunder's house carrying a pair of shears and offered to solve his romantic problems by castration. During tea with Carmel Myers, Scott went even further and boiled a couple of watches and assorted jewelry belonging to several of the guests in a can of tomato soup. No one could understand why he behaved in such a bizarre fashion, nor did anyone taste the stew. These antics reinforced Fitzgerald's reputation as an alcoholic, hurt his professional standing in Hollywood, and made it more difficult for him to get lucrative film work, thus indicating that the slow maturing of his immature personality was now deteriorating as a result of his alcoholism.

The Fitzgeralds married in April 1920 and Scott published *The Great Gatsby* in April 1925 and Zelda—following the momentous five-year pattern—had her first mental breakdown in April 1930. Fitzgerald identified himself with the Jazz Age, which he helped to define and called it "the most expensive orgy in history." If, as Arthur Miller observed, "the 30s were the price that had to be paid for the 20s," then that decade was far more costly than Fitzgerald had imagined. Just as his literary career spanned the twenties and the thirties, so his personal life— which began to collapse at the same time as Zelda's breakdown, soon after the Wall Street Crash of October 1929—ran precisely parallel to the boom and bust phases of the decades between World War I and World War II.

Perhaps because of his strong Catholic conscience, his superego, that probably made him feel at least partly responsible for Zelda's illness, Scott was intimately involved in her treatment for the rest of his life. Bonds of love and guilt inextricably connected him to her, by the hope that she would eventually recover and they could resume their life together and by his fear that she would remain ill and he would continue to suffer with her. Scott's artistic career was also bound up with Zelda, who had provided inspiration for so much of his work. His novel *Tender Is the Night* would soon draw upon her insanity and his stories would be written to provide for the best of treatment for her. All paths seemed to lead directly to Zelda from the destructiveness of the past, the sterility of their present, to the uncertainty of their future. No matter where he was geographically in relation to where Zelda was institutionalized over the next ten years, Fitzgerald lived in the phases of her madness and remained deeply involved in the specifics of her treatment. He wanted to be involved with the individual doctors, the different psychiatric approaches, the particular settings and atmospheres of each clinic. Zelda, whose apparent recovery was always followed by another breakdown and who constantly sought a way back to sanity, was treated in seven different hospitals in only six years. She repeatedly had to adjust to new people and strange surroundings while suffering hallucinations, depression, and suicidal impulses.

Needless to say, the period of sexual abstinence during Zelda's hospitalization was used as an excuse by Scott for the worsening of his drinking problem. He now drank more than ever. Samuel Johnson once explained how alcohol compensated for sexual deprivation. When asked what he thought was the greatest pleasure in life, he replied: "Sex and the second was drinking. He wondered why "there were not more drunkards, for all could drink although all could not perform sexually."

With all the chaos inherent in loving and caring for someone with schizophrenia, Fitzgerald even felt in danger of losing his own reasoning when torn by the agonizing, never-ending swings between hope and despair. Paradoxically, his participation in Zelda's treatment matured and strengthened his character. Though he could be irritating and self indulgent, he now achieved, through emotional isolation and intense self-scrutiny, a sweeter temperament, a deeper understanding of others, and a more dignified demeanor (personality conversion through positive changes in his defense mechanisms).

John Dos Passos, who had perceived of Zelda's insanity before her breakdown and criticized Fitzgerald's madcap life at Ellerslie, a thirty room mansion near Wilmington, Delaware, spoke for many of Scott's friends who discerned his nobility of character when confronted with personal tragedy:

"Scott was meeting adversity with a competency of purpose that I found admirable. He was trying to raise Scottie, keep a flow of stories into the magazines to raise the enormous sums that Zelda's illness cost. At the same time he was determined to continue writing first-rate novels. With age and experience his literary standards were rising. I never admired a man more."

Scott always wanted to give Zelda the very best medical care that was available. In late November 1930, Dr. Forel wished to call in the famous Eugen Bleuler—professor at Zurich (and teacher of Carl Jung), who had coined the word "schizophrenia" in a famous paper of 1911—to confirm his diagnosis and treatment. Scott agreed to pay the $500 consultation fee, a staggering sum at that time. Bleuler agreed with the current treatment and said that Zelda had borderline insanity (not to be confused with term used today for a different condition, borderline personality). No one knew the cause of her illness or how to cure it. He vaguely suggested rest and recreation, and said Zelda should be allowed to go skiing in the nearby mountains and to visit the shops, theaters, and operas in Geneva. Bleuler also told Fitzgerald that three out of four patients like Zelda were eventually discharged: one recovered completely and two others remained delicate and slightly eccentric. Zelda, however, eventually joined the unfortunate quarter that never recovered. She would end her days in an asylum for the insane.

In January 1931 Fitzgerald sailed home from Europe to attend the funeral of his father-in-law in Rockville, Maryland. Despite his bereavement, he received more hostility than sympathy from her family. They could not conceive how much he had suffered, and they secretly thought that Scott was the crazy one. They had no compunction in maintaining this attitude in spite of the fact that they were the ones that had concealed from him the deep and pervasive family history of mental illness. Ignoring that history, the Sayres held him to blame for Zelda's illness and accused him of putting her in an asylum in order to get rid of her. Personal humiliation seemed to inspire Fitzgerald's greatest art, and he managed a story as well as a check from his unhappy experiences in Hollywood. He completed *The Great Gatsby* while Zelda was cuckolding him with Jozan. He had transformed the accusations of the Sayre family and his guilt about Zelda into *Babylon Revisited*. Now he used his degrading experience of Irving Thalberg's party as the central episode in *Crazy Sunday* (1932).[1] These two stories in the early 1930s represent Fitzgerald's greatest work in this period. A few years later, he would transfigure his alcoholism and decline into *Tender Is the Night* and his own nervous break-down into the *Crack-Up* essays. Fitzgerald wrote three stories for *Esquire* for issues published in February 1936, March 1936, and April 1936, describing the subjective feelings he experienced during his own mental "crack-up." The following is an excerpt from the April 1936 issue entitled "Pasting It Together."

I have spoken in these pages how an exceptionally optimistic young man experienced a crack-up of values, a crack-up that he scarcely knew of until long after it occurred. I told of the succeeding period of desolation and of the necessity of going on, but without benefit of Henley's familiar heroics, "my head is bloody but unbowed." For a check-up of my spiritual liabilities indicated that I had no particular head to be bowed or unbowed. Once I had had a heart but that was about all I was sure of.

This was at least a starting place out of the morass in which I floundered: "I felt—therefore I was." At one time or another there had been many people who had leaned on me. Come to me in difficulties or written me from afar, believed implicitly in my advice and my attitude toward life. The dullest platitude monger or the most unscrupulous Rasputin who can influence the destinies of many people must have some individuality, so the question became one of finding why and where I had changed, where was the leak through which, unknown to myself, my enthusiasm and my vitality had been steadily and prematurely trickling away.

One harassed and despairing night I packed a briefcase and went off a thousand miles to think it over. I took a dollar room in a drab little town where I knew no one and sunk all of the money I had with me in a stock of potted meat, crackers and apples. But don't let me suggest that the change from a rather overstuffed world to a comparative asceticism was any Research Magnificent—I only wanted absolute quiet to think out why I had developed a sad attitude toward sadness, a melancholy attitude toward melancholy and a tragic attitude toward tragedy—*why I had become identified with the objects of my horror or compassion.*

The "crack-up" years were 1935–1937 and were years of social isolation for Fitzgerald that included the three articles for *Esquire* describing his rapid demise from alcohol and pills. They were associated with Zelda's own mental decline that included the gamut of mental symptoms from a catatonic state to multiple suicide attempts. Her psychiatrist, Dr. William Elgin at Sheppard-Pratt—found Zelda confused, withdrawn, and expressionless. The once active and vibrant woman now seemed to him a colorless "blob" who moved in slow motion and felt threatened by hallucinatory voices. Yet, her tender and poignant letter of June 1935 to Scott revealed that Zelda was all too aware of the devastation her illness had caused. She showed considerable insight into her emotional hollowness and expressed great sadness about all they had sacrificed. She also returned to the themes of lost identity and negation of self that Scott considered in his *Crack-Up* essays:

> *Dearest and always Dearest Scott:*
> *I am sorry too that there should be nothing to greet you but an empty shell. The thought of the effort you have made over me, the suffering this nothing has caused would be unendurable to any save a completely vacuous mechanism. Had I any feelings they would all be bent in gratitude to you and in sorrow that all of my life there should not even be the smallest relic of the love and beauty that we started with to offer you at the end....*
>
> *Now that there isn't any more happiness and home is gone and there isn't any past and no emotions but those that were yours where there could be comfort—it is a shame that we should have met in harshness and coldness where there was once so much tenderness and so many dreams.... I love you anyway even if there isn't any me or any love or even any life.*

Scott was fundamentally a moralist and was raised a very religious (Catholic) person and it kept him from completely enjoying his efforts at alcoholism and from experiencing sexual sensations normally. Scott, no doubt as a result of his brain toxicity from his alcoholism, could not decipher the prime paradoxical beliefs that he held. That is, he firmly believed in his own mind that Zelda was permanently insane but that she would recover, and that he was a hopeless failure but he would eventually succeed.

In mid-November he explained that he had become severely depressed and had suffered a mild nervous breakdown. Like all alcoholics, he rationalized the reasons for his drinking, which he was doing now more than ever—thirty-seven bottles of beer a day or its equivalent in liquor and taking Phenobarbital to help him sleep and Benzedrine to help him awaken in the morning. He also at this time attempted suicide twice. Once with morphine and once with Phenobarbital. He complained that he couldn't even succeed at suicide.

Fitzgerald confesses in the *Crack-Up* essays, "My life had been drawing on resources that I did not posses.... I had been mortgaging myself physically and spiritually my vitality had been steadily and prematurely ticking away." In short, he had been overcome by emotional exhaustion. The symptoms of his condition were a desire to be alone, a rejection of people, listlessness, apathy and lack of feelings, as well as a purely physiological response to alcohol addiction that includes hypersensitivity to both noise and silence, irritation, irrational prejudice (paranoia), and a sense of being emotionally impoverished. "In a real dark night of the soul," writes the insomniac Fitzgerald, alluding to the Spanish mystic St. John of the Cross, "it is always three o'clock in the morning, day after day." Of course, each one of these symptoms is a typical symptom of alcohol intoxication or alcohol withdrawal. Fitzgerald also makes a connection between insomnia, frequent changes of drenched pajamas, and the torment of writing that Lowell adopts and elaborates on in "Night Sweats."

> For ten nights now I've felt the creeping damp
> float over my pajamas' wilted white...
> Sweet salt embalms me and my head is wet,
> everything streams and tells me this is right;
> my life's fever is soaking in night sweats—
> one life, one writing!

His rationalization continued in many different veins with his friends: "Can you imagine a single American artist except James and Whistler (who lived in England) who didn't die of drink?" He frequently saw himself in the destructive yet romantic tradition of Edgar Allan Poe, who he much admired and who wrote his own self-analysis in his short story *The Imp of the Perverse* (see Chapter 4). Fitzgerald often compared his emotional symptoms and psychological vulnerability with those of Hemingway: "He is quite as nervously broken down as I am but it manifests itself in different ways. His inclination is toward megalomania and mine toward melancholia." Fitzgerald's diagnosis was off the mark a little in his conclusion. Fitzgerald was *hypomanic* and *depressed* whereas Hemingway was a *megalomaniac* and *depressed* (manic depressive).

Critics have been intrigued by what Glenway Wescott called Fitzgerald's "self autopsy and funeral sermon." Scottie, his daughter, who picked up this clinical metaphor, compared her father to a "surgeon performing an operation upon himself, hurting terribly but watching the process with a fascinated detachment." In 1945 Joseph Wood Krutch praised *Crack-Up* for its intelligence, sophistication, and artistic sincerity. And Mark Schorer, one of Fitzgerald's most perceptive readers, called it "a beautiful and moving confession; without a hint of self-pity, it is one of the most extraordinary self-revelations in literature."

Fitzgerald acknowledged in *Crack-Up* that, "there are always those to whom all self-revelations are contemptible." And he explained to Beatrice Dance that many friends—from Hemingway and Dos Passos to Perkins and Ober—thought that he had done himself great harm, when the articles were published in *Esquire* in the spring of 1936, by announcing to the world that he was morally and artistically bankrupt. Amid all this criticism of Fitzgerald, Arnold Gingrich, the editor of *Esquire,* was a persuasive, dissenting voice. He felt that Fitzgerald had indeed hit rock bottom, but that *any* publicity—good or bad—was helpful and that the *Crack-Up* essays actually had a beneficial effect on Scott's career: "Can't feel that it did any damage. So it got him a brutal letter from Ernest Hemingway and a rather hoity-toity one from Dos Passos. And an interviewer from the *New York Post*, stimulated by it to look him up, did a nasty piece about him that Marjorie Kinnan Rawlings deplored. But don't forget, at this point, sixteen years after his first fame, a lot of people thought he was dead. So the publicity occasioned by the publication of the *Crack-Up* series undoubtedly reminded Hollywood that he was still around, and led either directly or indirectly to his getting a second chance out there, with his contract that took him out there in July of 1937." At the "crack-up" stage nothing could harm his career—it could only help.

The personal revelations in *Crack-Up* seemed to start an avalanche in the American literature of writers who followed Fitzgerald's innovative path. Like Fitzgerald, Truman Capote, Tennessee Williams, and Norman Mailer deliberately provoked bad publicity in order to gain attention and revealed their pathetic or violent alcoholism. More significantly, *Crack-Up* had a powerful impact on confessional poets like W. D. Snodgrass, Robert Lowell, John Berryman, Anne Sexton, and Sylvia Plath, who wrote openly about their anguish and mental breakdowns, as well as on literary accounts of alcoholism, drugs, and depression that culminated in works like William Styron's *Darkness Visible* (1980) and Kay Redfield Jamison's revealing, scientific, and professionally educational autobiography, *An Unquiet Mind* (1996).

There was another miraculous social movement that literally was born during the same chronological period of time—mainly 1935 and 1936. I am speaking here of the self-help program of Alcoholics Anonymous. The birth of this fellowship historically began on June 10, 1935, when a stock-broker by the name of Bill Wilson made a phone call to a surgeon, Dr. Bob Smith, with the motivation that two or more alcoholics could abstain from alcohol together more easily than a single alcoholic could do it alone. That meeting between Bill Wilson and Dr. Bob Smith was held in Akron, Ohio and that same month a group of alcoholics started the first meeting of Alcoholics Anonymous. The first edition of the book of Alcoholics Anonymous was printed in 1939 and there were already 2,000 members. Then Jack Anderson wrote a feature article in the *Saturday Evening Post* about Alcoholics Anonymous in March 1941 that caused a deluge of new members that has continued until this day.

Why these unrelated events occurred more or less spontaneously and in the same decade or two I am not able to fully explain. It is just an idea whose time has come or an idea that was critically needed. Obviously, these two phenomena share a single common problem—alcoholism. In any event the convergence of two separate phenomena is compatible with one of the general concepts of this book. As new and better medications and treatments are discovered more and more individuals are able to recover from their afflictions.

Fitzgerald was able to acquire an unusual calm after a lifetime of flamboyancy and restlessness. Some of this may have been because his declining physical health (heart disease and his tuberculosis) was taking its toll. Fitzgerald was disciplined when it came to work. He could work whenever he needed the money in the past, but he began to realize that he could not work and drink at the same time, and he would shift to Coca-Cola when he had to write. As Frances Knoll, whose duties included disposing of Scott's gin bottles, told Mizener, "Drink in small quantities acted as a stimulus and did not affect the quality of his writing. Although he continued to write when he was roaring drunk, as well, most of that effort had to be discarded, though it had a kind of humor that would be hard to duplicate under normal conditions."

Fitzgerald gradually began to realize that alcohol hurt his work, damaged his reputation, ruined his health, and almost destroyed his intimate relationships.

Remembering the sad fate of the original Edgar Allan Poe, he told his Princeton classmates: "It seems to be the fate of all drunks that in the end they have to give up not only liquor but a whole lot of other good things." Refusing at first to admit that he was an alcoholic, Fitzgerald drank secretly or switched to just beer or wine, falling prey to the false belief of many at that time that beer or wine contained no alcohol. He also tried every conceivable method to cure his disease—stopping suddenly or gradually, smoking or eating candy when he got the urge—but nothing worked. Finally, he hired a doctor and nurses, forced himself to endure an agonizing three-day cure, was fed intravenously, could not sleep, and retched miserably throughout the night. At last he was able to report that even a single drink made him deathly sick. In May 1937 he proudly (if prematurely) told Ober: "Since I stopping drinking I've gained from just over 140 to over 160 pounds. I sleep at last and though my hair's gray I feel younger than for four years." Despite all these efforts, he was unable to give up drink completely until the last year of his life, when he raced against time to complete *The Last Tycoon*. Hemingway said, "The stuff he wrote at the end was the best of all. Poor bastard."

DEVELOPMENTAL AND CHILDHOOD HISTORY

Probably the most influential event of his childhood took place before F. Scott Fitzgerald was born. His two older sisters, Mary and Louise, suddenly died of an epidemic at the ages of one and three while their mother was still pregnant with Scott. Another infant, born four years later in 1900, lived only one hour. The Fitzgeralds were, needless to say, devastated by these losses. (Mollie kept Louise's dolls in tissue paper until the end of her life.) The death of his sisters may have made Scott feel guilty about surviving. It certainly placed a high value on Scott's life and led to an unnaturally close connection between the overprotective, middle-aged parents and their precious, delicate, and spoiled child. The family tragedy also strengthened the bond between Scott and the father, who tried to protect the boy from his mother's grief-stricken hysteria. Scott could not miss the fact that he was "the survivor" and he was made to feel that he was indeed precious and that it was up to him to compensate for his siblings' absence.

Scott was a robust infant, weighing ten pounds, six ounces at birth, but he became a sickly and much coddled child. When he was two years old he developed a persistent cough that his mother feared might lead to consumption. She promptly took him to a health resort. The following year his parents took him to infants' school, but he wept and wailed so much that they took him out again after one morning. The family physician, M. R. Ramsey, recalled that the stubborn and spoiled young Scott "was a patient of [his] when he was a small boy and until he went off to prep school. He was a very difficult and temperamental patient and refused to accept any regime which was not to his liking. This attitude he preserved throughout his life."

Scott's only surviving sibling, Annabel, was born in Syracuse in July 1901, and his first childhood memory of her was the sight of her howling on a bed. The self-absorbed boy was not close to her as a child, although he was gracious enough to give her substantial advice about how to attract boys as a teenager. She married and had two children and went on to lead a conventional life as a wife and mother.

Scott's father, Edward, was preoccupied with money because of his manifest inability to earn it. The most traumatic incident of Scott's childhood took place in Buffalo in March 1908, and, according to him, suddenly transformed his father from an elegant gentleman to a hopeless wreck:

> One afternoon—I was ten or eleven—the phone rang and my mother answered it. I didn't understand what she said but I felt that disaster had come upon us. My mother, a little while before, had given me a quarter to go swimming. I gave the money back to her. I knew something terrible had happened and I thought she could not spare the money now. Then I began to pray, "Dear God," I prayed, "please don't let us go to the poorhouse." A little while later my father came home, I had been right. He had lost his job. That morning he had gone out a comparatively young man, and a man full of strength, full of confidence. He came home that evening, an old man, and a completely broken man. He had lost his essential drive, his immaculateness of purpose. He was a failure the rest of his days.

Mollie remained locked in her own hysterical world. She looked down on her husband, who began to drink too much. His father frequently asked young Scott: "If it weren't for your Grandfather McQuillan, where would we be now?" Isn't it telling that the fathers of most of Fitzgerald's fictional heroes are dead before his novels begin?

Three crucial entries in Scott's autobiographical *Ledger* of his boyhood years from 1901 to 1904 expressed his acute anxiety and shame about his feet, which he associated with fear of exposure, with filth, and with perversion (foot fetish). Scott's bizarre obsession with and phobias about his feet were closely connected not only to his childhood guilt about sex and revulsion when kissing girls—the result of what he called "a New England conscience, developed in Minnesota"—but also to adult doubts about his masculinity and fears about his sexual inadequacy:

> He went to Atlantic City—where some Freudian complex refused to let him display his feet, so he refused to swim, concealing the real reason. They thought he feared the water.

> There was a boy named Arnold who went barefooted in his yard and peeled plums. Scott's Freudian shame about his feet kept him from joining in.

> He took off John Wylie's shoes. He began to hear "dirty" words. He had this curious dream of perversion.

The sight of his own feet filled him with embarrassment and horror. No amount of persuasion could entice him to permit others to see his naked feet and up until he was twelve. This fear caused him a great deal of misery. This complex suddenly disappeared on some undocumented day without any definite explanation—so we are left to conjecture through analytical means what psychiatric symptom this fetish was replaced with or what mature defense mechanism he learned that replaced the fetish.

Frances Knoll, Fitzgerald's secretary in Hollywood, observed that he was slightly pigeon-toed, always wore slippers, and never went about in bare feet. Sheilah Graham, Fitzgerald's companion during the last years of his life, wrote that he had mentioned his "mysterious shyness" about his feet and during the years that she knew him always refused to take off his shoes and socks on the beach. When Tony Buttitta, who visited Fitzgerald's hotel room in Asheville in 1935, noticed his "stubby and unattractive feet," Fitzgerald "fumbled for his slippers and hid his feet in them." Most significantly, Lottie, a prostitute who became Fitzgerald's mistress that summer, described his foot fetishism and said that he "caressed her feet, the toes, instep, and heel, and got an odd pleasure out of it...." It seems that the sight of women's feet had excited him since he first started thinking about sex. This may be related to his mother's manic-depressive disorder and her unusual habit of wearing a pair of mismatched shoes. In this regard it may be important to recall that another symptom of mania is *hypersexuality*. Then there is the symbolic episode of Scott giving back the quarter to his mother that she had given to him to go swimming when they learned that his father had been fired from his job with Procter & Gamble and Scott's association of that event with eminent poverty.

Fitzgerald's childhood phobia perhaps evolved from his subconscious "Freudian feelings." Though revolted by his own feet, the feet of women sexually excited him. His fearful associations with feet—which stuck out stiffly and were strongly associated with sex—both displaced and expressed his adolescent and adult fears about his masculinity. His deep-rooted insecurity later led him to seek embarrassing reassurance not only from the "crack-up" years (1935–1937), which also were years of social isolation for Fitzgerald, the three articles for *Esquire* describing his rapid demise from alcohol and his mistresses of the 1930s, but also from personal friends, about the size and potency of his sexual organ.

A FAMILY HISTORY
(PSYCHIATRIC, MEDICAL, AND ADDICTIONS)

Scott's father became an alcoholic after his furniture business failed and he lost his job with Proctor & Gamble. As an alcoholic, he became dependent on his wife's inherited fortune, but he was a proud and educated Southern gentleman.

Scott's mother had many symptoms of having manic-depressive disorder including flamboyant dressing and mood swings including hysteria. She was known for her "peculiar behavior" and Scott called her a neurotic, half insane with pathological nervous worry, and she remained locked in her own histrionic world after the death of her two young daughters during an epidemic before Scott was born.

Scott's maternal grandfather died from consumption (tuberculosis). Scott was also diagnosed as having pulmonary tuberculosis and hypoglycemia and at one time, the hypoglycemia was thought to be the cause of his alcoholism. However, whatever hypoglycemia occurs in relationship to alcoholism is caused by the alcoholism and not vice versa. His deceased literary hero, Edgar Allan Poe, was also diagnosed with hypoglycemia and alcoholism and Phenobarbital and morphine abuse, but the latter was never proven. Fitzgerald apparently never had withdrawal seizures although alcohol liver disease was diagnosed.

PSYCHIATRIC HISTORY OF
ZELDA SAYRE FITZGERALD'S FAMILY

The solid respectability of the Sayre family kept hidden the dangerous currents swirling beneath the calm surface of their lives. Zelda's father, Anthony Sayre, son of the editor of the *Montgomery Post,* was born in Tuskegee, Alabama in 1858 and graduated from Roanoke College in Virginia and was admitted to the bar in 1881. He married three years later and was elected and reelected associate justice of the Supreme Court of Alabama from 1909 until 1931. A man of fanatically regular habits, Judge Sayre always took the streetcar to and from work at exactly the same time every day and always retired for the night at exactly eight o'clock (obsessive-compulsive personality disorder?). Cold, humorless, and hypercritical, the judge became increasingly unsociable and remote from his family. Zelda considered him inhumanely perfect and desperately tried to penetrate his stony reserve. One day when Fitzgerald was visiting, Zelda goaded her father into such a rage that he picked up a carving knife and chased her around the dining room table while the rest of the family ignored them. Fitzgerald, nervous, and infatuated with Zelda, failed to perceive that this was a familiar occurrence, that the judge was not as self-controlled as he appeared to be and that all was not well in the Sayre household.

Zelda's mother, Minnie Machen, the daughter of a Kentucky senator, was born in 1860 and had in her youth cherished hopes of an operatic career. The Sayres had three older daughters—Marjorie, Rosalind, and Clothilde—whose ages ranged from nine to eighteen when Zelda was born, and a son Anthony, who was then six. Minnie nursed Zelda, her youngest and favorite child till the age of four.

Minnie's mother and sister had both committed suicide. Marjorie had had a mental breakdown and suffered from a nervous illness throughout her life. Young Anthony became notorious for his immoral and licentious behavior and left Auburn University without earning his degree. In 1933, after recurrent nightmares about killing his mother, he would also commit suicide by leaping from the window of his hotel room in Mobile (paranoid schizophrenia or psychotic depression?). No one ever told Fitzgerald when he was courting Zelda about the terrifying history of insanity and suicides in her family.

EDUCATIONAL EXPERIENCE

When his family returned to Minnesota from Syracuse, New York after Edwin was terminated from Procter & Gamble, the twelve-year old Scott entered a non-sectarian school, St. Paul Academy, which had forty boys between the ages of ten and eighteen. During his three years there, he energetically began his literary apprenticeship. He would memorize titles in bookstores and confidently discuss works he had not read with the same kind of pretentiousness that permeated his first novel. He attempted to achieve popularity with his classmates, as he had in Buffalo and at summer camp, but failed abysmally because he observed and criticized their faults. As he would do later at Princeton and in the army, he ignored his studies and "wrote all through every class in school in the back of [his] geography book and during first year Latin and on the margins of themes and declensions and mathematical problems." Even with all of these early attempts at writing it has been written that he never really learned how to spell even into his adult professional life.

He wrote many juvenile adventure stories for the school newspaper and melodramatic plays for the Elizabethan Dramatic Club. Scott's first published story, "The Mystery of the Raymond Mortgage" (1909) echoed the title and imitated the characters and themes of Poe's "The Murders in the Rue Morgue." Though he neglected to bring the mortgage into the story, no one seemed to notice.

Fitzgerald apparently saw the similarities between himself and Edgar Allan Poe, and certainly was aware that they shared alcoholism, insanity, and as Scott was convinced, genius. The similarities ended there since Poe was modest and lived in abject poverty and Fitzgerald was conceited and lived flamboyantly with the elite of the world, both at home in the United States and abroad.

Scott's poor performance at St. Paul Academy prompted his parents to send him to a stricter Eastern Catholic boarding school. This would, they hoped, provide a more rigorous academic program, expose him to a more sophisticated way of life and increase his chances of gaining admission to a good college. The Newman School in Hackensack, New Jersey (across the Hudson River and about ten miles northwest of midtown Manhattan) had been founded in 1890 by Cardinal Gibbons of Baltimore to attract the sons of Catholic "gentlemen" and taught sixty boys from well-off Catholic families throughout the country. Scott, brought up with the traditional values of his paternal ancestors in Maryland, had always yearned for an Eastern education.

Scott's hope and happiness, however, were short lived. As he entered Newman in September 1911, he naively overrated his appearance and athletic ability, social graces, and intellectual power, which he felt would lead him to success in school and retrospectively make him honestly admit that he lacked the fundamental elements of good character. However, his narcissistic personality prevented him from gaining insights from his honest list of character defects and instead, he listed them as assets that would be useful for him to take advantage of others:

> First: Physically—I marked myself handsome; of great athletic possibilities and an extremely good dancer.... Second: Socially...I was convinced that I had personality, charm, magnetism, poise, and ability to dominate others. Also I was sure that I exercised a subtle influence over women. Third: Mentally...I was vain of having so much, of being so talented, ingenious and quick to learn.... Generally—I knew that at bottom I lacked essentials. At the last crisis, I knew I had no real courage, perseverance or self-respect.

This paradox no doubt resulted from the conflict between him being treated as "an especially precious" child by his parents and as a "guilty sinner" by the Catholic Church. He had the unusual characteristics of feeling narcissistic and omnipotent on the one hand while at the same moment feeling worthless with an incredibly low self-esteem.

For his university, Fitzgerald chose Princeton. With an additional inheritance his mother received when his grandmother McQuillan died he was able to enter Princeton without financial constraints, which was another difference between himself and the financial problems Poe's foster father imposed on him at the University of Virginia. The way Fitzgerald saw it, Harvard was associated with New England puritans and brainy Jews, and seemed too "indoors" and intellectual. On the other hand, Yale men were too brawny and brutal and seemed to possess dumb energy just like the original Yale Bull Dog. Fitzgerald imagined the Princeton man to be just like him.

He managed to survive his freshman year. The dazzlingly handsome Fitzgerald had an imaginative and intuitive mind, and a spontaneous and impetuous approach to experience.

After idling away the spring of 1916 in St. Paul, he returned to Princeton to repeat his junior year. But his spirit was crushed. He felt it was stupid to spend four hours a day in his tutor's stuffy room enduring the infinite boredom. He had been deprived of the recognition he craved and had lost all chance of winning honors during his final years. "After a few months of rest I went back to college," he explained in the *Crack-Up*, "but I had lost certain offices, the chief one was the presidency of the Triangle Club...a musical comedy idea, and also I dropped back a class. To me college would never be the same. There were to be no badges of pride, no medals, after all." Fitzgerald dedicated the summer of 1917 to drinking gin and reading Schopenhauer, Bergen, and William James. But the gin had a more powerful effect than the philosophy, and he returned to Princeton to await his commission in the army rather than to get his degree. He never graduated. Though bitter about his failures, he always remained intensely idealistic about and deeply devoted to Princeton.

MILITARY SERVICE

Fitzgerald joined the army for the same reasons that he went to Princeton. It was the fashionable thing to do. He imagined himself as a war hero just as he had once pictured himself as a football star and wanted to prove his courage in combat. The army was also a convenient way to escape his recurrent failures in college.

Fitzgerald did as badly as an army officer as he did as a college student. Just as his classes seemed to interfere with his theatrical career at Princeton, so drills and marches became an irritating interruption of the novel he wanted to write. He never made it into combat because the Armistice of November 11, 1918, ended the war before he was sent overseas. The "unusually dispensable" Fitzgerald, one of the first officers to be discharged from his unit in February 1919, returned to New York hoping to duplicate the bohemian life of Edmund Wilson. He would always cherish the notion of himself as a tested and knowledgeable army veteran, wise in the ways of war.

MARITAL HISTORY

There was an instant physical attraction between Zelda and Scott, that was beyond sexual but definitely physical. They looked enough alike to be brother and sister and there were many instances reported when they both acted out in a bisexual manner. Scott had a narcissistic personality disorder and Zelda probably did too, but she tried to adapt to Scott's narcissism by becoming a *complementary narcissist* meaning she tried to live through his glory by playing the role of Mrs. Scott Fitzgerald, most, but not all of the time. Zelda also often rebelled against being Scott's complementary narcissist by acting out her own narcissistic personality disorder roles. She even tried being a writer and achieved some modest success for her supreme efforts, but often Scott accused her of plagiarizing his own novels. Frequently, she became jealous of Scott's top billing and would act out to refocus attention on herself in her own narcissistic way. Their public performances, which resembled the Marx Brothers at a debutantes cotillion, expressed their desire to act up to their reputation, be seen to lead the revolt against boring conventions and transform a dull experience into a lively occasion. Zelda had few inhibitions and would do almost anything. She had always been the star performer in Montgomery, and her shocking pranks in the North, which she called "exploring her abysses in public," were meant to compete with Scott. Needless to say, it was a rocky marriage, but they never divorced or even separated for any long period. In fact, in spite of her developing a mental illness (schizophrenia) and spending ten years in an out of expensive institutions and perishing in one by a fire that demolished the hospital, Scott never abandoned her while he was alive. Zelda was forty-eight when she died in the accidental hospital fire on March 10, 1948. However, Scott preceded her in death by eight years and Zelda perceived this as abandonment.

Most, if not all, of these extroverted behaviors were present before the marriage as well as after. Nevertheless, although Zelda was Protestant and Scott was no longer a practicing Catholic, they were married on April 3, 1920—eight days after the publication of Fitzgerald's first novel—in the rectory of St. Patrick's Cathedral on Fifth Avenue. But as if to emphasize the break the young couple had made with their backgrounds, neither Scott's nor Zelda's parents attended the wedding. The only witnesses were Scott's Princeton friend and best man, Ludlow Fowler, and Zelda's three older sisters, who were then married and living in New York. Scott, who was nervous, insisted the ceremony begin before her sister Clothilde arrived. There was no lunch or party after the wedding, which her sister Rosalind considered rude and never forgave her for, and the couple promptly left for their honeymoon at the Biltmore Hotel.

Zelda, who later became a model for fashionable women in the 1920s, had no taste or style when she first came north. She was even considered a bit cheap and "tacky." Horrified by her girlish, Southern frills, Fitzgerald anxiously asked Marie Hersey—his St. Paul friend, Ginevra King's roommate at Westover School and a graduate of Vassar—to buy Zelda the proper clothes for New York.

The marriage lasted, in spite of a few extra-marital affairs by both parties, until Scott died of his third heart attack on December 21, 1940, at forty-four years of age, eight years before Zelda's death on March 10, 1948, in an accidental hospital fire.

OCCUPATIONAL EXPERIENCES

Fitzgerald did not like his first salaried job, writing advertising copy at Barron Collier advertising agency, so he quit and moved back to his family home in St. Paul to begin writing his first novel, *This Side of Paradise.* His motivation to work as hard as he did writing that novel was to become a successful writer, become rich, and marry Zelda Sayre.

In early September 1919, Fitzgerald completed the second version of his novel, sent the manuscript to Perkins, and—eager to work outdoors—took a job repairing train roofs for James J. Hill's Northern Pacific Railroad. Instructed to wear old clothes, Fitzgerald turned up in elegant white flannels, irritated the foreman by sitting down when he tried to hammer nails, and despite his experience in dealing with ordinary soldiers, complained he was unable to talk to the working men. Fitzgerald lasted no longer as a rude mechanical workman than he had as a writer of slogans. On September 16, 1919, Perkins freed him from his job with an enthusiastic letter: "I am very glad, personally, to be able to write to you that we are all for publishing your book, *This Side of Paradise....* I think you have improved enormously. As the first manuscript did, it abounds with energy and life and it seems to me to be in much better proportion.... The book is so different that it is hard to prophesy how it will sell but we are all for taking a chance and supporting it with vigor."

While he was waiting for the novel to be published he was transformed from an unemployed amateur into a professional writer as a result of the work he had done on the rewriting of *This Side of Paradise*. During that period of time he discovered his subject, his voice, and his style. When he returned to New York he began to turn out amusing, cleverly plotted, and at times absurd tales about the innocent adventures of bright upper-class teenagers and young people. Instead of the massive series of rejections he had suffered in the spring, he found that his stories were accepted as fast as he could produce them. *Scribner's Magazine* paid $150 each for more didactic pieces—"The Cut-Glass Bowl" and "The Four Fists"—from the firm's new author. Slight pieces like "The Debutante," "Porcelain and Pink," "Dalrymple Goes Wrong," and "Benediction," (one of his few overtly Catholic works) were gobbled up by the *Smart Set* in the fall of 1919. Fitzgerald also sold "Head and Shoulders" to the *Saturday Evening Post.* He energetically poured out five other stories between November 1919 and February 1920, that included the "Ice Palace," "May Day," and "The Camel-Back."

Fitzgerald's novel, *This Side of Paradise,* was published on March 26, 1920, and Zelda and he were married eight days later. With his marriage and the tremendous success of his first novel, Zelda and Scott slowly but surely began their extravagant lifestyle. Scott was searching for material for his novels and stories and Zelda was in search of exotic things to do and buy and try. To a large extent they were complementary to each other's purposes. Except for their first trip to Europe for three months in May 1921, while Zelda was pregnant, they contented themselves with frequent moves around the United States. After a riotous summer in Westport, Connecticut, the Fitzgeralds took an apartment in New York City where he wrote his second novel, *The Beautiful and the Dammed.* After their daughter Frances Scott Fitzgerald (Scottie) was born in St. Paul on October 26, 1921, they rented a mansion in Great Neck, Long Island to be near Broadway where his play, *The Vegetable* was to be performed, but it failed at its tryouts in November 1923. Fitzgerald wrote his way out of debt with short stories. The distractions of Great Neck and New York prevented Fitzgerald from making progress on his third novel. During this time his drinking increased. Fitzgerald was an alcoholic, but he wrote sober. Zelda regularly "got tight," but she was not an alcoholic. There were frequent domestic rows, usually triggered by drinking bouts. As a social historian Fitzgerald became identified with the Jazz Age: "It was an age of miracles, it was an age of art, it was an age of excess, and it was an age of satire." Fitzgerald's lifestyle fit that description perfectly and Zelda became the stereo-typical "flapper," and in September 1922 Scott published *Tales of the Jazz Age.*

The Fitzgeralds went to France in the spring of 1924 seeking tranquillity and inspiration for his work. He wrote *The Great Gatsby* during the summer and the fall in Valescure near St. Raphael. They then went to Rome in the winter of 1924-1925 where he revised *The Great Gatsby;* they were en route when the novel was published in April. *The Great Gatsby* proved to be Scott's first masterpiece and it marked a striking advance in Fitzgerald's technique, utilizing a complex structure and a controlled narrative point of view. Fitzgerald's achievement received critical praise, but the sales of *Gatsby* were disappointing, though the stage and movie rights brought additional income.

On the Riviera, the Fitzgeralds formed a close friendship with Gerald and Sara Murphy, as well as Ernest Hemingway who Scott admired for his personality and genius. Fitzgerald made little progress on his next novels, studies of American expatriates in France provisionally titled "*The Boy Who Killed His Mother,*" "*Our Type,*" and "*The Worlds Fair.*"

The Fitzgeralds remained in France until the end of 1926 alternating between Paris and the Riviera. During these years Zelda's behavior became increasingly eccentric. The Fitzgeralds returned to America to escape the distractions of France.

After a short, unsuccessful stint as a screenwriter in Hollywood, Fitzgerald rented the estate, Ellerslie, for two years interrupted by a visit to Paris in the summer of 1928, but he was still unable to make significant progress on his novel. While in Paris, Zelda was stressed because of her attempt to become a ballet dancer, and she suffered her first breakdown. Zelda was treated at Prangins Clinic in Switzerland until September 1931, while Fitzgerald lived in Swiss hotels. Work on the novel was again suspended as he wrote short stories to pay for psychiatric treatment.

Fitzgerald's peak story fee of $4,000 from *The Saturday Evening Post* may have had the purchasing power of $50,000 a year in today's dollars. Nonetheless, the general view of his affluence is distorted. Fitzgerald was not among the highest-paid writers of his time; his novels earned comparatively little, and most of his income came from 160 magazine stories. During the 1920s, his income for all sources averaged under $25,000 a year—good money at a time when a schoolteacher's average annual salary was $1,300, but not a fortune. Scott and Zelda spent money faster than he earned it; the author who wrote so eloquently about the effects of money on character was unable to manage his own finances.

The Fitzgeralds returned to America in the fall of 1931 and rented a house in Montgomery. Fitzgerald made a second unsuccessful trip to Hollywood in 1931. Zelda suffered a relapse in February 1932 and entered Johns Hopkins Hospital in Baltimore. She spent the rest of her life as a resident or outpatient of sanitariums for treatment of her schizophrenia.

Fitzgerald rented *La Paix*, a house outside Baltimore, where he completed his fourth novel, *Tender Is the Night*. Published in 1934, his most ambitious novel was a commercial failure, and its merits were matters of critical dispute. Set in France during the 1920s, *Tender Is the Night* examines the deterioration of Dick Dever, a brilliant American psychiatrist, during the course of his marriage to a wealthy mental patient.

The 1936–1937 period is known as the "crack-up" from the title of three essays Fitzgerald wrote in 1936 for *Esquire*. Ill, drunk, in debt, and unable to write commercial stories, he lived in hotels in the region near Asheville, North Carolina, where Zelda entered Highland Hospital. After Baltimore, Fitzgerald did not maintain a home for Scottie. When she was fourteen she went to a boarding school, and the Obers became her surrogate family. Nonetheless, Fitzgerald functioned as a concerned father by mail, attempting to supervise Scottie's education and to shape her social values.

Fitzgerald went to Hollywood alone in the summer of 1937 with a six-month Metro-Goldwyn-Mayer contract at $1,000 a week when a new Ford cost $550. He received his only screen credit for adapting *Three Comrades* (1938), and his contract was renewed for a year. Although Fitzgerald paid off most of his debts, he was unable to save any money. His trips East to visit Zelda were disastrous. In California Fitzgerald fell in love with movie columnist Sheilah Graham. Their relationship endured despite his drinking, and she tried, with some success, to control hers. After MGM dropped his option at the end of 1938, Fitzgerald worked as a freelance scriptwriter and wrote short stories for *Esquire*. He began his Hollywood novel, *The Love of the Last Tycoon*, in 1939 and had written more than half of a working draft when he died of a heart attack in Graham's apartment on December 21, 1940.

F. Scott Fitzgerald died believing himself a failure. The obituaries were condescending, and he seemed destined for literary obscurity. The first phase of the Fitzgerald revival occurred between 1945 and 1950. By 1960 he had achieved a secure place among America's enduring writers: *The Great Gatsby*, a work that seriously examines the theme of aspiration in an American setting, defines the classic American novel and is a masterpiece.

ALCOHOL AND DRUG ABUSE HISTORY

Many recovering alcoholics and drug addicts who, when sober, are law abiding individuals with a high moral value system are shocked to learn about the bizarre and amoral behavior they participated in when they were under the influence. Their sober friends who were observing this shameful behavior would say that they acted, in front of the public eyes, as if they were invisible and could not be seen. When they would tell their friends in recovery, alcoholics and addicts getting well, that they could not remember doing those things, they were told, "Oh! You were just in an alcoholic blackout." This is not a state of unconsciousness or immobility but a state of amnesia during which the person with a "blackout" looks, acts, talks, and drives as if he were sober or almost sober.

William James observed: "Sobriety diminishes, discriminates, and says no; drunkenness expands, unites, and says yes." While this type of bizarre and shocking behavior may not happen predictably or often with some problem drinkers or alcoholics, it was a constant with Scott and Zelda and in fact became their trademark. I believe that both Zelda and Scott had more than the average number of these flamboyant episodes because they both had narcissistic personality disorders, and during their periods of intoxication, they were "free" to expand upon and dramatize these when drinking. In addition, I believe that Scott also had intermittent hypomanic episodes that he inherited from his mother who probably had an undiagnosed but full-blown case of manic-depressive disorder. Unlike Edgar Allan Poe, John Berryman, and Kay Redfield Jamison— Scott Fitzgerald had to abstain from alcohol before he could do good creative writing. The previously mentioned creative artists felt, at times, that alcohol allowed them to be creative because it slowed, at least for a while, their overactive, racing minds brought about by their intermittent mania. However, we must remember that Zelda had also inherited a psychotic schizophrenia that made it easier for them to have a shared psychotic disorder (*folie à deux*). In this situation they did not have the consistently normal or traditional marital partners who would be in a position to easily check on each other's reality testing.

Early on, Scott deliberately encouraged Zelda's wildly impulsive role so that he could write about the bizarre things she had done. He was attracted by the behaviors that were, at first, essential to his work but then later helped to destroy it. Writing about what had happened to them seemed to define—or help them develop—their real selves, which were hidden beneath their immature role-playing and image-making personalities. As he ingenuously observed: "I don't know whether Zelda and I are real or whether we are characters in one of my novels." After he had created the public personae which he and Zelda felt obliged to imitate, and which revealed the disparity between their projected and actual lives, he admitted: "We scarcely knew any more who we were and we hadn't a notion what we were." The above statements define the behavior of the alcoholic and the thinking of the mentally and emotionally ill from both the objective and the subjective points of view. Fitzgerald's alcoholism was diagnosed medically during his many hospitalizations for detoxification. Mencken's doctor, Benjamin Baker, treated him for his alcoholism. Between 1933 and 1937, Scott entered Johns Hopkins Hospital eight different times to recover from alcoholic binges or to seek treatment for mild bouts of tuberculosis. According to Dr. Baker, Fitzgerald did not blame his drinking on Zelda's illness and took responsibility for it himself. He did not deny that he was an alcoholic but, despite frequent medical treatments, he was unable to control his drinking—or his behavior.

Friends and admirers, including Tony Buttitta, who ran a small book shop in the arcade of the George Vanderbilt Hotel in downtown Asheville in 1935, and later published a memoir about Fitzgerald, observed: "That summer in Asheville everything had crushed down about him," Buttitta wrote. "He was a physical, emotional, and financial bankrupt. He smoked and drank steadily, but ate very little; he took pills to sleep a few hours.... Often when I saw him he cried, suddenly, as if he were an overwrought, indulged child."

When Laura Guthrie rejected his advances at the George Vanderbilt Hotel, he hired her as a secretary and companion. According to Laura, who also kept an elaborate record of his behavior and conversation, he was extremely dictatorial and expected to be instantly obeyed. He smoked heavily, never ate a decent meal, was ashamed of his drinking but could not control it, consumed (beginning at breakfast) as many as thirty-seven beers a day, and took pills in order to sleep. He trembled, was desperately lonely and tried to acquire a suntan to hide the effects of his dissipation.

In 1938, while Sheilah Graham was living with Fitzgerald and taking care of him, she also reported that he was addicted to barbiturates and that he took a very heavy dose of chloral hydrate and two or more Nembutals to put himself to sleep, and he needed several Benzedrine pills to wake up.

PSYCHIATRIC HISTORY

F. Scott Fitzgerald had, in addition to his diagnosis of alcoholism and substance abuse, multiple psychiatric diagnoses with symptoms, some of which could mimic many of the typical symptoms frequently associated with alcoholism and substance abuse as well as fulfilling many of the criteria for several separate psychiatric diagnoses. Fitzgerald was highly unusual in this regard because his personality disorder (narcissism) was of a relatively immature and primitive type stemming from his unusual developmental experiences. He also inherited two genetic or familial psychiatric disorders from his parents. They were manic-depressive disorder from his mother, and alcohol dependence from his father. In addition to his own vulnerability, he married a woman, unbeknownst to him at the time, who had a strong family history of mental illness—probably schizophrenia. Thus, this newly-married couple living together, each with their individual vulnerabilities and weaknesses, found it easy to escape reality when it was convenient or necessary through a shared psychotic disorder (*folie à deux*).

DIAGNOSTIC CRITERIA FOR *DSM-IV* (297.3), SHARED PSYCHOTIC DISORDER:

A. A delusion develops in an individual in the contest of a close relationship with another person(s), who has already an established delusion.

B. The delusion is similar in content to that of the person who already has an established delusion.

C. The delusion is not better accounted for by another Psychotic Disorder (e.g., schizophrenia) or a Mood Disorder With Psychotic Features and is not due to the direct physiological effects of a substance (e.g., a drug of abuse, a medication) or a general medical condition.

Scott always suffered from sadness and depression because of the primary depression he inherited from his mother as well as the secondary depression from his alcoholism, or because of the reactive depression resulting from his narcissistic personality disorder. He was never satisfied with how others viewed his precious status in this world that did not recognize that he was "entitled" to a place of eminence. The resulting sadness would feel to him like a crushing rejection of his persona that was further fed by his hypomanic grandiosity. Scott, on the other hand, believed he was entitled because of his proven talent as a highly celebrated writer, but the truth is, it was no less apparent in his later years of disappointment and seeming failure than it was during the zenith of his success.

But mostly, it was an attitude he exuded as a result of his narcissistic personality disorder that rooted in early childhood because his only two siblings died in an epidemic before he was born. He was left as an only child for the first five years of his life until his sister and only surviving sibling, Annabel, was born. Therefore, from infancy, Scott was always aware of his special place in his parents' affection and protection, and he definitely held to and nurtured an idea of his unique "specialness" long after he grew from childhood. He was an especially precious child to his parents.

Zelda, too, was her mother's favorite child and because of mental illnesses in Zelda's siblings, she was also her most protected child. Her mother nursed her until she was four years old. Symptoms of many different psychiatric disorders can be found in abundance in the attitudes and behaviors that both Scott and Zelda exhibited during their relatively short lives and that many of their friends and acquaintances observed in their entertaining yet shocking attitudes and behaviors. Scott and Zelda started out their lives by having a lot in common. After he had created the public personae that he and Zelda felt obliged to imitate, and which revealed the disparity between their projected and actual lives, he admitted, "Neither our public or our personal personae felt real to either of us."

From his three *Esquire* articles known as the *Crack-Up*, that were revealingly confessional, he noted that he was often limited as a writer by his inability to get outside or beyond himself. "I never did anything but live the life I wrote about," he declared. "My characters are all Scott Fitzgerald. Even the feminine characters are feminine Scott Fitzgeralds."

In 1932 he had told his editor: "Five years have rolled away from me and I can't decide exactly who I am, if anyone." In the *Crack-Up* (1936) he proclaimed, "There was not an 'I' any more." And in the summer of 1937, soon after he arrived in Hollywood, he emphasized his loneliness and the

Poe-like split in his personality by writing a strange and disturbing postcard to himself: "Dear Scott—How are you? Have been meaning to come in and see you. I have [been] living at the Garden of Allah. Yours, Scott Fitzgerald."

During this period that Fitzgerald referred to as his "crack-up," he attempted suicide at least two times in 1936 and 1937. All attempts were made by taking overdoses of his prescribed medications, mainly Nembutal, morphine, and chloral hydrate. They all seemed to be serious suicide attempts during periods of major depression and they all were thwarted by inadvertently vomiting the medication. None of them appeared to be overtly manipulative in that there were no witnesses present when he attempted suicide and he never warned anyone of his intent.

Although this is a posthumous summary of the potential psychiatric differential diagnoses of F. Scott Fitzgerald, there is enough historical information to document the possibilities now that can be clarified when we address these issues in the Psychiatric Formulation below. He no doubt did have a narcissistic personality disorder as did his wife Zelda. Their combined narcissistic personality disorders plus Zelda's presumed diagnosis of a hereditary psychosis, probably schizophrenia, warrants the diagnosis of a shared psychotic disorder (*folie à deux*). Scott's maternal family history of a manic-depressive disorder along with his depressions, suicide attempts, and episodic flamboyant behavior is sufficient to make one suspicious that he had at least a major depression and intermittent hypomanic episodes. By his own admission, he had alcohol dependence and was also cross addicted to Phenobarbital, chloral hydrate, Nembutal, and Benzedrine, and probably morphine abuse also. There was sufficient alcohol and sedative use to confirm a diagnosis of intermittent acute alcohol and sedative withdrawal, toxic psychosis from the same drugs and alcohol, and at least one bout of frank *delirium tremens*.

Although the illness was unknown during his generation, I feel that today there would be sufficient evidence to diagnosis Scott with *dyslexia* (developmental reading disorder, *DSM-IV* (315.0) because of his spelling difficulties.

PSYCHIATRIC SYMPTOMS DUE TO GENERAL MEDICAL CONDITIONS

I hesitate to mention the medical condition of low blood sugar (hypoglycemia) as a serious cause of psychiatric symptoms for reasons that I will document shortly. However, I would be remiss in the purpose of this book if I did not mention this condition. Whatever truth there is in the diagnosis of hypoglycemia either as a true disease or as a syndrome, the diagnosis has been in use for at least three centuries to explain various psychiatric illnesses. Therefore, hypoglycemia could be an explanation of many of the *masquerades* cited in this book. However, they are rare and for the most part they consist of only two legitimate causes of hypoglycemia: (1) tumors of the pancreas glands *Islets of Langerhans*, and (2) accidental or intentional overdoses of the insulin used to treat diabetes mellitus. There is a third cause of hypoglycemia, but it is also rare and does not usually cause any psychiatric symptoms or illnesses and is functional or idiopathic in etiology and can be treated with a high protein and low carbohydrate diet.

With F. Scott Fitzgerald, as well as with Edgar Allan Poe, *hypoglycemia* was used as a medical explanation for their peculiar form of alcoholism. Both writers were purported to have suffered from hypoglycemia, or low sugar in the blood, which interfered with the supply of glucose to the brain and gave Fitzgerald and Poe a purported abnormal craving and sensitivity to alcohol when they were drinking, and for chocolate and Coca-Cola when they were not drinking. There is some truth to the latter part of this theory because many alcoholics, when in withdrawal, crave either sweet or sour foods. The theory then goes on to say that this disease made it difficult for them to metabolize and tolerate alcohol, which always had an immediate and catastrophic effect of their system. Both Poe and Fitzgerald manifested many of the symptoms of hypoglycemia: insomnia, pallor, and fatigue, as well as pressured speech, excessive sweating, visual blurring, muscular tremor, a sense of uncertainty, increasing confusion, and, finally, unconsciousness. All of these are symptoms of low blood sugar, but what is important to know is that they are also symptoms of alcohol intoxication and alcohol withdrawal. However, this medical crisis could never be mistaken for the transient hypoglycemia attacks experienced by Poe and Fitzgerald if they experienced them at all, which is extremely unlikely. Many alcoholics, if they don't eat normally and stop drinking their typically large doses of alcohol, will almost always experience some of these symptoms in a relatively mild form frequently from low blood sugars as a result of alcohol liver disease.

Other medical illnesses can and do cause hypoglycemic symptoms such as traumatic brain injury, pituitary tumors, the overdose of exogenous insulin, hyperthyroidism, alcoholism in the late stages, and even diabetes mellitus in the early stages. However, neither Poe nor Fitzgerald was ever suspected of having any of these conditions. Therefore, they are not part of the differential diagnosis for either Poe or Fitzgerald. It is important to point out for clarification that hypoglycemia is a symptom of many illnesses and should not be used as a primary medical diagnosis but rather to describe a symptom complex for many primary medical illnesses such as those just mentioned above.

PSYCHIATRIC FORMULATION

Scott Fitzgerald had the developmental experiences that laid the groundwork for his narcissistic personality when his only two siblings died from an epidemic before he was born. Not only was this enough to make him a "precious child" in the eyes of his parents but he looked the part as a very handsome, blond, green-eyed boy with an idyllic face and head. He was raised to believe that he was an "entitled" child. His less than pretty mother had manic-depressive disorder and contributed the genetic makeup to Scott that enhanced his feelings of "entitlement" by adding the hypomanic attitude of power and omnipotence that gave him a posture of being someone very special. Of course his brilliant to genius Intelligence Quotient did not detract from his physical appearance. If you add narcissistic personality, manic-depressive disorder manifested usually as hypomanic episodes, and a genius level I.Q. together, you have all the makings of a creative individual, or at least, that was what was suggested by Ruth Richards and Kay Jamison in their separate works investigating the etiology of creativity. As if those "assets" were not enough to stimulate Fitzgerald's creativity, he was also "lucky" enough to find a wife (Zelda) who was his mirror image in looks and also had a narcissistic personality and suffered from a genetic mental illness (schizophrenia or manic-depressive disorder), as well as a high Intelligence Quotient, and was also creative. As a matter of fact, there have been discussions by experts over the last eighty years whether Zelda plagiarized Scott, or Scott plagiarized Zelda, or, as Scott more frequently claimed, they were both mutually creative. The latter might well have occurred intermittently if they did also have a shared psychotic episode.

Another illness Zelda and Scott shared, although not of equal severity, was acute and chronic alcoholism and drug abuse that definitely detracted from their creativity. Scott could not write when he was drinking heavily. There is no information available about Zelda's creativity when she was under the influence, and she was about as often as Scott was except when she was hospitalized, as she often was, during the last ten years of her life. Scott frequently suffered from the typical complications of alcoholism and drug abuse that included diaphoresis (night sweats), tremors, insomnia, hallucinations and delusions (all symptoms of *delirium tremens*), and heart disease at forty-four years of age. His heart disease was probably alcoholic myocardiopathy for which he was taking digitalis medication.

They also suffered from depression, either as a part of the cyclic swings of manic depression, or as part of Zelda's schizophrenia. It was usually disabling and both Zelda and Scott had multiple suicide attempts.

Scott also suffered from two medical conditions. One was serious and potentially lethal, Pulmonary Tuberculosis with cavitation, and the other, interesting considering he was a brilliant professional writer and author, was an inability to spell properly as a result of his dyslexia.

DIAGNOSTIC IMPRESSIONS ON F. SCOTT FITZGERALD

AXIS I:
1. Bipolar I Disorder (manic-depressive disorder) with Intermittent Hypomanic Episodes, *DSM-IV* (296.40)
2. Alcohol Dependence One Year Past Physiological Dependence at Time of Death, *DSM-IV* (303.90)
3. Intermittent Barbiturate, Chloral Hydrate, Morphine and Amphetamine Dependence, *DSM-IV* (304.80)
4. Shared Psychotic Disorder by History (*folie à deux*), *DSM-IV* (297.3)
5. Intermittent Hypoglycemia Causing Personality Changes Due to Alcohol Dependence Unspecified Type, *DSM-IV* (310.1) (very doubtful)
6. Foot Fetishism, *DSM-IV* (302.81)

AXIS II:
1. Developmental Reading Disorder (Dyslexia), *DSM-IV* (315.0)
2. Narcissistic Personality Disorder, *DSM-IV* (301.81)

AXIS III:
  1. Pulmonary Tuberculosis with Cavitation, ICD-9-CM
  2. Alcohol Cardiomyopathy as Cause of Death, ICD-9-CM
  3. Idiopathic Hypoglycemia (doubtful)

AXIS IV:
  1. Problems related to social environment
  2. Problems related to occupation
  3. Problems related to economics

AXIS V:
  1. GAF: 75

AVAILABLE TREATMENTS

F. Scott Fitzgerald had available to him essentially the same medications that were available to Edgar Allan Poe through a medical doctor's routine medical care. These medications included Phenobarbital, chloral hydrate, and Nembutal and laudanum. In addition, Fitzgerald's generation had invented Benzedrine. This was the first of the amphetamine (speed) category of drugs. In a similar category was cocaine. Cocaine was available in Europe, especially in the area where Fitzgerald lived in France and was being made popular through the research of Freud who was touting it as a cure for morphine addiction. There is no mention in the archives of Fitzgerald ever having used it medicinally although at the beginning of the twentieth century cocaine was one of the original ingredients of Coca-Cola until 1903, when the Coca-Cola manufacturers voluntarily replaced the cocaine with caffeine. The formula for Coca-Cola was devised by druggist, John Pemberton around the mid-1880s. If Fitzgerald ever used cocaine it was probably through his contacts in France and Italy when he lived there in the early part of the twentieth century and cocaine was being endorsed by Freud as a treatment for morphine addiction. However, there is nothing in his biography that suggests that this was true other than his impulsive behavior, his extravagance, his chronic shortage of money, and his hypersexuality, all of which are commonly found in individuals who abuse cocaine, back then as well as now. However, everything about the biography of Fitzgerald suggests that he had found his drug of choice—alcohol—early in life and used it with impunity until one year before he died of heart disease.

Fitzgerald did use morphine, Phenobarbital, chloral hydrate, Nembutal, and Benzedrine, but it appears that he primarily used the sedative drugs medicinally to treat alcohol withdrawal, insomnia caused by alcohol, and that he used Benzedrine to treat the fatigue, also caused by the insomnia of alcoholism. However it is naïve to believe that Fitzgerald, because of his keen interest in Freud, would not have known about its medicinal use. There were no medications available during his lifetime to treat the mania or hypomania that resulted from his inherited psychiatric illness presumed to be manic-depressive disorder and/or intermittent hypomanic episodes. In other words, none of the anti-psychotic medications had been discovered yet and medications for mania and hypomania were not yet available either. However, it is conceivable that he was using cocaine to self-medicate himself out of his depressions so he could return to his productive hypomanic phase. Insulin shock treatments, Pentylenetetrazol-induced convulsions, and electro-convulsive therapy were not introduced until 1927, 1934, and 1938 respectively and only the insulin shock treatments were being used in 1927. (Later they were used for treatment of the psychosis of schizophrenia.) Zelda started receiving electro-convulsive therapy about 1927 and continued until her death in 1948.

Fitzgerald had more than a passing interest in the new self-confession treatment for mental and emotional interests. His three essays in *Esquire* during 1936, called the *Crack-Up* stories, were all about confessions and renewal and recovery. Knowledge of this self-help method may have contributed tremendously to his one year of sobriety immediately before his death in 1940, and that was before Alcoholics Anonymous really got started.

We also know he had a healthy interest in the developmental causation of personality dysfunction, as Freud was famous for expounding during Fitzgerald's most productive years. Fitzgerald was able to demonstrate how Jay Gatsby and Nick Carroway in *The Great Gatsby* were able to complement each other in the ego ideal and ego alien terms.

In summary, Fitzgerald was on the brink of understanding himself and had the fundamental knowledge to accomplish this. Fitzgerald understood that he had an *immature personality* and needed to develop healthy defense mechanisms to become a *mature personality*. The lethal effects of alcoholism did not give him enough time on earth to accomplish this. To quote Ernest Hemingway, "Poor Bastard."

CHAPTER SIX

Drugs, Depression, and Dream Songs: A Case History of John Berryman

BIOGRAPHY

John Berryman was born in rural Oklahoma Territory in 1914 to John Allyn Smith, and Martha ("Peggy") Little, whose family hailed from Arkansas. From the time John Berryman was twelve years old he believed that fate had control of his life. It had not always been so, for his life was more secure and happy when his name was John Allyn Smith Jr., and that was when John Allyn Smith Sr., his biological father, committed suicide by drowning. That was the act that opened the way for his father's rival, a man named John Berryman, to step in and take over the identities of John Allyn Smith, father and son. Father was buried and the son's name was changed at the age of twelve to that of his stepfather, John Berryman. In spite of prolonged psychoanalysis and extensive psychotherapy treatment, with introspection into his markedly depressed psyche that he himself described as a world of "complete darkness," and in spite of his extensive professional dream analysis and his ability to write about them in his own poems—his *Dream Songs*—and in spite of liquor, drugs, and the intimacy of fifty women, and last but not least, in spite of multiple opportunities to recover from his alcoholism through the program of Alcoholics Anonymous, he never managed to get beyond the trauma of that early expulsion from the family garden or from the family genes. He achieved the creation of a great body of poetry that often bespeaks of lifelong agony, and committed suicide on January 7, 1972, at the age of fifty-seven.

FORMAL EDUCATION, ACCOMPLISHMENTS, AND ACCLAIMS

John Berryman's schooling came easily to him and he spent most of his free time reading pulp magazines. When he graduated from the eighth grade in 1928, he was voted "the most studious boy" and he looked every bit the part. He was near-sighted, wore thick horned-rimmed glasses and was nicknamed "Blears." His physique and his near-sightedness thrust him into the role of a student and out of that of an athlete.

Following the eighth grade, Berryman was accepted to South Kent School in South Kent, Connecticut, a small private boys' school run by Episcopalian priests. The school prided itself on a form of Emersonian self-help and taught the boys to live a rugged and monastic life, requiring them to perform daily chores such as mandatory dishwashing, snow shoveling, and the like. The school was not a good choice for someone as non-athletic and emotionally dependent as Berryman. Its goal to make young men out of its boys made it a cross between "purgatory" and "hell" for young Berryman.

Soon, Berryman began asking questions about the nature and origin of the universe. He wrote to his mother asking her about the origin of the human race as well as the problem of evil and the reality of Adam and Eve, to give a few examples of the thousands of questions that he had about life in general. He said he was asking her "because nobody at South Kent seemed to have the answers."

His prep years behind him, he kept in touch with the headmaster of the school for the next thirty years to keep him abreast of the honors he was to receive. He probably did this because he suffered too much at Kent School just to let his record close with graduation. If he had had an undistinguished career there (except for his grades which seemed to matter precious little), the ugly-duckling would one day demand attention as the "swan-bright" alumnus he had (correctly) dreamed he was to become.

Berryman was determined not to repeat his dismal South Kent experience at Columbia University. He converted himself to an extrovert instead of an introvert. From the beginning he tried to make himself popular. He memorized all of the names of the freshman class. He went out of his way to meet as many of the coeds at the neighboring Barnard's University as he could. He ran track and rowed crew and went into college politics, but he cut as many classes as he dared because he was unconvinced of the value of higher education.

Prohibition was repealed while he was a freshman at Columbia. This led to an increase in his drinking, accident proneness, and contacts with women. In turn, all of these changes led to some new strange behaviors. He began going without shaving and showering; he cut even more classes so he would have more time for drinking and chasing women—a harbinger of more serious, but related problems to come.

Berryman became enthralled with literature and poetry because of the influence of a dedicated and disciplined professor at Columbia, Mark Van Doren, who introduced him to the magic of the classics in literature and poetry. From this time forward he divided his time between poetry, women, and alcohol, but not necessarily in that order of importance.

Berryman was accepted at Cambridge University in England for two years (1936–1937). Before sailing to England aboard the Cunard Line's *Britannic*, he admitted himself to a spa in Williamsburg, Ontario, Canada for his first treatment, at age twenty-two, for a nervous disorder that he attributed to "the stress caused by his last semester at Columbia." He was unimpressed by a one-week treatment of foot manipulation by a Dr. Locke.

When he arrived in Cambridge on October 1, 1936, he found it even better than he had dreamed. His room was magnificent with a porter to carry his luggage, and a "gyp" served him strong hot tea while he sat before a fire reading Keats. All of this made him feel very welcome in the economic depression years. By December he had quit attending lectures altogether because he felt they were a waste of time. He read Henry James and Menchen on *The American Language*, listening for subtle differences in English and American speech rhythms.

Also, by this time he was again suffering from nerves and wild mood swings, which may have been manic-depressive symptoms. He diagnosed himself as having a mild form of manic depression with "mental instability, fits of terrific gloom and loneliness and artistic despair alternating with irrepressible exultation." One moment he was serious and the next moment he was frivolous.

He experienced periods of hyper-religiosity. He pondered, "by the fire for hours over the question of time and life and God...reading Revelations and Job and the New Testament" and wondering if he could ever accept Christianity. He passionately wished he could.

Berryman voluntarily discarded his self-imposed sexual abstinence and he became hypersexual with multiple heterosexual relationships (another symptom of the manic phase of manic-depressive disorder). He started writing plays and "burned" hundreds of his recent and old poems (in the depressive phase). When the crisis passed, he again started writing, revising, and reshaping his poems. He began drinking alcohol more and more heavily, again going without sleep; he was probably trying to induce sleep caused by the insomnia of the manic phase with alcohol. Finally, he collapsed and his doctor told him he would have to stop drinking and rest or he would risk a "nervous breakdown." Berryman, however, ignored the advice and continued drinking, believing that to be the only way he could recover his creativity.

This "magical thinking" is a common phenomenon in problem drinkers who attribute to alcohol a power it does not have. What actually happens is that in the manic phase the mind is racing and disorganized and the depressant alcohol can slow down the racing mind. This self-medicating with alcohol can be effective early on in drinking, before one becomes addicted to alcohol. Once addiction is in place, the withdrawal symptoms from alcohol can actually make the addicted person more hyperactive than before drinking was taken up. Berryman's sexual impulses, also a symptom of mania, became more and more uncontrollable; he confessed he "nearly raped the wife of his best friend." He confronted friend and foe alike with his "nasty" poems and excused himself by explaining that he was going "mad" at Cambridge. This explanation was probably closer to the truth than he himself believed. He was experiencing constant bouts of hysteria between intense bouts of work and heavy drinking.

Berryman spent the last few months of his time at Cambridge romping Europe and England in a vain attempt at shaking his emotional depression. Some might call this an attempt at a "geographical cure" for his aberrant behavior, caused by his mood swings and his alcoholism. But not surprisingly, he was getting more and more depressed and not drinking any less. He was also becoming deeper and deeper in debt, and in general making his life more and more unmanageable while planning to marry his pregnant fiancée, Beryl. Although he did not recognize it, his behavior was making him eligible to qualify for the first step of Alcoholics Anonymous: "We admitted we were powerless over alcohol and our lives had become unmanageable."

A few days before his final exams, Berryman finally "woke up" and began to study. Suddenly, doing well on his exams and getting his Master's of Arts degree mattered very much to him and he graduated with his Master's from Cambridge. But because of his "acute financial strain" he was forced to leave behind most of the new and very valuable library he had acquired; it would be years before he would be able to retrieve it.

Berryman also had a severe problem adjusting to life in the United States on his return from Cambridge. Part of the difficulty was adjusting to his mother. Always a somewhat disturbed woman, in his two-year abstinence she had become more coquettish and odd in her behavior. She wanted to be introduced as his sister and not his mother. Three weeks after returning to live in his mother's apartment, he wrote to his mentor Mark Van Doren, that "the heat in the apartment together with the strain, anxiety, and loneliness," made him so claustrophobic that he had "hysterical fits" and he was afraid of going "mad." What had caused the "fit" he did not say, but in fact, he had discovered that the only way to stop his mother's monologue was to faint. As her verbal barrages intensified, Berryman would suddenly stop arguing and his eyelids would flutter, his eyes would dilate, and he would collapse. His mother, forced to stop talking, would begin to take care of him, chafing his wrists and trying to move him to the couch or bed to make him comfortable. After a few minutes, pale and drawn, he would regain consciousness and retreat to his bedroom. This is more or less a classical example of a "pseudoseizure" and can be found in other mental disorders, mainly factitious disorder and malingering as well as with histrionic personality disorder. As we will see in the Psychiatric Formulation following later in this biography, there is a good possibility that both of these (factitious and malingering) coexist as symptoms of a primary histrionic personality disorder. Berryman's nervous collapses continued for months whenever his mother visited him, including in the presence of his fiancée, Beryl.

That Berryman had not yet managed to find a job by then was due as much to Berryman never having earned a Ph.D., as to his emotional depression, his recently acquired British accent and British mannerisms, and his disdain for anything American, which continued to alienate him everywhere he went. For instance, when he interviewed for a position at *Time* magazine in October, he made it clear that while journalistic work was beneath him, he might consider such a job should one be offered. But, he added, this being asked impertinent questions by strangers was "an incredible exercise." With the publication of *Homage to Mistress Bradstreet* in 1956, when he was already in his forties, Berryman won widespread recognition and acclaim as a boldly original and innovative poet. No one was prepared, however, for the innovations that were to follow in a collection of poems that would seal his reputation as an essential American original. Seventy-seven *Dream Songs*, published in 1964, and awarded a Pulitzer Prize, unveiled the unforgettable and irrepressible alter ego "Henry" and "Mr. Bones." Adrienne Rich wrote a brilliant review in *The Nation,* noting that the book was a series of sonnet-like poems whose "wretched syntax, scrambled diction, extraordinary leaps of language and tone, and a wild mixture of high lyricism and low comedy plumbed the extreme reaches of a human soul and psyche." In succeeding years Berryman added nearly four hundred poems to his collection of *The Dream Songs.*

Berryman taught at Wayne State University in Detroit, Michigan and went on to occupy posts at Harvard and Princeton. From 1955 until his death in 1972, he was a tenured professor at the University of Minnesota. Though he never earned a Ph.D., he did receive, near the close of his life, an honorary doctorate from Drake University. At the high point of his remarkable career as a poet and writer, and after several belated and unsuccessful yet extraordinary attempts to recover from his now acknowledged alcoholism that was associated with an inadvertent use of early antipsychotic medications for his yet undiagnosed manic-depressive disorder, Berryman ended his life by suicide at the age of fifty-seven. On January 7, 1972, he jumped off the Washington Avenue Bridge in Minneapolis, near the campus of his academic home, the University of Minnesota.

BERRYMAN'S OCCUPATIONS, ROMANCES, ADDICTIONS, AND PSYCHIATRIC DISORDERS

John Berryman's first academic position was as an instructor in English at Wayne State University in Detroit; the year was 1939. He would have three classes at ten, eleven, and six on Mondays, Wednesdays, and Fridays, besides evening classes on Tuesdays and Thursdays, for a total of thirteen classroom hours a week. Frightened by the prospect, Berryman went to see his Columbia mentor, Mark Van Doren, who advised him to work hard, keep steady, and not let himself get depressed. At age twenty-five, Berryman took the train to Michigan and began teaching; he also enrolled as a graduate student at the University of Michigan in Ann Arbor.

He worried about his fiancée, Beryl, who was living in war-torn London, and borrowed five hundred dollars from a bank to help her through a rough time, pay for his mother's move to a new apartment, and repay Columbia University for some of the tuition bills still owed. He began to lose weight and withdrew more and more into himself. Unable to sleep, he walked the streets until early hours in the morning, drank alone, then slept a few hours before classes began. Once more he had mood swings that he thought were brought on by his self-enforced sexual abstinence; but, of course, he did not realize that sleep deprivation is both a symptom and a cause of manic episodes. This was no doubt the beginning of his symptoms of manic-depressive disorder (bipolar disorder). He was also using alcohol to self-medicate his physiological symptoms of depression, mania, and anxiety. His "seizures" returned more and more frequently. There is no evidence that he had any true seizures but there could have been some *grand mal* seizures brought on by hyperventilation during his hysterical pseudoseizures. After each attack he would retreat to his bedroom for several days. He became more and more tired, lonely, and anxious. He would write poetry compulsively in the middle of the night. Then, in early December Berryman "collapsed."

When his mother did not hear from her son for six weeks, she flew to Detroit and was shocked to find him pale, emaciated, feverish, and depressed. Several medical specialists were brought in to examine him. In February 1940, he was diagnosed as having a mild form of epilepsy called *petit mal*. This diagnosis is highly suspect because *petit mal* seizures never occur after adolescence. However, this diagnosis seemed to have relieved Berryman's mind about the seizures, but his real complaints now were insomnia and fatigue. His married housemates moved out because the wife became afraid of Berryman's antics caused by "nightmares" and his nightly wrestling with "grief." A dear friend of Berryman's, Robert Bhain Campbell, who was dying from carcinoma of the testicle said, "Berryman's real problem was that he was at odds with the world and it did not seem likely that the contest would ever be settled." Then he added, "At least the world did not seem to cry uncle and no other possibility seemed to be in the offering." When Bhain heard that liquid calcium lactate was prescribed for Berryman's diarrhea and seizures, he called it "the milk of the mother, I take it, which has set him at war with the world." Bhain was a poet, not a psychiatrist, but at least he sensed the real source of Berryman's troubles. He, of course, was referring to mother's milk being a metaphor for the calcium lactate because milk does have high calcium lactate content.

Bhain was also implying that Berryman had a personality disorder based on Freud's theory on personalities and the Oral/Anal and Oedipal Stages of development. This would be consistent with his symptoms of mistrust, dependence, compulsions, and obsessions, inferiority, pseudoseizures, and conversion hysteria that were manifested by Berryman, along with and probably because of his mixed personality disorder (dependent and histrionic). At the end of February the "mysterious seizures" were cured with the two teaspoons of calcium lactate a day. Berryman said at that time, if it was not for his fiancée, Beryl, he would prefer to be dead. His suicidal threats and suicidal ideation were negative hallmarks of his existence throughout his life.

In September 1940, Berryman was driven to Cambridge, Massachusetts to begin teaching at Harvard. His mentor, Mark Van Doren, again gave him sage advice: "Don't anticipate too much evil at Harvard—there may be less there than you think." Soon he was feeling every bit as exploited at Harvard as he had felt at Wayne State. Could this be the paranoia that is as common a symptom in manic depression as it is in alcoholism? Van Doren advised him to take the world a bit more like it was and to try to sound less hysterical. Paranoia was creeping more and more into Berryman's thoughts. One night he got drunk at a local bar and was soon arguing with a stranger over the state of poetry. When he sobered up he resolved never to let that happen again. He was admitting that he had a loss of control when he drank, but he did not recognize the significance of this at that time and it would be almost three decades before he did. Finally, admitting his alcoholism, he never publicly acknowledged that he might have manic-depressive disorder, although in his poetry he described the symptoms so accurately that one knew he had firsthand knowledge of the disorder.

On New Year's Day, 1941, Berryman began another unsent letter to Beryl: "For two weeks I did nothing whatever except drink and wander from party to party—not for pleasure, I promise you, but desperately to avoid thought." He was probably searching for oblivion while paradoxically he continued to wait to start living and become happy. Seeking oblivion is a common immature defense mechanism used by alcoholics and drug addicts as well as people with other personality disorders. Alcohol prevents them from accepting responsibility and resolving their unhappiness and anxiety by avoiding learning the mature defense mechanisms and coping skills.

Later that year, Berryman received an RCA radiogram from London from Beryl on his twenty-seventh birthday. "HAPPY BIRTHDAY, ANGEL," it read. That evening he wrote Beryl, "The completely happy man would never act, never speak, never think—least of all measure or confess his happiness." For years he believed he would die young but wanted to live with her and write. In spite of his depression, he believed he had it in him to be happy because as a boy he had been happy, but had lost that happiness when he lost his father. Then at twenty, finding Beryl, he had found happiness once more. He was determined to find it again. But the monotonous repetition of teaching was paralyzing him. Here he was "qualified as few men in the country are to lecture Shakespeare, on seventeenth-century verse, and on modern verse," but unable to advance at Harvard because he was without a doctorate. So it would be freshman, freshman, freshman "until they fired [him] or [he] cut [his] throat." This letter was never mailed either.

At one point during that year it appeared that he was having a hypomanic episode that he described in his own words as, "my imagination being in a state of frenzied activity." He said he read Dostoevsky's *Crime and Punishment* as if he were driving a pack of hounds through a wood, feverishly. Everything about the book he found unbearably interesting. He told his mother that he "wanted to stop and examine it for a long time," except that, "the hounds are off ahead and won't let [him] stop." Even his "unhappiness," he added, seemed "acute, sharp, and engaging."

One of Berryman's friends, the poet Delmore Schwartz, advised him that the best thing that could happen to him would be for him to lose his job so that he could get back to his writing. That was fine, Berryman complained, until it came time to eat. Delmore also had his own opinions about Berryman's poor state of health. The only thing wrong with Berryman, he wrote Van Doren, was "some kind of hysteria. The fainting fits he has occur when he is spoken to sternly or contradicted." Delmore felt that if Beryl would only come to America and marry him, it would do Berryman a world of good. "Living alone as he does in Boston instead of Cambridge, and seeing no one for days at a time, he really is not well off; and being improvident, he sometimes spends all his money and then tries to feed himself on chocolate bars, until the first of the month." This type of impulsive spending is also a symptom of mania and was a constant with both John and his mother. Delmore did not mention the use of alcohol as a contributing factor to Berryman's medical problems but there is little doubt that it was a problem also.

Berryman, on the other hand, concluded that the worldwide suffering caused by World War II to the masses of citizens around the globe disturbed him. This included his fiancée Beryl, and the enormously elite he would see at Boston parties living in luxury and apparently oblivious to the suffering of others. He rationalized his drinking by saying that to comfort himself in the face of all of these worries he had taken to Scotch with ice and water. "The new Trinity," he called them.

To help himself to survive he asked Beryl to come to the United States and marry him. She said she could not desert her war post during London's worst crisis. She called off their engagement. What Berryman had most feared and yet hoped for had happened. Ten days later, in a Connecticut restaurant, he asked another woman acquaintance to marry him, and Eileen Mulligan accepted. Although they both had misgivings, they were married at St. Patrick's Cathedral on October 24, 1942, with both of them in a state of financial distress. If Eileen and Berryman married to learn survival techniques, they learned them of necessity and fast.

Eileen quickly found employment in Boston in the legal department of Liberty Mutual Insurance Company. Berryman was still employed as an instructor at Harvard but he was spurred to earn extra income through his poetry, and he did. But their combined incomes nevertheless left them constantly short of funds. If their finances were in disarray, however, they were models of order compared to his mother's finances. Uncontrolled spending is a common symptom of manic-depressive disorder and both Berryman and his mother were perpetually in financial chaos through such spending. One morning in May he was shaken to find two Internal Revenue Service agents knocking at his apartment door in search of his mother. He was himself in dire financial straits; he could not find a job and he could not sell any of his poetry. So here it was, "in the middle of one of the greatest employment booms of our time," wrote Berryman, and he was without a job. He had nothing but contempt for the employment interviewers who rejected his applications with equal contempt. The worst of it was watching Eileen suffer from weight loss, headache, fatigue, and colds. "What kind of man am I," he asked himself, "that I can't make money, write, or care for Eileen's health or prevent her unhappiness?"

What troubled him even more, however, was that Eileen believed, as had his mother, that he could control his nervous seizures if he wanted to. To him his "epileptic seizures" were things of "undifferentiated terror, inadequacy, and weakness," that took hold of him when they wanted. He had become so afraid of the seizures that he considered taking his own life. Eileen made him promise not to dwell on such thoughts. Still, there were times when he longed for oblivion (classic alcoholic thinking under stress). He knew alcohol would help, but that was one of the things he could no longer afford financially. The only thing that comforted him was he knew nothing—not even life—lasted forever.

In October, finally rescue came in the form of an offer from Princeton University for a four-month term teaching position beginning on November 1. On October 24, they had a wonderful time celebrating their first wedding anniversary. As luck would have it, just after he had accepted the job at Princeton, several other university positions opened up including one at Duke University. It was too late to worry about that. Eileen, flush with hope, took him to a fashionable clothier's to get him a new suit and overcoat. After she and Berryman had spent the year worrying about their future, a bright new world was suddenly beckoning to them.

From 1943 to 1947 John Berryman began making progress in his work as a poet. His position at Princeton was progressing and he was growing in stature. He was getting published and was invited to give lectures at several institutions. In 1947, as his literary successes accumulated, he found himself developing an obsession with a beautiful married woman named Chris, and a torrid affair ensued. Berryman calculated that he had slept with Chris about fourteen times. There had, of course, been days of "unspeakable happiness," but he was ready to let her go. There were after all, the sonnets that their affair had helped him create and the fact that the affair had given him new insights into women. As for what the affair had cost his marriage, he had no way of gauging.

During this time Berryman attended several parties without Eileen, mostly with colleagues and all for semi-professional reasons. He drank heavily and returned to Eileen more and more moody than ever. And, as the amounts he drank increased, so did the ferocity of their arguments. She worried about what was happening to him and could not forget how drunk he had let himself get at Chris's house. Berryman confided to his journal, "Eileen talked violently about my drinking now and during the past year." He noted that he was hurt that she had taken his social drinking as a sign that he might actually have a problem with alcohol. But in his heart he must have known Eileen was right.

Berryman's depression, which had been deepening since August, now became so pronounced that he decided to seek professional help. He began seeing a psychiatrist in New York, Dr. James Shea, who helped him uncover the reasons for his obsessions with Chris. By then he realized that even Eileen was treating him as if he was ill. There is little doubt that his heavy drinking was making his depression worse, but there is also no doubt that his depression would not have been adequately treated just by him stopping drinking.

Berryman's type of depression is an example of a particular Dual Diagnosis that is one of the most common of the masquerades. Alcoholism can cause depression, but there is no doubt that alcoholism can occur in people who have a primary depression. Both types of depressions need distinctly different treatment and they need to be given simultaneously, preferably in the same setting by the same staff.

John Berryman had manic-depressive disorder before he ever began drinking in such a self-destructive and addictive way; he probably inherited alcoholism from his father and manic depression from his mother. Had his first attempt at treatment been in an alcohol treatment center, any treatment that he would have received there would have been inadequate because his manic-depressive disorder would also have needed to be treated simultaneously. Also, neither of his early psychiatrists treated his alcoholism adequately, and in fact they both may have made his alcoholism worse by prescribing sedative medication while not addressing his alcoholism as the primary disease that it was, along with his second primary disease, manic-depressive disorder.

John Berryman thus became involved in a revolving door or merry-go-round for both illnesses. This is a very sad but very common occurrence, costing many valuable lives and careers, as well as depriving the world of many of its geniuses.

Berryman's sessions with Dr. Shea at first revolved around how he was continuously abandoned by those he loved: by his biological father in suicide, by Beryl, by Bhain with testicular cancer, and by Chris's rejection of him. Up until then he had been unwilling to examine his past, partly because all he could see when he looked there was a "hopeless fool," and partly because there were things he did not want to think about. Dr. Shea convinced him that the epileptic attacks that Eileen had long since dismissed as merely "hysteroid," were his way of dealing with a difficult mother, and were in fact probably just that. One of the things that bothered Berryman about his mother was the number of suitors that he had caught her with, including his stepfather. To him, it was like she was spitting on his father's grave.

After the first visit in late September, Berryman took to jotting down things to tell Shea. He saw clearly now that he hated women in direct proportion to how much he could use them, even for art, and he was soon showing Shea the sonnets he had written that summer, wanting some indication that they were too good to destroy. Shea advised him that at least for the next two months it would be better for him to stay away from his mother and work instead on cementing his relationship with his wife. After all, he had to remember Eileen was *not* his mother. He followed Dr. Shea's suggestion, for the most part, and he did mend some fences with Eileen and he was becoming more sober.

The sessions with Shea turned now to an examination of Berryman's relationship to his father. Actually, he could remember almost nothing of his father anymore, and most of what he did remember his mother had told him. According to his mother, Berryman's father cared nothing about living, had almost no sexual vigor, and he looked, with his little trim beard, rather like a French homosexual. But as the memories began flooding in, he wondered if his mother might actually have killed his father, at least by insisting on a divorce at a time when his father's world was collapsing upon him. And what of his own betrayal by taking Uncle Jack's name? But the more he looked at the hell within, the more he feared he might already be beyond Shea's or anyone's help.

Berryman, although not yet financially successful, said , "All I want is *time* and I will be a great poet still." Berryman knew that this was a fact. He was receiving praise for many of his works from friend and foe alike. On February 13, 1948, he read and recorded four poems for the Library of Congress: "The Statue," "The Narcissus Moving," "Rock-Study with Wanderer," and "New Year's Eve." He was very prolific and was published in many literary journals, but he was still broke until he started teaching at Princeton that fall.

In mid-July Eileen had a severe relapse of her back problem and moved to her sister Marie's home nearby. It seemed now as if Eileen was going to need back surgery. Whether it was an excuse or because he was fragile, Berryman was unable to cope with the stress and he became more anxious and depressed. Broke, he drank more and more heavily and twice borrowed money from his mother to tide him over. His depression deepened with the drinking but, for financial reasons, he decided to stop seeing Shea. Not only was he drinking heavily again, but he was also involved with another woman. He was horrified that he could give Eileen so little support in her illness. Again his thoughts turned to suicide.

About that time one of Berryman's promoters, James Laughlin, stopped by his apartment to check on the progress of an assignment he had given him for pay. He heard a faint croak telling him to come in, only to find Berryman hiding under the covers, muttering weakly that he was dying. Alarmed, Laughlin called in an internist who, after examining him, took Laughlin aside and told him he could find nothing wrong with him. Was this a factitious disorder, a conversion disorder, or just plain malingering? These same three questions keep coming up concerning Berryman's difficult to diagnose disabilities and illnesses.

That Christmas Berryman and Eileen went to New York to see his mother and some friends. One of them was Milton Halliday, whom Berryman called, asking him to meet him in Penn Station before Berryman took the train back to Princeton. When Berryman showed up, half an hour late, he was already drunk. Out of the blue, Berryman told Halliday that he had recently been talking to his friend Bhain Campbell, who at that point had already died of carcinoma of the testicle with metastases to the brain—Halliday knew that he had attended his funeral. Did he mean in his imagination, Halliday asked him? "He calls me on the phone," Berryman slurred, "very late at night. It happened several times lately. It's Bhain, no mistake. You know how recognizable his voice is." Halliday walked Berryman to the platform and watched him disappear in the crowd. It was the last time Halliday ever saw him. This was unlikely *delirium tremens* because he was actively drinking and there was no fear or panic or confusion as to person, time, or place. The more probable cause is hallucinations and delusions caused by the manic phase of his manic-depressive disorder. Berryman, in the manic phase, could believe it natural to talk to Bhain on the telephone. This is grandiosity that is the opposite of paranoia, and a manic person can have either grandiose or paranoid delusions.

Early in February, Berryman confided to his diary that at least he had "all of the best help science could give...." What Berryman was calling "science's best" was Shea's prescription of Dexedrine (speed) morning and afternoon, martinis before dinner, Nembutal (sleeping pills), and sherry after midnight to wash down the Nembutal. At that time both of these medications were considered quite benign. As a matter of fact, several drug companies mixed Dexedrine and Nembutal into a capsule and sold the mixture to millions of obese women and overweight males as a diet pill for years. They were not then and are not now benign—far from it. Today such prescriptions would be considered malpractice.

Interestingly, current research by Bemi Mayfield suggests that when psychiatric patients self-medicate (Dual-Diagnosis patients), the drugs they choose tend to mimic their psychiatric symptoms. This is the opposite of what one might expect. Berryman, for instance, had manic-depressive disorder and Dexedrine would duplicate, to some extent, his emotions when he was in a manic phase. The sedative Nembutal would duplicate his symptoms when he was in his depressed phase. Exactly how Berryman manipulated his moods with these medications is unknown. He probably had a hard time getting all of the Dexedrine he wanted and he might have tried to fill in with alcohol. Of course this type of medicating would make him worse in a short period of time. The best medications for his manic phase had not been discovered yet, as his doctors were unaware of Lithium, Depakote, and Tegretol and the new-generation anticonvulsants as mood stabilizers and the new-generation anti-depressants, which are almost without side effects. Current treatment is *not* aimed at neutralizing the manic phase with Nembutal and stimulating the depressive phase with Dexadrine, but rather using the proper combination of the newer medications to try to prevent or abort the manic phases and the depressive phases altogether. One theory that explains why many patients choose street drugs that resemble their psychiatric symptoms is that the street drugs may give them a sense of control over their disturbing symptoms. For instance, it may be less alarming to have hallucinations when taking a medication voluntarily, rather than having hallucinations without a known cause.

That very same month he was awarded the Shelly Memorial Award for 1948 for his overall contributions to poetry. The award came to $650, money he found "very useful." He bought himself some books and paid off some bills. He also treated himself to a bottle of Scotch and then demolished it at one setting. He was drinking more and more heavily and talking nonstop. His pressured speech reflected the "flight of ideas" of the manic-depressive patients in their manic phases. His doctor "had to double [his] sedatives to slow down [his] racing mind!"

Meanwhile he struggled to finish the Crane assignment, bolstering himself with sedatives and alcohol and becoming more and more depressed. "My conscience gets worse and worse," he wrote; "My mind and body fouled and I cut myself off from my only source of help—Eileen—by my own conscience."

One evening in August, he got into an argument with Eileen and his friends while on vacation at Cape Cod. Berryman stormed down to the beach, walking directly into the ocean, clothes and all. For the next half-hour his friends frantically searched the beaches looking for him. Finally he reappeared, sullen and thoroughly soaked, but alive.

During his stay at The Cape, Berryman managed to outline several essays. One was a response to Geoffrey Gorer's much-talked-about essay, "The American Character," published in *Life*. Berryman focused on the economic insecurities of the American intellectual. What did America do to her writers and artists that made some like Vachel Lindsay, Sara Teasdale, and Hart Crane take their own lives, and others like Pound, go crazy? But Berryman failed to note the problem of emotional and mental illness and suicides and insanity is not exclusively an American trait among American artists. Aristotle, Socrates, and Plato all focused on the relationship between melancholia, madness, inspiration, and creativity. "Why is it," Aristotle asked, "that all men who are outstanding in philosophy, poetry, or the arts are melancholic?" Kraepelin, like Benjamin Rush a century earlier, likened increased artistic productivity more specifically to manic-depressive disorder.

The genetic nature of mood disorders is underscored by the family history of many of the poets for depression, mania, suicide, violence, or insanity (psychosis). Of course there are many more poets and creative minds that are not afflicted with any mental illness and are normal mentally and so their families were unaffected. But in the families of Byron, Gray, Cowper, Chatterton, and the Coleridges, there is definite evidence of a hereditary link, and in the families of Crabbe, Blake, Clare, Beddoes, and Mangan, a high probability existed indicating a genetic relationship. The incidence of alcoholism and drug abuse is common among any list of creative individuals and their families. Hemingway, Poe, Fitzgerald, John Berryman, Tennessee Williams, and Lowell were all alcoholics. However, like mental illness, alcoholism is not a criterion for creativity. There are many creative artists who are neither alcoholic nor do they have a mental illness or for that matter, a personality disorder, and they function normally all of their lives.

In speaking of the genetic or familial aspects of mental illness in general and manic-depressive disorder in particular, in September Berryman, once again in New York, had an "angry, long, insufferable session" with his mother. Dr. Shea had warned him that he would need at least a year of intensive psychoanalytic treatment to deal with his *mother fixation*, and now Berryman could see that Shea was right. For the first time he spoke freely to his psychiatrist about his mother's flamboyant sexuality and about his own relations with women. Hypersexuality is also a symptom of manic-depressive disorder; he shared this symptom as well as a number of other behaviors commonly found in the disorder, such as shopping sprees and financial indiscretions, with his mother. They also both could talk emotionally and excessively in patterns of speech that psychiatrists call *pressured speech* with *flight of ideas*. Berryman would start many political papers, poems, and essays but leave them unfinished; this, too, is characteristic of persons with this disorder. When he tried to register his reactions to world and national affairs he turned awkward, verbose, and bizarre, all symptoms of mania.

Berryman's drunkenness had progressed to the point where Eileen left him. He was having affairs with several women. He was having many and varied physical injuries in 1953, and in the year following he was in deep trouble again with his drinking and had accident proneness, no doubt related to his drinking. He had fractures, lacerations, contusions, and hospitalizations for these injuries. He barely managed to hold down his teaching position at the University of Iowa, to which he had been appointed following his several years at Princeton.

Although he did prove to be an excellent teacher in writing there, he was having many "alcoholic blackouts" and could not remember many days and most evenings, although he was "awake" and "functioning" on these occasions.

Finally, following a newspaper report of his being arrested for drunkenness and disorderly conduct, he was summoned to the office of the Dean and Provost, where he was dismissed from the University of Iowa. Now he understood he really had hit the bottom and wondered where he was going to turn next. Berryman, in the midst of shame and confusion, contrived to have another father figure rescue him and call him home. Jobless and desperate, he phoned Allen Tate, a fellow poet at the University of Minnesota, who told him to come to Minneapolis and he would try to find him a teaching position there. Tate took Berryman to meet Ralph Ross at the University of Minnesota where he headed the Humanities Program in the Department of Interdisciplinary Studies. Ross promised to find him a job there as soon as possible.

For the first time in weeks he was able to sleep soundly. He rented a room in a private home within walking distance of Tate. He told himself that he would start all over again, and since his drinking had led to his dismissal at Iowa, he resolved to limit his drinking to beer and an occasional martini, a resolution that no addict could keep (pathetic rationalization).

It is safe to say that as of 1954 John Berryman had absolutely no insight into either of his two illnesses—alcoholism and manic-depressive disorder. Certainly, his promised approach to what he admitted was his drinking problem was a far cry from the theories then being promulgated in Minnesota in particular, and in the United States in general, as the *Minnesota Model* for the treatment of alcoholism and drug addiction. The Minnesota Model supported the theory of total abstinence from alcohol and/or addictive drugs as promoted by the rapidly growing program of Alcoholics Anonymous.

Berryman even began keeping a record of his drinking. He promised himself to answer his mail and wrote a literary agent asking about freelance work. Within a week he heard from Ross. The term would begin just after New Year's and Ross was offering him a full time job lecturing a section in Medieval Literature and a seminar in Modern Literature. Berryman accepted.

Then the nightmares returned, and he found himself staying up all night again. Alcohol withdrawal or the beginning of another manic episode could have caused either or both the nightmares and the insomnia. He was writing what he himself recognized as worthless dribble about Shakespeare. In spite of his resolve to control his alcohol intake, he was soon drinking heavily again.

He took to writing down his dreams and nightmares in an obsessive fashion, and since Dr. Shea was ill and fifteen hundred miles away, he resolved to analyze his dreams himself, which he did in his obsessive and grandiose manner over the next six months.

The Minnesota gloom piled seasonal affective disorder onto his already chronic depression. Overnight, as winter gave way to summer, Berryman's depression lifted. Berryman was very productive at the University of Minnesota and was producing voluminously. He was in big demand and his students loved him and knew they had a "live one." Berryman was, drunk or sober, an extraordinarily gifted teacher.

When Berryman was forty, "it was two twenties" he was really after. He began seeing a graduate student, Elizabeth Ann Levine, a New Yorker—not that he considered their relationship exclusive, as he was seeing many young women. But when Ann Levine returned from New York that September, she was carrying Berryman's child. He was prepared to marry her, the only problem was, he was still married to Eileen, and Eileen was hoping for a reconciliation. The divorce was very emotionally traumatic for both of them.

Afterwards Berryman and Ann headed for South Dakota and were married in Sioux Falls the morning after Christmas by a justice of the peace in 1956. With the baby due in two months, he made another New Year's resolution to take better care of his health, and for a while stopped his chain smoking and his drinking. When his body reacted violently to the double withdrawal, however, he was sure it was because he was on the mend and his smoker's cough was beginning to resolve. However, he was having his teeth "ripped out" twice a week by his dentist. The narcotic medication prescribed for pain by his dentist (codeine) probably had a lot to do with both his cough improving as well as his relapse into active alcoholism.

In June he wrote his mother to say that the baby had cast a "cold eye on his first vegetables." He hoped she would come out and see her new grandson, and he enclosed fifty dollars toward her airfare as a peace offering.

Finally, he was granted tenure at the University of Minnesota in January 1957 and promoted to associate professor. On his return to the university in January, his new salary would be eight thousand dollars annually.

In July, totally exhausted, he started an official business, lecture, and educational tour in Tokyo. Typically, after settling himself up into his hotel, he rewarded himself with a Japanese massage performed expertly by a geisha, and later bought the services of a prostitute. The other sights he saw in Japan he described as austere beauty. His tour brought him to India and the Taj Mahal and hundreds of the world's wonders in between.

Two months after the start of his tour he arrived at the Rome Airport. He checked into the Hotel Regina and slept for fifteen hours. A few hours later he was on a train heading for Levanto to be reunited with his wife, Ann, and their six-month-old son. He took long swims in the sea at Levanto and long walks with the Scott and Zelda Fitzgerald and spent lazy afternoons playing chess on the beach. He spent hours telling Ann of all he'd seen in India and admiring his son, who looked exactly like him. He loved Levanto, with its beautiful beach and surrounding mountains. After having spent two months in Kyoto and Calcutta and Bombay, everyone in Levanto seemed "impossibly white and big and prosperous and energetic."

Naturally, on their way home to America, waiting to embark from Seville, Berryman got himself so drunk that he passed out in the alley, discovering only the following morning that he had lost his wallet and his watch and had been hurt. As usual, he could remember nothing. Still, he could not admit to himself that he was an alcoholic with a bad temper and proclivity to have periods of amnesia brought on by alcohol.

Another incident in Lisbon during the month of December brought that bitter truth as least closer to realization. He and Ann had a terrible fight, "marked by extended and ultimate recriminations." As tempers flared, he struck her across the face and then left. That night he roamed the streets of Lisbon and, once again, drank himself into oblivion. When he sobered up he was terrified that the university would learn that he had disgraced himself in a foreign country. If he lost his job that would be the *"final irretrievable disgrace"* he knew he had been courting for years. There was absolutely no evidence that he had any insight that his alcoholism was making his life so utterly unmanageable.

On the first of April, Dr. Boyd Thomas, his astute physician, had him admitted to a private room at the Abbott Hospital, where he was treated for "exhaustion," a euphemism for alcohol poisoning. The medical staff tried to get his weight up and get him rested, and in a week he was discharged.

That Good Friday, Dorati's *Canata Dramatica* made its world premier on the university campus. Four thousand people heard 230 voices sing the music for which Berryman had provided the English lyrics. But Berryman, salted away in a hospital room two miles from campus, was busy gestating a poem that would in time exceed the fourteen stations of the cantata many times over.

The following evening he fought with Ann and concluded it was not good for him to talk to anyone at night. He may have been correct in this assumption because he was usually the most drunk in the evening, but he did not have any insight into the connection. The truth was, he raged at everyone: at Ann, the nurses, at anyone within shouting distance, which, in his case meant several houses down the block. Sedated from alcohol, he began examining his behavior, getting it wrong from the start. He could see no relationship between his behavior and his drinking, but his friends and family did not agree with him on that subject.

Berryman thought he drank merely to lift his spirits so he could tolerate other people. Why was it, though, that liquor would begin by calming him, only to leave him more irritable than ever? Berryman blamed this phenomenon on his nervous system. Ironically, he was more correct than he realized. Since he had manic-depressive disorder, when he was manic or hypomanic, alcohol would calm the mania or hypomania for a short while. However, when the alcohol was metabolized, withdrawal from the intoxication would be added to the mania and hypomania. This combination would not only make him more hyperactive and anxious than before he drank, but it would cause him to be paranoid, grandiose, and hallucinatory. For all of his psychoanalysis and self-analysis, he had learned nothing about the symptoms of alcoholism and manic-depressive disorder that he was constantly manifesting.

The Sparine medication that Dr. Boyd Thomas was prescribing for Berryman's detoxification from alcohol and for his "nervous condition" was actually an anti-psychotic medication that was popular and was being widely used for alcohol detoxification around the country at that time. It was *not* particularly a good choice for detoxification since it was an anti-psychotic medication, but it was—inadvertently—a good medication for reducing the psychotic symptoms of his manic-depressive disorder. Almost by accident it was helping his mania and his psychotic behavior, hallucinations, as well as his grandiosity. Sparine has lost its popularity for detoxification because it frequently caused severe hypotension.

One night in early February 1959, Berryman said to himself, "I have not slept for four nights," as he found himself alone drinking in a Minneapolis bar. He was dangerously on the edge again, and he knew it. He told himself that he had to take it easy, and "do as little as possible and avoid all strain and deci-sions." He had not yet learned the connection between manic-depressive disorder and alcoholism and sleep deprivation. In the manic phase of manic-depressive disorder the mind races so much that sleep is almost impossible. If alcohol is consumed in large quantities to induce sleep, it probably will not help much, but it can cause insomnia during the alcohol withdrawal phase and the confusion increases. Decreased sleep is both a symptom and a cause of mania. In this complex situation, the patient feels both paranoid (alcoholic paranoia) and grandiose (manic grandiosity). Berryman began to feel that he was there merely to supply other people's needs: his wife and baby, Ross and Tate, students and readers (here and abroad), publishers, editors, and the English Department. No one saw him as a human being anymore so that his roles as a "husband, father, lover, and friend" had died. He felt so bad for himself that one night he broke down in the Waikiki Room and a few nights later in another bar. Rationalization and resentments fostered by sleep deprivation can cause "stinking thinking" as they say at Alcoholics Anonymous meetings.

By then Ann had taken Paul and their second born son Rudolph and left Berryman to work out a settlement divorce with her lawyer. Berryman was feeling very tired and he knew it was time to get back in the hospital so he began drinking more to bring on oblivion. This type of thinking could also be a symptom of his dependent personality, his need for someone to take care of him. Finally, Dr. Boyd Thomas had him admitted to Glenwood Hills Hospital, in the closed ward for alcoholics.

After three-and-a-half weeks in the hospital, Berryman was sent home. Most of that time he had been able to meet his classes, going to and from the university by taxi. Sometimes he would stop in between the hospital and the university at a local bar for a "pick-me-up." When he was discharged from Glenwood Hills Hospital he was far from cured of his various medical and psychiatric conditions or from his alcoholism. He was still depressed and exhausted, was still drinking, and was not going to Alcoholics Anonymous meetings. He moved into a small apartment at 1917 Fourth Street, just a block from where he had lived two years before. Once again he was within a few minutes' walking distance from his office and back again to the Seven Corners section of the city, with its twenty working class bars to keep him company and where he continued his drinking and depression.

During the fall term he had himself readmitted to Glenwood Hills Hospital by Dr. Boyd Thomas for the second time in eight months. The hospital became his base of operation; from it he was taken by taxi to teach his classes, back to it he would be taken to be fed and cared for by the nurses. Here, he could indulge in yelling and screaming at the staff. This type of wanton living certainly qualifies him for the diagnosis of a dependent personality as well as for a histrionic personality disorder. "After four days in and I ain't well yet!" he wrote Boyd on the fifth day. "Christ! Can't thou medicine to a mind diseased? Yes? Yes! It was all a matter of nerves, nerves, nerves." He could barely stand the doctors and nurses who kept interrupting him. He needed heavier and heavier doses of Sparine to calm himself. As I mentioned before, the Sparine was a good medication for his as yet undiagnosed manic-depressive disorder but certainly not an optimal medication for alcohol detoxification.

Two weeks later he was back in bars drinking and picking up women. He would then go back to his small apartment with visitors who flocked to him nightly, among them Campbell, Thomas, and many others of his long dead friends (hallucinations and delusions).

Berryman spent Christmas 1959 with his mother in New York. It was becoming more apparent all the time that his mother's mania was increasing, and she began talking or rather babbling in a loud reverberating voice with pressured speech without content (flight of ideas). Others had used these symptoms of manic-depressive disorder for years to describe his mother as well as her other symptoms such as compulsive spending, uncontrolled indebtedness, and hyper-sexuality. There is no recorded evidence that she was ever diagnosed or treated for manic-depressive disorder, and her biological father, having committed suicide, may have carried the gene for major depression. If this was so, Berryman could have inherited manic-depressive disorder from both sides of his family.

Berryman had been invited to teach the spring semester in the speech department at Berkeley and he had accepted the offer. At a party for him, held by his chairman, Berryman was grandiose and recited by memory a litany of poems for six hours while he was drunk. Similar drunkenness with bizarre behavior continued throughout that semester at Berkeley.

On May 8, Mother's Day, he wrote a letter that was intended to be a letter of apology to his mother but ended up being a diatribe about her behavior on the previous Christmas when he had visited her in New York. He wrote that he was too old to be "smothered by talk" by anyone. "Thirty times I tried to make conversation out of it but on you rushed." He insisted "there was some-thing intensely neurotic and aggressive" about her obsessive monologue speech. He did not mention the possibility of her having manic-depressive disorder, and he was unable to see similar, if not identical, behavior in himself.

He returned to the University of Minnesota and taught there in the summer semester. He taught his courses sometimes inspired and sometimes drunk while bragging that he had limited his drinking to one quart of bourbon per day. After the semester was over he drank steadily, lost more weight, began incontinence of urine at night, and again became an insomniac.

On Friday, September 1, 1961, Berryman and twenty-one-year-old Katherine Ann Donahue were married while he was absent without leave from another hospital where he was admitted for detoxification from alcohol. After marrying Kate he simply stopped making child support payments to Ann and threatened to commit suicide if she took legal action against him, but Ann's lawyer served him a summons at the university despite his threats.

He was, after his triumphal readings, admitted to McLean Hospital outside of Boston. By the third day, Berryman was swearing to never again combine liquor with the writing of his poems. Sick and sweating, he tried once more to bring order into his frazzled life. That day he wrote a "coon" song:

"Disaster-prone Henry in the Observation Room," asking why so much seemed to happen to Henry? To which his interlocutor answers with another unanswerable question, like Job's God out of the whirlwind: "Mr. Bones, as say de Book, when de waters swirled/was you there with the sieve?"

Berryman was kept heavily sedated and slept much of the time. He played chess, had a physical exam, and was visited daily by doctors. Then he had a bout of *delirium tremens*, which upset him greatly because he thought he was getting better. He told friends and family that he was in the hospital because of "violent overwork" on his long poem, although he expected to be out by the time of Kate's "babying." He was not pleased to have the hospital psychiatrist tell him that he would probably "crack up" when the baby was born.

On the first of December he was allowed to leave the hospital with a promise that he would not drink. The next day Kate was admitted to Providence Lying-In Hospital and gave birth to a seven-pound, four-ounce daughter that they named Martha.

On the fourth he went to see Kate and the baby and then visited friends afterwards. They noted he was drinking but that he did not seem drunk at the time they put him in a taxi and sent him home. When Berryman got out of the taxi, however, he was very unsteady, and somehow the cab backed over his left foot snapping his ankle. Twenty-four hours later his friend got a call from Berryman's psychiatrist at McLean's Hospital. Berryman had missed his appointment that afternoon and was not answering the phone. They found him in his upstairs bedroom, his foot mangled and already beginning to fester. The ambulance was summoned and took him to Providence Hospital and he was admitted for three days. When his friends went to visit him he admonished them not to give him "any tenth-grade Freud" about his being in one hospital and his wife being in another, as though he was competing with Kate over who was more in need of attention. On the seventh he was released from the hospital on crutches with his leg in a cast.

The fame that Berryman had so longed for and dreamed of began now to seek him out. On the twenty-ninth of January 1963, he learned that Robert Frost had died, and with the great man gone, Berryman wondered who was "number one" among the poets. To David Hughes, who brought him the news about Frost's passing, Berryman suggested Robert Lowell, hoping that Hughes would contradict him and tell him that Berryman was. A few days later Berryman read what Phillip Toynbee had said in *The Observer*, that Frost had been "the greatest American poet alive even in the age that had produced Robert Lowell and John Berryman." The contest brought about even more effort by Berryman to earn the title of "number one." He went on a spree of productivity until his mother came to visit him to celebrate her sixty-ninth birthday. Her presence had once again kept him from sleeping or getting anything done. "Throw me more, please, 50 mg Sparine," he begged Boyd. He did not enjoy gorging on drugs, but he was going crazy watching his mother's interactions with his baby daughter. (As mentioned above, Sparine was a reasonable medication, among the ones available at that time, for manic-depressive disorder. Lithium and Depakote were not available yet and Tegretol, though available, was thought to be efficacious only for back pain as a muscle relaxant and was unknown at that time to be a benefit for mania.)

During this year of high productivity for Berryman he had lost many friends from his field of poetry and literature including the great Robert Frost who died a natural death, Theodore Roethke who passed away in a drowning accident, as well as the suicides of Sylvia Plath in London, Ernest Hemingway, and William Faulkner.

In January 1964 Berryman got back the corrected manuscripts of *77 Dream Songs*. He was still dissatisfied, and this year was to show less of his inspired work than the previous two years. In March he won another prize, the Russell Loines Award, of one thousand dollars from the National Institute of Arts and Letters. The prize would be formally awarded in New York on May 20, with Lowell as the presenter.

He began a fourth book, an *Opus Posthumous* sequence that would hinge the first three and the last three books of his poems together. A few days later he left Washington for a reading tour through California. But by then he was in very poor physical condition, suffering from bronchitis, an ear infection, and hallucinations either from the fever, too much alcohol, or a manic episode. All were a possibility. He telephoned Dr. Thomas to get him back into Abbott Hospital just as soon as he was done with the readings. But on March 16 he collapsed and had to be rushed by ambulance to Riverside Community Hospital where he was diagnosed as suffering from "influenza syndrome complicated by acute infection of the left ear and exhaustion." After three days at Riverside Community hospital, he promised them that he would return home immediately "for further hospitalization and treatment" and was discharged. While waiting at home for a hospital room to become available he nursed himself with whiskey. After four days in the hospital, sedated and isolated, he received an advance copy of *77 Dream Songs*, and he felt a need to celebrate. With Dr. Thomas' express permission, he left the hospital and went shopping, "stopping at the Brass Rail on the way back to the hospital for four martinis." He wrote to Kate, "The shopping spree and the drinks left me with an electric sense of liberty, restoration and normality." At that time he was probably in a manic phase of his disorder. Dr. Thomas was apparently leaning toward that diagnosis too because he prescribed large doses of Thorazine (chloropromazine), 150 mg and more, but he was leaving the hospital every day for "a few drinks to steady [himself]." In fact, Berryman was coming to the conclusion that "maybe a toot every fortnight or so" was a sound conception as long as he kept out of trouble. But after three weeks in the hospital he was still so excitable (manic) that he couldn't watch television. *Why did he drink so much?* he asked himself in *Dream Song 96*. And he answered:

> *That last was stunning*
> *The flagon had breasts. Some men grow down cursed.*
> *Why drink so, two days running?*
> *Two months, O seasons, years, two decades running?*
> *I answer (smiles) my question on the cuff:*
> *Man, I been thirsty.*

Berryman managed to convince Boyd that he was never going to get off booze unless he got more drugs, and Boyd wisely put him back on higher doses of the non-addicting neuroleptic medication that had been keeping him alive and sane for these many years (Sparine and Thorazine). Dr. Thomas was probably treating his depression and his mania as well as his psychiatric illness could be treated at that time and in that era of psychiatric knowledge.

When Berryman wrote Kate that evening, he complained how "dead tired" he was, working forty-eight hours on two new Songs with only two hours of sleep. This also would indicate that he was in a manic state. On publication day, Berryman lay in the hospital, his brain still "boiling" with Songs. His chief rival for "King of American Poetry," Robert Lowell, did not give Berryman's newest publication a good review. Berryman stayed awake all night again, going through his book convinced that Lowell was wrong. Many of his poet friends, like James Wright, James Dickey, James Merrill, and Adrienne Rich, stopped by the hospital or wrote him to say how much they admired his Songs.

The longer he stayed in the hospital, the more paranoid Berryman became. One day, standing in an elevator, he asked a police officer why there were so many police around the hospital. The officer turned and stared at him. Enraged at having been fixed "insect-like" by a man armed with a gun, Berryman returned to his room to write *Dream Song 95*, damning the guard to hell:

> *A meathead, and of course he was armed to creep*
> *across my nervous system some time ago wrecked.*
> *I saw the point of Loeb*
> *at last, to give oneself over to crime wholly,*
> *baffle, torment, roar laughter, or without sound*
> *attend while he is cooked.*
> *Until with trembling hands hoist I my true*
> *& legal ax, to get at the brains. I never liked brains*
> *it's the texture & the thought—*
> *but I will like them now, spooning at you,*
> *my guardian, slowly, until at length the rains*
> *lose heart and the sun flames out.*

Finally, on May 8, still unsteady, he paid his hospital bill and was taken to the airport for the trip back to Washington. Berryman continued in this year, 1966, to be productive in his writing and successful in getting his poetry accepted for publication. He also continued to lose close friends to death: Delmore Schwartz by myocardial infarction at the age of fifty-one and Randal Jarrell by suicide in October. He also continued going in and out of Abbott Hospital under Dr. Thomas so often that his friends quit visiting him there.

Berryman's frequent hospitalizations at Abbott were for alcoholism and for some other psychiatric conditions that were never identified. However, the medications he was receiving for treatment at Abbott were not the typical medications used for detoxification at that period. Although Sparine continued to be popular with some physicians, most had stopped using it because it frequently caused hypotension (low blood pressure) and syncope (fainting). The two medications Berryman received most often were Sparine and Thorazine, which are neuroleptics that were used for schizophrenia and the mania of manic-depressive disorder and other psychotic episodes including *delirium tremens* from alcoholism. Apparently these medications were helping him because he returned to Abbott many times requesting them by name. Neither of them are addictive medications nor do they produce euphoria like alcohol, sedatives, and tranquilizers do. For a brief period they were called "major tranquilizers," but that classification was changed to "neuroleptics" because it was realized their mechanism of action was not through tranquilization.

Years before, Berryman had been prescribed Dexadrine and Nembutal, a stimulant and a depressant respectively, by his psychoanalyst, Dr. Shea, for insomnia and fatigue, but there is no evidence that these medications were continued by Dr. Thomas. The medications prescribed by Dr. Thomas were appropriate for the symptoms of a racing mind, delusions, hallucinations, insomnia, grandiosity, and paranoia, all of which Berryman manifested and all of which can occur in manic-depressive disorder. These same medications would also be appropriate to treat an organic mental disorder such as dementia that can occur with Korsakoff's psychosis that is associated with chronic alcoholism, but there was absolutely no evidence that Berryman was demented. He remained brilliant and productive right up to his suicide.

There is also no doubt that Berryman was having frequent bouts of acute and subacute alcoholism complicating his chronic alcoholism, and therefore there were many times he suffered from *toxic brain* disease with delirium. Any one of these conditions could have caused many of his hospital admissions. However, he also had the concurrent manic-depressive disorder (Dual Diagnosis) that is associated with intermittent depression and mania. It would appear that Dr. Thomas's treatment kept him alive for a longer period of time than if he had been admitted for detoxification from alcoholism and then promptly discharged. But it would have been better still if Dr. Thomas had included an alcohol rehabilitation program along with his psychiatric treatment and prescribed Berryman to go to Alcoholics Anonymous meetings.

In mid-March Berryman was awarded his second Guggenheim. Now he could take Kate and little Martha and go off to Dublin at the end of August 1966 for a year. Berryman was ready to leave the United States. He was calling America the "country of the dead" because of the passing of so many of his poet friends, and he was ready to sail to Ireland on *The Carmania*. By the fifth day at sea he had become a familiar face at the bar, but what he saw staring back from the mirror behind the ship's bar was wreckage. After a mild crossing, the Berrymans disembarked on September 1 at Cobb where the journalist and photographers met them. They took the five-hour train trip to Dublin, arriving in mid-afternoon at the Majestic Hotel. The couple was exhausted and little Martha was suffering from the flu. There were letters from America awaiting him, showering professional praise for his many successful, recent accomplishments.

By the end of October, the "blaze" (mania) that had fired Berryman for the previous four months began to subside. He had written seventy-five Songs in Ireland by November and was now feeling "invincibly tired." But the Songs were still coming at him unbidden, so that he had "fifty new ones" in his head. Now he was willing to confront the terrifying and unadorned facts of life and death. By his estimation he had long ago moved beyond Yeats; now he was willing to get on with the hilarious tragedy life had become for him. Comedy and tragedy were nouns that described the Berryman paradox.

New Year's 1967 at midnight, the Berrymans could hear ships like ghosts blowing their foghorns through the mist. Berryman knew it was time to be going through the 300 *Dream Songs* he had collected. But that night he fell again, hurting his right side so badly that at first Kate thought he had broken his back. Thorazine and not alcohol, he complained, was responsible. Berryman was more defensive of his disease of alcoholism than he was of his manic-depressive disorder—a very common attitude in people with a Dual Diagnosis. He preferred to blame anything except alcohol for his unmanageable life. Perhaps he had never been informed about his diagnosis of manic-depressive disorder, but he was such a brilliant man and so highly educated that it seems like a conspiracy of silence by the feigning ignorance of both himself and his doctors. But in spite of his pain, he stuck to his schedule, passing judgment as to which of the new Songs would live and which had to die.

Finally, toward the end of January, Kate had him committed to Grangegorman, the forbidding-looking Dublin Mental Hospital he had visited thirty years before. The place was no Abbott, and after a week of it, Berryman was begging Kate to sign papers for his release. He was discharged in mid-February.

On August 24, 1967, the day Berryman's *Sonnets* were published, he was back in New York. H. Wendell Howard would remember walking through Kennedy Airport being frozen by Berryman's voice roaring at him. He had just spent a year in Ireland, he told Howard, "right on the edge of Europe," a place crawling with "delicious people who spoke English and are blazing with self respect." He wished ol' Howard had been with him in those pubs "where everybody sings, they do not sing well but they sing together," and where he had been received "like Sam Johnson in the court of the Dauphin." He was still showing the symptoms of the grandiosity of mania that carried him to the readings of the *Dream Songs* at the American Academy and at the Guggenheim back in New York. His jacket looked as if he had walked all over it before putting it on. Shortly after his reading at the Guggenheim, he was rushed to the French Hospital with alcohol poisoning. Kate and Martha were still in Dublin and he returned there in mid-May with Jane Howard who was doing a feature story of him for *Life* magazine.

The Berrymans went on to spend five days in Paris, and then they traveled on to Italy, taking in all the sights, and then on to a five-day cruise of the Greek islands. Needless to say, there was excessive drinking at all of these places for Berryman. Cutting their Greek holiday short, the Berrymans flew from Athens to Liverpool to embark for the return trip to Montreal and then home.

For three days and three nights Berryman remained confined to his state room, suffering from *delirium tremens* and muttering through his vomit while the steward tried to get into the darkened room to clean it.

Back in Minneapolis, Berryman was admitted to Abbott Hospital, and on his release he returned to his classes—and drinking—once again. Berryman continued working, doing his readings and lecturing, drinking all the while.

Just after Thanksgiving he was back in Abbott's Mental Health Unit. Terrence Collins, an English major at the university who worked at the hospital, was on duty when Berryman was admitted. "He was fairly well intoxicated" that night, Collins recalled, but as he followed the routine admission procedures of blood pressure, temperature, and the like, Collins began talking "about literature, and specifically about *The Scarlet Letter*," for which he had a paper due the following morning. Amazed, he listened as Berryman talked about Dimmesdale's crisis and his realization of his hidden guilt. It was, Berryman assured him, "the high point in American fiction of the nineteenth century." On his break, Collins wrote down everything he could remember of what Berryman told him; he got an A-plus for his paper. This truly gives testimony to the fact that the remote memory can remain intact in the presence of toxic brain damage at a minimum. In addition, it supports the deduced conclusion that the manic brain can function well and on some occasions even better while it is sedated. This is truly a remarkable phenomenon that has shown itself repeatedly throughout Berryman's life. At the same time, Berryman's lifestyle of heavy daily drinking speaks volumes that its effect on his judgment and social etiquette were disastrous as were the effects of alcohol and cigarettes on his physical health.

Berryman managed a month without drinking alcohol, going over the *Dream Songs* a final time at the rate of ten a day. He organized his books, read Shakespeare, cut back on his cigarettes and coffee, and started exercising. But he knew arranging his life in this manner was like arranging the deck chairs on the *Titanic*. He had made similar resolutions fifty or a hundred times during his lifetime, held to them for a week or two and occasionally even a month, and then always found himself drinking with a new vengeance. He knew that alcohol and drugs had rendered him a very old fifty-three, and he was still plagued by suicidal ideation and plans. Now even his drive for extra-marital sex, obviously a dubious benefit of his manic-depressive disorder, was losing its charm for him. "What was this extra-marital sex thing after all," he wrote, "but a matter of two minutes where one lowers the lights and lets the genitals have full play, where I go up and down, you go up and down and nothing much happens after all." This sounds like Berryman was suffering from premature ejaculation and perhaps he found that alcohol and drugs, at times perhaps, gave him the benefit of retarded ejaculation. Could this have been the original reason for starting his heavy drinking in the very beginning? The real issue was alcohol and drugs. That June he wrote:

> *Haldol and*
> *Serax and Phenobarbital*
> *Vivactil, by day: by deep night*
> *Tuinal & Thorazine*
> *Kept Henry going, like a natural man.*

Vivactil is a potent antidepressant for treating a major depression. Haldol and Thorazine are potent antipsychotic medications and are frequently needed in manic-depressive disorder. Serax, Phenobarbital, and Tuinal are a benzodiazepine and barbiturates respectively, and today they all are frequently used for detoxification from alcohol and sedatives. Henry was a name Berryman frequently used in poems to represent himself.

There can be little doubt that Berryman (alias Henry) had extensive experience with all of these medications and that he eventually understood, in a non-scientific way, that he did have what has now become known as a Dual

Diagnosis consisting of manic-depressive disorder and alcoholism. *His problem was that he was born too soon to benefit from the use of lithium, which could have totally changed his life.*

In the fall of 1968, Berryman taught two seminars, one on "The American Character," with readings by de Tocquevill, Santayana, D. H. Lawrence, D.W. Brogan, and others; the second on "The Meaning of Life," with readings from the Buddhist text, Saint Mark, Tolstoy, Freud, Norman O. Brown, and *The Tempest.* At the start of the semester, Daniel Hughes spent a weekend with Berryman. There was no liquor when he first arrived, he remembered, but soon a "substantial delivery" was made. An advanced copy of *His Toy, His Dream, His Rest* had just arrived, and Berryman insisted on Hughes having it. But in spite of Berryman's friendliness, Hughes did not feel comfortable. There was just too much smoking and drinking, too many long silences interrupted by Berryman's sudden boisterous presence, and his sudden unexplained absences. Nor could he help observing the tensions between Berryman and Kate. And then there was little Martha, almost seven years old, who sang and colored with crayons and played house and was Daddy's little "Twiss," blossoming before them.

When Lowell received a copy of *His Toy*, he wrote Berryman immediately: "They add up enormously and are much clearer, are perfectly clear. Either they are really so, or I am much more at home with your idiom." Lowell's new book and Berryman's shared what he thought was much of "the same world," though their styles were not alike. "They seemed to have only the character of Jarrell in common," he added. But three days later Lowell wrote again, "dumfounded at how many of the same things" the two poets shared. What particularly astonished Lowell was how Berryman had continued to grow even as time ravaged them both. He did not mention their shared problem with alcohol that was causing their demise prematurely.

Lowell did think the difference in their vision was that Lowell was more tragic and Berryman was more comic. I am not as familiar with Lowell's life and poetry, but I personally found Berryman's poetry laced with plenty of tragedy as well as comedy. The result was a life of paradoxes.

A week later, in the winter of 1969, Berryman was admitted to Hazelden with symptoms of acute alcoholism. He had taken Thorazine and Tuinal and, disoriented, had fallen down and hurt himself. X-rays were taken at a nearby hospital, and then he was transferred back to Hazelden, where the admitting doctor described him as "a well-developed, poorly nourished, bearded male," weak, but "alert and cooperative...[suffering from] chronic severe alcoholism, alcohol-induced peripheral neuritis, drug abuse, and the beginnings of acute withdrawal." He did not make any mention of manic-depressive disorder or any other psychiatric disorder other than his alcoholism.

For a week Berryman stayed in the acute detoxification unit. This time there would be no more trips to the Brass Rail. At the beginning of his second week, he was assigned to Thiboult Hall with twenty-one other alcoholics in a similar state of need for education about their alcoholism. At first, he followed their program patiently, but soon he insisted on getting back to his teaching. This time he was told flatly that he would have to stay put. He had already paid for the treatment, and if he chose to leave the hospital early—as he had every right to do—he would not be permitted to return. He would also forfeit his five hundred dollars. Berryman roared, but then submitted.

By the end of the second week, he was convinced that he was feeling better than he had in years. Sunday afternoon Kate brought Martha out to visit him, and the next day, November 16, she wrote William Meredith asking for a favor. John was in Hazelden Alcohol Rehabilitation Unit and he was having a very hard time of it. Almost no one knew he was there and she asked Meredith to write to him. Finally John had been made to understand that he would have to give up drinking. Then she added that "God alone knew if the treatment would work."

At the end of the month Berryman was assigned a counselor, who began to uncover Berryman's history of alcoholism. "It was not until 1947 that I actually realized I might have a drinking problem," Berryman explained to the counselor. That was at Princeton, during a time when he was having an intense affair. Since then, the longest time he had gone without a drink was three months, and that was from September to December of the previous year. As for drugs, he had taken sleeping pills "irregularly" since 1949, and pills for his nervous condition since 1955 on an irregular basis. It had seemed so natural at the time. He had seen a psychiatrist from 1947–1953 and every other week for the past year for marriage problems and alcoholism. He was willing, finally, to admit that he was indeed an alcoholic.

There was no psychiatrist on staff at that time at Hazelden. That was the era that will be referred to as the "great divide," meaning that this country had separated alcoholism treatment from mental illness treatment by design. Alcoholism was believed at that time to be a biological medical illness and treatment was generally on the Minnesota Model that embraced the principles of Alcoholics Anonymous. A "physical allergy" to alcohol was a term used in the Big Book of AA and at AA meetings and alcohol rehabilitation centers such as Hazelden and Brighton. They taught the need for total abstinence from alcohol and addictive drugs, one day at a time, and the need to work the AA Twelve-Step program while attending Alcoholics Anonymous meetings regularly: that would bring about a physical, psychological, and spiritual recovery.

The concept of Dual Diagnosis, which is that an individual may have two or more psychological, emotional, or addiction illnesses concomitantly or simultaneously, was never taught or even considered. The reason for this was that alcoholism was just beginning to be correctly understood, and Alcoholics Anonymous meetings were still relatively new and had growing pains. Furthermore, the alcohol treatment centers that were in existence, such as Hazelden and Brighton Hospitals, were not licensed or equipped to treat psychiatric disorders, and therefore could not safely or legally treat Dually-Diagnosed patients. Inasmuch as there were no psychiatrists on staff in alcohol rehabilitation centers, and there were likewise no addiction specialists in the psychiatric hospitals, the patient's formal diagnosis depended on which of the two types of treatment center the patient was admitted to. It is true that at least some of the symptoms of alcoholism and some of the symptoms of psychiatric illness masquerade or mimic each other. Simply put, the symptoms of alcoholism may appear at certain stages to be identical to a personality disorder, manic-depressive disorder, psychotic disorder, or one of the many forms of anxiety disorders. For an individual to have a Dual Diagnosis, it implies that the patient will need two separate and distinct mental, addiction, or emotional diagnoses and two separate and distinct treatment plans, one for each diagnosis. Furthermore, it implies that all of their diagnoses will be found in the *Diagnostic and Statistical Manual of Mental Disorders* (*DSM-IV*), or subsequent editions, of the American Psychiatric Association. If a patient with a Dual Diagnosis went to an alcohol and other addiction rehabilitation center, he would be diagnosed and treated only for his addictions, and that was by design. If a Dual-Diagnosis patient went to a psychiatric hospital he would be diagnosed and treated only with his psychiatric diagnosis, and this, too, would be by design.

The theory behind this misguided hypothesis was that whichever illness was treated as the primary problem would respond to the treatment, and it was assumed that the other would go away spontaneously or naturally. Why was this considered a logical treatment policy? Perhaps it was the result of a fall-out from over-specialization that resulted in limited general medical knowledge as frequently happens with Dual-Diagnosis patients.

John Berryman was a victim of this dichotomy of treatments. He had a difficult time accepting his diagnosis of alcoholism and drug abuse and only received treatment for it during the last few years of his life. Furthermore, the psychiatrists he was seeing never made the diagnosis of manic-depressive disorder. Although they were treating him for mania and depression, it was probably inadequate because the medications that were available during Berryman's era were neither optimal nor adequate for his psychiatric illnesses.

Also, some of the psychiatrists were not addressing his alcoholism sufficiently to give him insights into his alcoholism, and it appears they were contributing to his drug abuse problem by prescribing addictive medications for him to use at home. I would like to add that the majority of patients being admitted to alcohol rehabilitation centers were probably not Dual-Diagnosis patients and therefore were, in most cases, receiving proper treatment for their alcoholism.

The one big exception to the above disclaimer are the patients in the alcohol treatment centers who had a severe psychotic or suicidal depression and were not given treatment for their depression. It was common at that period of time to diagnose depression present in alcoholics or drug addicts during withdrawal and during alcohol rehabilitation as *reactive depression,* believing their depression was a secondary depression to the social complications of their alcoholism or other addictions and would resolve spontaneously in a few weeks to a few months. The possibility of a Dual Diagnosis during the 1950s through 1970s was rarely considered. This was definitely so during John Berryman's era.

Today, quality research is being carried out at the world medical schools and pharmaceutical companies, and researchers are finding that most depressions either preexist the addictions or are caused by the addiction, and if they are not in remission after six days of detoxification they most likely need treatment with psychotherapy and/or medication.

On December 19, six weeks after being admitted, Berryman was released. "I feel marvelous," he wrote Ross, his chairman, that day. "Better than I have felt for many years." Then Berryman proceeded to describe the Hazelden program very accurately. He said, "The staff were almost as much interested in your character defects [personality disorders] as they are in your drinking problem. I corrected some of my wrong thinking about myself, helped by the lectures (three a day)." There had also been group therapy sessions, reality therapy sessions, as well as "various excellent books they give you to read, and interviews with a counselor, a psychologist, & a priest." Please note that there is no mention of an evaluation or treatment by a psychiatrist. The first four days, he confessed to his mother after Christmas, had been "pure hell," and it had seemed "hard and ridiculous to expect to reform one's character, morally and spiritually, in just three weeks' time." Nevertheless, he was convinced it was his fellow alcoholics, his friends—eight or ten of them, regular, nondescript people he normally would have ignored or avoided—who had helped him pull through.

However, as we shall see shortly, Berryman did not "pull through." All too often, when an alcoholic or drug addict does not recover after being in a treatment center, the attitude of the treatment center, the employer, the family, and the world is that it is the patient's fault. More times than not one can explain failures in treatment programs as related to the failure to diagnose and treat one of the patient's Dual Diagnoses. Fortunately these attitudes and oversights are improving—but slowly. The Hazelden Foundation Butler Center for Research released a statement in April 2000 that describes the Hazelden Experience: "A large proportion of patients have coexisting mental health problems, most often depression or anxiety disorders (including post traumatic stress disorders) and eating disorders, particularly bulimia. The Hazelden model of treatment now incorporates mental health staff as co-case managers with chemical dependency counselors to develop special and group therapy for the mental illness and the medical management." Obviously this is a dramatic step forward and Hazelden is to be congratulated for making these changes in their treatment model.

Berryman spent Christmas at home with his family. Kate, Martha, and John exchanged gifts. When Kate's "lousy and worthless brothers, with her sad grandmother" had made their annual visit that afternoon, Berryman had become so upset that he considered having a drink, but somehow he managed to stick to coffee. This is an example of the classic defense mechanism of projection often used by alcoholics and drug addicts to blame all of their problems on others rather than attempting to use introspection to look at themselves to discover what they are contributing to any animosity in relationships.

He wrote a hopeful and confident letter to Adrienne Rich: "As one who took a bottle away from me in New Haven," he wrote, "you deserve to hear that I have just spent a whole month in intensive treatment...and am a new man in fifty ways." He was preparing his proseminar on *Hamlet* for the winter term, his first-ever regularly scheduled course for the English Department, and he was anxious to do a good job. When preparations for that were out of the way, he would begin "branching out" into a comprehensive overview of the current studies of Shakespeare to bring himself up to date on the subject. He still had that critical biography of Shakespeare to finish, and this time he meant to finish it.

Berryman's new sobriety, in spite of his apparently honest, new-gained insight from Hazelden, lasted just twelve days. He took his first drink at a party New Year's Eve, explaining away the horror of what he was doing by telling himself that he needed a stiff one to get some work done and this time he would drink only in moderation. Kate was almost in despair. One cannot help but wonder if the results of his treatment at Hazelden would have worked out differently if his diagnosis of manic-depressive disorder had been made there and if he had been started on medication appropriate to that diagnosis as well. But Berryman continued to produce scholarly work and read scholarly books. He read up on Mexico, planning to vacation there with Kate that summer.

As long as classes continued, he felt free to drink. Afterwards he would enter Hazelden and get cured again. But his nervous system could not wait. Late Saturday night in May he was rushed to the Intensive Alcohol Treatment Center at St. Mary's Hospital in Minneapolis. Chris Fall was on duty that night and saw a drunk with a ragged, untrimmed beard and large, raw blisters on his hands from cigarette burns, looking like "a disheveled Moses." He sat there in the nursing station, quoting from various Greek and Japanese poets, then stood up and in a loud voice sang one of Bessie Smith's blues numbers.

Berryman spent the next three weeks going through withdrawal again, by turn arrogant and humble, until he feared he was actually going insane. He paced up and down his room all night long, threatening to kill himself because he could not eat, then because he could not sleep. But just ten days after his admission, he felt strong enough to plan to take a taxi to the university to lecture on St. John's Gospel before being brought back to St. Mary's to continue his treatment in the Intensive Alcohol Treatment Center. This was the "normal" treatment he was accustomed to at Abbott. No one on the staff at St. Mary's noted that he was exhibiting symptoms typical of manic-depressive disorder during the days before his planned leave of absence. One cannot help but wonder if they had made the diagnosis of manic-depressive disorder at St. Mary's Alcohol Treatment Center, or if he had been in St. Mary's Psychiatric Unit, would they perhaps have started him on the proper medication? This is just another example of the *masquerades of psychiatry* that hinder proper diagnoses for some cases. But at ten o'clock on the appointed morning, permission to leave the hospital was withdrawn; Jim Zosel, one of his counselors, an Episcopal minister who had training in New Testament theology, offered to take over his class for him.

While Berryman was hospitalized at St. Mary's there had been disclosures that American troops in Vietnam had widened the war by crossing into Laos and Cambodia, and the news had resulted in an outbreak of student uprising around the country, including the University of Minnesota. Berryman was horrified to learn some of his students were wearing red arm bands in support of the Viet Cong and was chagrined at his absence from the scene, missing the opportunity to influence his students in debate and dialogue. He felt terror and helplessness, new emotions for him. In spite of his personal collapse, however, Berryman was not about to witness the collapse of the one place left for reasoned discussion. He felt driven to get out of the hospital and go over there to do what he could. His insistence was typical of his grandiose and omnipotent thinking in the manic phase of his mental disorder. His grandiosity was probably enhanced by his thirst for a martini while he was on the trip over to the university, or back, or both. But the decision at St. Mary's would not be changed; he was not allowed to leave.

Suddenly, something happened that Berryman would later call "a sort of a religious experience," changing him from his previous belief in a transcendent God controlling the universe, to a more benevolent God who cared about the individual fates of human beings and who would intercede for them. He did the only thing that he knew how to do when confronted with a "higher power,"—in this case the administration of St. Mary's Hospital—he retreated to the place where he was king—his poetry. Beginning May 21 and extending over the next two weeks, while he continued his recovery at St. Mary's, Berryman wrote a series of poems that became his "Eleven Addresses to the Lord." His poetry would tell his story of having always tried in the past to go the journey alone. Ever since his father had abandoned him, he had experienced signs of God's presence and love, but nothing like this. Now he had the sense of some incredible weight being lifted from him, and his poetry seemed to reflect his own thinking rather than his alter ego, Henry's.

The "Eleven Addresses to the Lord" turned out to be a complex orchestration of pleadings and responses to the Lord, ranging from awe and qualified belief to a new understanding of love and fame from a less ego-centered perspective. *Let me only get on with my work*, Berryman prayed, *and let God decide its worth*. After all, the poems had always been a gift from God to him.

Zosel could see that Berryman was not surrendering himself to his higher power that recovering alcoholics finally come to call on. Berryman's statement indicated that he was willing to surrender only his creative abilities, and they were a special gift to him from God anyway. In other words, he was God's chosen one. At the end of five weeks, Berryman still drew the line as to how much he was willing to change. He had heard the cliché at St. Mary's, "we alcoholics are as sick as we are secret," that he later wrote about in his book, *Recovery,* that was published posthumously. Berryman believed his life was "an open poem." Perhaps he meant poems open to anyone's interpretation but itself exclusive to its maker. In his willingness to counsel others in whatever way he could, the grandiosity of the manic was still present; for himself he still saw suicide as his only way out (the ultimate leverage of the manipulator).

Zosel noted Berryman's unconscious habit of playing over and over again the timeless version of the same song that dated back to 1926, the year Berryman's father had killed himself. He played the same tune in a letter to his mother in June, when he wrote what had frightened him was that, "three weeks into withdrawal, [he] had a seizure and that was very unusual and threatening." He was trying to convince his mother that "this time [his] body was warning [him he] might not survive another such period of drinking." This is information that Berryman needed to understand and believe himself: there was no need or purpose to inform anyone else, including his mother, of his possible demise from drinking. It is on the one hand a perfectly obvious likelihood that death could have occured, and had occurred to some who had been close to him. On the other hand, it was on his part an obvious emotional threat of tyranny. Furthermore, a seizure three weeks into withdrawal probably indicated that part of his withdrawal included withdrawal from the barbiturates (Phenobarbital and Tuinal) that he was known to be addicted to, in addition to alcohol.

On June 12, he was discharged *uncured.* He had lost nineteen pounds in the hospital and he could sleep only sporadically. There had been some progress Zosel noted, but Berryman began to retreat into his former "hostile, arrogant and defiant behavior."

Berryman is a classical example of why an individual with a Dual Diagnosis has a more difficult time recovering from either his psychiatric disorder or his addiction disorder unless both diagnoses are treated specifically and simultaneously. A person with manic-depressive disorder, who understands his disease is aware that he may well have been given a "gift" as well as a "curse" from the resulting mania that enables. The "gift" is realized with the stimulation of the brain and the flow of creativity that occurs only when he is able to cooperate with the treatment and control the excesses that are causing the chaos.

The insightful manic person realizes that when he becomes overstimulated, usually in a cyclic fashion, creativity becomes inefficient. Due to the racing of the mind, the person may inadvertently discover that alcohol and sedatives can calm him down to the point that his creativity is more productive and usable. However, there is a high probability he may become physically addicted to the alcohol or sedatives used to level off his manic highs in his attempts to self-medicate.

Equally problematic is the fact that an untreated manic depressive can become physiologically addicted to his own manic highs (auto addiction) that he interprets as a "soothing euphoria." In other words, he becomes physiologically addicted to his own excessive norepinephrine and serotonin. He actually becomes physiologically and psychologically addicted to his manic highs. When the manic depressive is "high" or "euphoric" on his own excessive neurohormones, he is either grandiose and feels omnipotent with hyper-religiosity, or he may instead become aggressive, paranoid, and violent. He may feel grandiose because he feels he has special powers, he may feel hyper-religious because he has been chosen by God to be creative (which is, after all, especially to be "god-like"), or he may feel paranoid because people do not believe, recognize, or appreciate his special gifts.

If a person with manic-depressive disorder becomes an alcoholic or a sedative addict, as John Berryman did, he may attribute to the alcohol or sedative a power that it does not have. He could believe it is the alcohol that increases his creativity. Alcohol does not and cannot do that. What alcohol and sedatives can do, to some extent, is sedate the racing mind and give the creative person less scattered, more organized thinking and/or a subjective feeling that he is more organized, creative, and productive—which is never true, but may feel that way.

Drunkenness does not help anyone's creativity, productivity, or reputation, and it creates problems for the creative person with a Dual Diagnosis, just like drunkenness produces problems for the typical alcoholic or addict. Unfortunately, the public frequently overlooks the creative person's drunken

antics and attributes it to the creative person's eccentricity. The modern
medicines like lithium, Tegretol, or Depakote probably could have stabilized
Berryman's manic phases, but unfortunately these medications were not available
when Berryman was alive. He did have Sparine, Thorazine, and Haldol that
were helpful for the acute psychotic periods and helped the mood stabilization
when he was sober, but they also had side effects that made these medications
undesirable to Berryman. This left Berryman in the vulnerable position of
trying to titrate his manic episodes with alcohol, Phenobarbital, Thorazine,
Haldol, and Tuinal against his depressed episodes with Vivactil. This placed
him in a position that an addicted alcoholic cannot possibly handle without
humility and the willingness to surrender and accept his powerlessness over
alcohol and drugs, and turn control of those things over to his Higher Power,
his physicians, and Alcoholics Anonymous. In Berryman's case, he had made
some progress during his treatment at Hazelden and St. Mary's Hospital
treatment centers, but his progress was somewhat equivocal and was more in
the nature of his own personal hyper-religiosity than it was his surrender and
identification with a power greater than himself.

Just three weeks after discharge from St. Mary's, Berryman "having worked
that hard" rewarded himself with a drink, then another, then another, until once
more he was drunk. After many partial attempts to right himself he finally
decided to go into the hospital again after having a "fling" with another young
graduate student. One night he asked a woman to drive him home where, he
wrote, "every light in the house seemed on.... " Later, he wrote:

> He knew he was standing in his entry-hall. Wife facing him, cold eyes,
> her arm outstretched with a short glass—a little smaller than he liked—in
> her hand. Two cops to his left. His main Dean and wife off somewhere
> right.... The girl had gone. He was looking into his wife's eyes and he was
> hearing her say: "This is the last drink you will ever take." Even as some-
> where up in his feathery mind he said, "Screw that," somewhere he also
> had an unnerving and apocalyptic feeling that this might be true....

I would like to say parenthetically and emphatically now that having a
manic-depressive disorder or any other psychiatric diagnosis is not a prerequisite
for being a creative person or ending life by suicide. In most studies of creative
people, the manic-depressive disorder people are not in the majority.

However, their numbers are staggering. The highest percentage of creative people who have suffered from manic-depressive disorders, psychosis, depression, alcoholism and/or drug abuse, or have ended their life by suicide are the poets. Berryman is just one of many. Juda's study found that the highest rate of psychiatric abnormalities, including alcoholism, was found among poets (50 percent). Dr. Arnold Ludwig's recent study of individuals based on biographies studied over a thirty-year period (1960–1990) is impressive for both its scope and careful methodology and was favorably reviewed by the *New York Times Book Review*. Consistent with Juda's findings in German artists and Jamison's study on British writers and artists, Ludwig found the highest rates of mania, psychosis, and psychiatric hospitalizations in poets. A staggering 18 percent of poets had committed suicide. Because alcoholics, by intent or by error, frequently were included in studies like these, statistics may become somewhat inflated. I would agree that at least 50 percent of all artists, composers, writers, and poets have no mental disorders or alcohol or drug addiction disorders and therefore should be classified as "normal." These findings are highly suggestive of the fact that mental illness and especially manic-depressive disorder do play a major role in creativity if for no other reason than the increased energy it gives the afflicted individual. It also seems clear that alcohol and other addictive drugs are used by these creative people to self-medicate their psychiatric illnesses. These so-called recreational drugs are addictive and complicate their lives with loss of control and unmanageability and cause chaos to reign supreme. If, instead, they were to have their illness treated by legitimate non-addictive medications such as lithium, Tegretol, or Depakote they could level out their moods scientifically and retain their creativity without having it distorted or otherwise sedated by alcohol and other addicting drugs.

"Six weird days and nights" had come to their conclusion. Attended by two campus security guards, Berryman was strapped down and taken by ambulance across the Washington Avenue Bridge to the locked ward at St. Mary's.

This, his third formal and specialized treatment for alcoholism, he believed was different. It was "humbler but grander" than before. One morning during Transactional Analysis he had suddenly seen himself not as an actor in an amphitheater but as the amphitheater itself, watching the dreams of life unfold before him. Desperate for a cure, he tried harder than ever to level with himself—to be truly honest. He struggled to move outside himself and help other patients on the ward. When one of them left he applauded, wept, and cheered. He listened to the suggestions made to him in therapy. But he also composed extraordinary poems that told him he really was a man who for all his "yesses," was still saying no:

> *If after finite struggle, infinite aid,*
> *ever you come there, friend,*
> *remember backward me lost in defiance,*
> *as I remember those admitting and complying.*

After six-weeks in treatment and when he had been out of St. Mary's for ten days and was still sober, he was telling himself that he was feeling "just fine." He was planning outpatient treatment for an additional two years, but also planning that his next drink would be on his deathbed, thus indicating he still had some residual reservation about drinking again.

Berryman's mind was still racing with manic energy. He had planned to give readings at ten colleges in Wisconsin before going to New York to see plays and record his poetry. He invited Valerie Trueblood to come up from Washington to have dinner with him and then he was going to fly to Haiti for ten days to read. He decided, however, to cut the ten Wisconsin lectures to five and checked into the Chelsea Hotel in New York on December 13. By then, having passed through several airports, he was once again drinking heavily. He began what Alcoholics Anonymous calls "telephonitis," making many, many long distance phone calls to his friends during the night, including his ex-wife Eileen who was remarried and who told him he could visit them only if he was sober. He did not see her. For the next few weeks he managed to stay sober for a few days by going to AA meetings and did some political poetry, as well as some poetry about how and why he might drink again.

For example, in "Man Building Up to a Slip," he wrote:

> *I haven't downed whiskey for 4 months*
> *a girl for 4 years. Liebchen, I'm growing old,*
> *with seventeen thousand dollars in the bank*
> *and am restless, restless.*

By the end of September, when he finished his elegy for Dylan Thomas, "In Memoriam" (1914–1953), he was once more up to a quart of whiskey a day and the poem reflected how much he now wanted an end to his twenty-five-year struggle with alcohol.

In May 1971, Drake University awarded Berryman his first honorary degree. He and Kate flew to Des Moines on the fifteenth so he could give a reading. The following afternoon at the commencement exercises he was capped, hooded, and honored. Then on the twentieth, having successfully avoided the airport bars, he checked into the Shoreham Hotel in Hartford. That night, alone in his room, drinkless and rereading Graham Green's *The Power and the Glory*, Berryman sensed "someone" in his room with him. He wrote a religious poem he called "The Facts and Issues." It seemed to catch something of his fear and hysteria, expressive perhaps of alcoholic paranoia or manic delusions. If God wanted him to acknowledge the divine presence in the room, he was ready to, he shouted on the page. There were plenty of "smart cookies" out there who were ready to admit that God had suffered for humankind; then he too, with his "pathetic and disgusting vices," must be included. But why? So that John Berryman could be happy? Well, he was happy. In fact he was "so happy" he could scream. (This sounds like the grandiose and manic euphoria of the manic phase of manic-depressive disorder)."Its enough," he added. "I can't BEAR ANY MORE! *Let this be it.* I've had it. I can't wait." (Presumably he meant for his own death.) He called Kate at 4:00 in the morning to ask her to remind him "of any act of pure and costly giving" he had ever done. He explained that he'd had enough of "this heaven and hell thing." He was willing to settle for some middle ground where he could get some sleep when the ordeal of living was finally over.

This is a good description of the horrendous fatigue that settles on a manic person when his mind is racing and of the predictable despair that accompanies the inevitable depression that follows.

Later that morning, his friend Meredith arrived in his old Mercedes. They discussed alcoholism on their way to Bread Loaf and Berryman was proud of his AA medallion and his three months of sobriety. That night, as he and Meredith walked the quiet streets, Berryman began shouting the dates for his tombstone. "John Berryman: 1914–19..." But, he added, there was no particular hurry about filling in the blank.

On July 27, 1971, Berryman received his six-month sobriety chip at his AA meeting. He flew to Berkeley to try to work on his novel and to get away from his family. He was becoming more and more explosive with them and every-body else. His moods could still swing at a moment's notice from tenderness to rage. He had never learned coexistence and shared responsibility, and he was too old to start now. He had also stopped communicating with his poet friends by letter. Ralph Ross saw Berryman late that summer and remarked to Allen Tate, "He was friendly and courteous, but he was losing weight, up to four packs of cigarettes a day, keeping himself and his family awake by his coughing all night and was afraid to drink because it would kill him and he wanted to live." He was very depressed and hypercritical of everyone including Kate and his mother. Ross further noted, "There was no warmth shown to anyone and no excitement of mind [mania] and no ardor." Ross concluded that "the only John one could love was a John with two or three drinks in him, no more and no less, and such a John could not exist." This remark is reminiscent of a common saying at AA meetings, "One drink is too many and a thousand is not enough."

He continued to try to work, and on December 7, he taught his last class. The depression had been building up in him all summer and fall and it began to overwhelm him with the onset of winter. (He had for long time been subject to seasonal affective disorder.) He thought constantly of suicide now even as he told himself that way was a "cowardly, cruel, and wicked" way to die.

On the morning of the thirteenth of December, after Martha had gone to school and Kate and the baby had gone shopping, he thought of taking his Spanish knife and gun and checking into a hotel in Minneapolis and just doing it. He fell to his knees with the knife and gun in his hands, shaking and praying for help until the crisis passed.

Afterwards, he went downtown to do some Christmas shopping and clear his head. He would give up writing the novel after all, he decided, knowing he was not going to finish it to his satisfaction. When he told Kate, she merely shrugged. It was his business. He also decided then to quit seeing his psychiatrist since that route was getting him nowhere. Strangely, his depression lifted, something that often happens once a suicidal patient decides he is going to commit suicide. It was, he thought, as if God was stroking him for sacrificing everything.

Five days later, on Wednesday, January 5, Berryman bought himself a bottle of whiskey and drank half of it. This time Kate was too exhausted even to be disappointed. She had quit waiting for the other shoe to fall. He was going to have to turn to his AA meetings and friends to help him if that was what he still wanted. Before leaving the house that day he left a note on the kitchen table that read, "I am a nuisance." With classes about to begin, he once more contemplated taking his own life.

Now, at least, he knew how he would do it. He would climb over the railing of the upper walkway of the Washington Avenue Bridge, take his Spanish knife and slash his throat so that he would feel faint and have to pitch forward. He would not submit to another Iowa fiasco, with the cops locking him up and losing his proffesorship. This time it would be for keeps.

In any event, he found the strength to return home that day, where he wrote another poem. It was to be his last. "I didn't. And I didn't," he wrote, using *Henry's Dream Song* stanzas once again. He didn't, but he would, the way Hart Crane had prefigured for himself in the opening to "The Bridge" by simply tilting out from the railing and letting go:

> *Sharp the Spanish blade*
> *to gash my throat after I'd climbed across*
> *the high railing of the bridge*
> *to tilt out, with the knife in my right hand*
> *to slash me shocked or fainting till I'd fall*
> *unable to keep my skull down but fearless*
>
> *unless my wife wouldn't let me out of the house,*
> *unless the cops noticed me crossing the campus*
> *up to the bridge*
> *and clapped me in for observation, costing my job—*
> *I'd be now in a cell, costing my job—*
> *well, I missed that;*
>
> *but here's the terror of tomorrow's lectures*
> *bad in themselves, the students dropping the course,*
> *the Administration hearing*
> *and offering me either a medical leave of absence*
> *or resignation—Kitticat, they can't fire me—*

Nothing fired him anymore. He put a slash through the poem and tossed it into the wastebasket. Then he put the bottle of whiskey away and called a friend in AA and asked him to take over for him at the next meeting, since he did not think he would be able to make it.

The following day was Thursday. John Berryman walked across the

Washington Avenue Bridge again, this time on his way to the Wilson Library apparently to read a volume of James Hastings' *Encyclopaedia of Religion and Ethics.*

Friday morning, January 7, 1972, after another restless night, Berryman told Kate he was going to the office to put his things in order. Kate sent Martha to school, then bundled up Sarah to do some shopping. "You won't have to worry about me anymore," he told her as she went out. But she had heard that one before too. At half past eight, he put on his coat and scarf and walked down University Avenue. There he caught the shuttle bus heading out onto the upper level of the Washington Avenue Bridge. It was bitterly cold, but rather than use the glass-enclosed walkway, he began walking along the north side of the bridge toward the west-bank campus. Three quarters of the way across, he stopped and stared down.

A hundred feet below and to his right was the river that was narrow, gray, and half-frozen. In front of him were the snow covered cold-storage docks and directly below, the winter trees on a slight knoll rising like a grave. He climbed onto the chest-high metal railing and balanced himself. Several students inside the walkway stopped what they were doing when they saw him and stared in disbelief. He made a gesture as if waving but he did not look back. From that height he must have figured the blade seemed redundant after all. Then he leaned out and let go.

Three seconds later his body exploded against the knoll, recoiled from the earth, then rolled gently down the incline. The campus police were the first to arrive and found a package of Tareyton cigarettes, some change, and a blank check with the name Berryman on it. Inside the left temple of his shattered horn-rimmed glasses they found the name a second time. An ambulance took the body to the Hennepin County Morgue, where Berryman was officially pronounced dead. His body was taken to the Hanson-Nugent Funeral Home on Nicollet Avenue, prepared for burial, and placed in a sealed casket. Father Robert Hazel arranged for burial at Resurrection Cemetery after services at St. Frances Cabrini.

On Monday, January 10, at half-past four in the afternoon, Berryman's wife, mother, brother, and friends gathered for the Mass of the Resurrection. The pallbearers included Bob Ames, chairman of the Humanities Department, Robert Giroux, a lifelong friend in the publishing business, ex-mayor Art Naftalin, and Dr. Boyd Thomas, the man who had tried to keep him alive as long as possible. There were readings from the Psalms, Lamentations, and Luke, a Beethoven Quartet, and a reading of the twenty-seventh and seventy-seventh *Dream Songs*. Finally there was a reading of the eighth of the "Eleven Addresses to the Lord," Berryman's prayer for himself, where he had asked the Lord to help him understand his terrible secrets and to, "cushion the first the second shocks, will to a halt in mid-air there, demons who would at me."

PSYCHIATRIC AND SUBSTANCE ABUSE FORMULATION

John Berryman's Psychiatric and Substance Abuse Diagnostic Formulation is based on the following: physical characteristics, basic intelligence, developmental experiences, genetic inheritance, familial influences, and life experiences—all of which influenced the final person he became.

I. Physical characteristics—slight, ectomorphic build with near-sighted vision.
II. Very high intelligence with genius level I.Q.
III. Developmental interference in childhood with resulting personality disorder.
IV. Familial and/or genetic alcoholism in the biological family.
V. Genetic manic-depressive disorder in mother and major depression in father.

John Berryman's physical characteristics and weaknesses alone were enough to influence his social and educational responses to the world. He was very near-sighted and had to wear thick, horned-rimmed glasses from an early age and was tagged with the nickname "blears" because of his visual problems. Near-sighted people may naturally be more studious students, if for no other reason than they cannot see objects well at a distance. This makes it difficult for them to do well in most competitive sports because they cannot see goals, balls, or players at a distance, but they excel as "book worms," and in lone sports like jogging and swimming. In fact, Berryman did participate in jogging and swimming alone because ectomorphs are "loners" by temperament. So, his near-sighted vision and his slight body build conspired along with his genius intelligence to make him the best of students with a natural talent for academic success, but little interest in gregarious activity.

Berryman's genius intelligence quotient made school and higher education as easy as he wanted it to be. But being above average in intelligence may make recovery from addiction or mental illness harder or easier depending on the quality of medical/psychiatric treatment. Of equal importance is the presence or absence of support systems such as employers, family, friends, society, and individuals to help an addict or mentally ill person surrender to the principle of total abstinence from all mind-altering chemicals. Probably the worst advice to an alcoholic from his family or friends is to be told that all he needs to do is cut down on his drinking. For anyone with mental illness it is important that the treatment team and family expend as much effort as possible extending hope, faith, and expectation for recovery along with benevolent coercion in that direction. Paramount to dealing with this kind of situation is to keep evaluating for the presence of a Dual Diagnosis that will indicate the need for application of both of these treatment principles simultaneously.

The formation of an individual's personality traits and personality disorders are based, according to the majority of psychologists and psychiatrists, on the accumulated life experiences that the child has in his formative, preadolescent, adolescent, and very young adulthood years. John Berryman had sufficient developmental interference during his early and middle childhood and adolescent years that one could have predicted that there would be enough significant negative influence to cause a personality disorder. For one thing, his biological father was probably an alcoholic who caused chaos when he was home and insecurity when he was absent. Berryman's mother alternated between periods of excessive smothering of her son and periods of aloofness depending on her own emotional needs. She demeaned his biological father, Mr. Smith, by stating he did not have any sexual "vigor" and said he looked and acted like a "French homosexual." She had four husbands and as many business adventures and different careers that were both highly successful and moderately successful, but all of them eventually ended in failure. Just imagine the effect of all of this on Berryman, who was having problems with basic trust, control, and competition issues. He wrestled with inferiority because of his failure to resolve the first oedipal issues at five years of age by surrendering the forbidden incestuous love for his mother to his father, and then during the second oedipal period he was faced with the suicide of his father at the age of twelve. John won the battle with his father over the "love" of his mother, only to lose it again to his mother's new suitor and husband, John Berryman, Sr. Only this time he would also sacrifice his very name and identity by being forced to become legally adopted by the senior Berryman and having to change his birth name from John Smith to John Berryman. This led to an identity disorder as described in *DSM-III-R,* 313.82 as causing subjective distress regarding uncertainty about a variety of issues, "including three or more" of the following:

- long-term goals
- career choice
- friendship patterns
- sexual orientation and behavior
- religious identification
- moral value system
- group loyalties

John's early financial security oscillated between him being one of the privileged and one of the deprived. These oscillations in family wealth were probably more difficult on John because of his very high intelligence. He complained that he suffered a great deal of insecurity because of his changing economic stresses. Even before this traumatic event, Berryman, with the developmental interference of Freud's Oral and Anal stages of life, had already experienced a high probability that could have caused many of the multiple problems he had with basic trust, control, separation, and individuation. Certainly the combination of his high intelligence, his slight physical build, his near-sighted eyes, and his lack of a competitive spirit more or less forced him toward being a bookworm rather than an athlete. His objective symptoms ran the gamut from difficulty trusting people and projecting blame on others to having claustrophobia and suffering from "hysterical fits." He would also have fits of temper that were so violent that he would appear to feign seizures (pseudoseizures) and would manipulate his family by becoming mute—his eyelids would flutter and his pupils would dilate and he would collapse. This would end with his mother stopping the excessive talking that disturbed Berryman so much. Then, she would put John to bed and provide for all his needs for the rest of the day. Pseudoseizures can also be diagnosed as a physical or psychological factitious disorder, meaning that Berryman knew he was faking the seizure but did it for some ulterior motive. In Berryman's case, the ulterior motive would be to escape the hysterical reactions of his mother and possibly as an excuse to obtain or use mind-altering medications. All of these complex developmental experiences eventually led to two Axis I diagnoses, identity disorder and factitious disorder, and two Axis II diagnoses, mixed personality disorder (dependent personality and histrionic personality disorders).

As an adult, and while Berryman struggled to get better teaching positions, his drinking escalated. He may have inherited his alcoholism from his biological father. However, Berryman blamed his drinking on his inability to sleep. The insomnia actually resulted from his alcohol withdrawal and probably the onset of his undiagnosed cyclic manic-depressive disorder that caused mood swings with symptoms of depression, mania, paranoia, and grandiosity. He probably inherited the manic-depressive disorder from his mother who was also undiagnosed. Other possible causes of Berryman's mood swings may have been a traumatic brain injury, encephalitis, or drug-induced mood disorder, but his history does not suggest any cause other than inheritance. His hypersexuality (a symptom of mania and sometimes alcoholism and possibly a sexual identity disorder) was also a constant companion and contributed as much to his instability as his alcoholism and manic depression. From Berryman's own words we know that his eventual motivation for drinking had become to reach "oblivion," or, at least intermittently, "just to avoid thought." He would cite his personal problems as well as all the problems of the world as the reason for his great need to experience oblivion.

He inadvertently discovered that alcohol could "give [his] mind a rest" and sometimes "alcohol would make [him] creative." This was probably not exactly true, but alcohol may have, for a period of time, made him more productive because he couldn't produce anything in his manic states of high frenzy. Perhaps early on, before he became addicted to alcohol, alcohol did have the "power" to reduce that frenzy so he could write poetry or notes about future planned projects.

This was not new; it was typical Berryman. Most everyone who knew him, including Berryman himself, would (incorrectly) credit the bursts of energy and talent to his alcohol intake. He drank the same quantities and knew his alcoholism was worsening, as were his nightmares and his bouts of *delirium tremens*. This suggests a decreased tolerance to alcohol either from alcohol-induced brain damage or because of decreased rate of metabolism of the alcohol by his liver. "Reduce Booze," he would write despairingly in yet another creative and successful Song. The truth has to be that there were bursts of creativity and genius brought about during spontaneous manic phases for short periods during the rapid cycling of his disorder that would bring forth creative work even when he was drinking. He was also unknowingly self-medicating his manic psychosis with his supply of Sparine prescribed by Dr. Boyd Thomas.

He complained about his "sparingitis," which is a spasm of the vocal cords (dyskinesia) causing laryngitis-like symptoms that is not an uncommon side effect of the Sparine medication.

His alcoholism produced a new source of stress in his life. He began dating, marrying, divorcing, having children, and having extra-marital affairs with women half his age.

Inasmuch as Berryman never properly resolved his competitive issues with his father when he was four or five years old or during the pre-puberty period of eleven to twelve years of age (when his father committed suicide), he never learned how to compete in his interpersonal relationships or within his profession. He needed to be King or die! He did have a chance to be King of Poetry. This realistic but unrelenting goal seemed to help him compensate for the fact that he could not make enough money to care for his wives or his children. He continued to have seizures that neither his wives nor his mother thought were real.

Because he was brilliant and a genius, he continued to get good teaching positions at Harvard, Princeton, Berkeley, Wayne State, University of Iowa, and the University of Minnesota and received many, many awards, including the Pulitzer once and the Guggenheim twice. All the while he continued to have a sullied reputation because of his drunkenness, and he was fired from the University of Iowa position allegedly for that very reason. Although, his eccentric behavior and sexual misconduct could have contributed to that reputation as well as his alcoholism, sexual identity disorder, or his manic-depressive disorder.

He spent his mid-life in and out of psychiatric hospitals ostensibly to be detoxified for his alcoholism, but he never accepted the diagnosis of alcoholism until the last three years of his life. Likewise, there is no evidence that Berryman or his psychiatrist or medical doctors ever made the diagnosis of manic-depressive disorder. It appears that Berryman's reputation of being an eccentric genius was explanation enough for his bizarre and drunken behavior. Berryman himself frequently said he was depressed and constantly threatened to commit suicide. He often said he had manic periods, but he did not consider these episodes to be a result of a psychiatric illness, in spite of having been admitted and sometimes committed from forty to sixty psychiatric hospitals all over the world. His concept was that he was going into psychiatric hospitals for his "nervous condition" and for "detoxification from alcohol," but mostly for "a needed rest." He apparently never saw any inconsistency with his way of thinking and the world's opinion of normal behavior.

John Berryman had three admissions to two of the best treatment centers in the country at that time—Hazelden and St. Mary's, both in Minnesota. He did accept his alcoholism with the fateful reservation about the extent of his disease and he did manage to acquire six months of sobriety during the last year of his life.

It is difficult to understand why John Berryman never accepted that he had a psychiatric diagnosis. It never seemed to concern him *why* he had a "nervous condition," with symptoms of anxiety, paranoia, grandiosity, pressured speech, flight of ideas, hypersexuality, uncontrolled spending, tirades of anger, depression, suicidal thoughts and plans, mood swings, hallucinations, delusions, and other psychotic escapes from reality. It is true that during his lifetime the medications for most psychiatric illnesses like his had enough side effects to be frightening. Lithium, Tegretol, and Depakote were not available or at least not in use for psychiatric illnesses during his era. He was taking the medications that were available, but not in a controlled way and not under a physician's supervision. He also did not accept all of the help that was available to him for treating his alcoholism through the program of Alcoholics Anonymous.

It is truly a tragedy that a genius who attained the epitome of his life goal and became the King of American Poetry would commit suicide while essentially sober and professionally successful. This alone suggests an escape from reality that can be explained best by a psychotic process like manic-depressive disorder or psychotic depression.

The big question is, did the alcoholism come first and cause the mental illness, or did the mental illness cause the alcoholism? It is the same old traditional cliché: which came first, the chicken or the egg? In the case of Berryman and Poe they both probably had manic-depressive disorder before they developed alcoholism, but only Poe seems to have recognized the connection. Poe wrote: "But I am constitutionally sensitive—nervous in a very unusual degree, I became insane, with long periods of horrible sanity.... During those fits of absolute unconsciousness I drank, God knows how much or how long. As a matter of course my enemies referred the insanity to the drink rather than the drink to the insanity."

These two great men and creative poets and authors suffered from alcoholism *and* mental illness. To a large extent, Poe recognized his mental illness and knew he was drinking to escape the horrors of his mental illness. His melancholia was part of a major depression, but he also had cyclic mania that at a minimum gave him spurts of energy, drove him to wanton gambling and explosive anger, and added to the difficulty he had managing his finances. Mania and melancholia in the time of Poe would today be called manic-depressive disorder or bipolar disorder.

Berryman definitely lived during an era when manic-depressive disorder was diagnosable, but he was never diagnosed accurately. He drank to slow down his racing mind and secondarily became an alcoholic. It is apparent that Berryman, like Poe, received some benefits from using alcohol as a medication. It is also evident that he, also like Poe, met his demise from the use of alcohol and drugs simply because it was the wrong "medicine." It also produced an addiction, with its inevitable loss of control. It is certain that both Poe and Berryman were exceptionally brilliant individuals who probably would not have died so young and would have had even more successful careers if they had taken medications that treated their psychiatric symptoms specifically rather than sedating themselves with alcohol. There were no Alcoholics Anonymous meetings nor any effective psychiatric medications at the time of Poe's death. There have been Alcoholics Anonymous meetings since 1935, and John Berryman did attend a few treatment centers and several AA meetings. It was his undiagnosed manic-depressive disease, no doubt, that precipitated his suicide.

John Berryman's behavior when drunk or sober portrays how alcoholism and manic-depressive disorder masquerade or mimic each other, making the diagnosis difficult for both the physician and the patient. His genius and creative abilities, when combined with alcohol and manic-depressive disorder, often were discounted by the public as the eccentricity common to artists, poets, composers, and writers or simply as "the madness that to genius is often near allied."

When a Dual Diagnosis occurs in a creative genius its diagnosis and treatment is frequently delayed simply because friends and associates are not aware of the struggle necessary for the artist to just stay alive. Invariably, his struggle is not rewarded financially in proportion to the academic recognition, and a life of relative poverty simply adds to the already difficult struggle. Life's tragedies seem to accompany his every move and, of course, suicides are all too common. Often, too, both the patient and his physician are reluctant to institute treatment for their eccentric behavior or mental disorders for fear treatment will eliminate or at least reduce creativity. Because of this attitude, important diagnostic clues are often overlooked: the possession of the high intelligent quotient of a genius is often considered sufficient explanation for the eccentric, depressed, manic, anxious, or drunken behavior of the patient.

In the case of Berryman, the death of his father when he was twelve years old along with the forced change in his identity to that of his new adoptive father, his proclivity to be a perpetual student in an ivy league environment, and his brilliance were seen by many, including his psychiatrist, Dr. Shea, as explanation enough for his drunken and eccentric behavior. The failure to recognize alcoholism and manic-depressive disorder early in his life, though both were definitely present, precluded the diagnosis and adequate treatment of both diseases.

Back in Minneapolis during the winter of 1958, Berryman returned to his *Dream Songs*, drinking heavily to sustain his "inspirations." Or perhaps his "inspirations" were racing through his brain too fast and furious because of his mania and he thought he needed alcohol to slow his brain down enough so that he could convert the "inspirations" to writing. By this time, however, John's drinking had become so heavy and so constant that he actually thought he might die.

Berryman struggled all of his life and died young, and our country was robbed of his genius far too soon.

John Berryman, born almost 100 years after Poe, had both of his diagnoses defined by the medical profession during his lifetime. But the medications for his mania were somewhat inadequate during his era, and mood stabilizers like lithium and anticonvulsants were not fully understood and the neuroleptic antipsychotics only became available in 1950. Alcoholics Anonymous was available and he did eventually try to make it work. The primary reason it didn't work was because neither his psychiatrist nor the medical doctors recognized that an individual could have two mental or emotional illnesses concurrently, and Berryman's two illnesses mimicked or masqueraded as each other. Each of his illnesses caused the same or very similar symptoms that affected his thinking and judgement, how he felt emotionally, and how he behaved. But, because the symptoms were caused by two separate illnesses and the treatment for each illness was different, he did not get the appropriate treatment for either of them simultaneously. He could never have totally recovered. This is why the concept of Dual Diagnosis is so important.

Berryman was making progress in alcohol treatment, but he was using two different types of doctors and two different types of hospitals. Unfortunately, John Berryman had to decide, with an intoxicated and mentally-deranged mind, what kind of doctor he needed and what kind of hospital he needed. He didn't even know or want to know that he had manic-depressive disorder. Berryman called that part of his illness "nerves" and "fatigue."

Most medical doctors working in alcohol treatment centers honestly believe that if an alcoholic stops drinking and goes to Alcoholics Anonymous meetings, his alcoholism and his mental problems will be controlled essentially with the one treatment program. This is *not* true if there is a Dual Diagnosis. The problem is that sometimes the symptoms of alcoholism masquerade as mental illness and vice versa. On the other hand, many psychiatrists and psychiatric hospitals honestly believe that if the underlying psychiatric problem is adequately treated then the patient will have no need to drink and will spontaneously stop drinking. Both concepts are in error. John Berryman almost certainly committed suicide because of his inadequately treated manic-depressive disorder, not entirely because of his alcoholism. He was taking his AA program seriously and was making significant progress. He was sober at the time of his suicide.

DIAGNOSTIC IMPRESSIONS ON JOHN BERRYMAN

AXIS I:
1. Manic-Depressive Disorder Mixed Psychotic Features with Seasonal Pattern, *DSM-IV* (296.64)
2. Alcohol Dependence in Early Remission, *DSM-IV* (303.90)
3. Alcohol Induced Intoxication Delirium, *DSM-IV* (291.0)
4. Factitious Disorder with Pseudoseizures, *DSM-IV* (301.19)
5. Rule Out Malingering, *DSM-IV* (V65.2)
6. Sexual Identity Disorder, *DSM-IV* (312.82)
    Possible Dual or Triple Diagnosis

AXIS II:
1. Primary Mixed Personality Disorder, (Dependent *DSM-IV* (301.6), Histrionic 301.5)

AXIS III:
1. Ectomorphic build with near-sightedness

AXIS IV:
1. Severe problems with primary support group (multiple), legal, occupational, and marital

AXIS V:

1. Global Assessment of Functioning (GAF) Scale = Variable + 75-100

    Because of Berryman's genius intellect, the only logical way to apply classical numbers to GAF would be to divide his functioning into four component parts:

    Work = 85   Love = 55   Play = 75   Creativity = 100

CHAPTER SEVEN

Life, Liberty, and Lithium:
The Story of Dr. Kay Redfield Jamison

In *An Unquiet Mind*, the autobiographical account of how she lived with and suffered from, struggled against, and finally came to cope with her bipolar (manic-depressive) disorder, Dr. Kay Redfield Jamison, professor at Johns Hopkins University writes: "Within a month of signing my appointment papers to become assistant professor of psychiatry at the University of California, Los Angeles, I was well on my way to madness; it was 1974, and I was twenty-eight years old. Within three months I was manic beyond recognition and just beginning a long, costly war against a medication that I would, in a few years' time, be strongly encouraging others to take. My illness and struggles against the drug that ultimately saved my life and restored my sanity had been years in the making."

Dr. Jamison describes her mood disorder as beginning rather benignly and escalating slowly as she matured. She remembers being intensely emotional as a child and mercurial as a young girl. During adolescence she experienced her first severe depression, and as she grew into adulthood and began to embark upon a professional career, she found herself living the cycles of a manic-depressive illness. Very conscious of and attentive to her mood swings throughout her childhood and adolescence, she deliberately became a professional student of moods, motivated by intellectual curiosity and personal necessity, and determined to understand and own her illness. Through research and knowledge, she would try to make a difference in the lives of others who suffered with mood disorders.

Kay Redfield Jamison grew up in a closely-knit, supportive family consisting of herself, an older brother and sister, and both parents. Her parents were able to provide her with a very stimulating atmosphere during her childhood. All of the children were encouraged to have pets, to investigate poetry, and participate in school plays. As their schooling progressed, they were encouraged to consider preparation for a career in science or in medicine, among other fields of endeavor. An emphasis on education came naturally; both her parents were graduates of the University of Chicago and well educated, her mother being a schoolteacher and her father a meteorologist in the Navy, his father a college physics professor. About the only apparent possible negative influence in her early years was that her father's position in the Navy required frequent geographical dislocations. The family lived in Florida, Puerto Rico, California, Tokyo, and twice in Washington, D.C. By the time Kay was in the fifth grade she had already attended four different elementary schools in as many cities. Nevertheless, Kay felt very protected by her older brother, her mother, and grandmother, all of whom she characterizes as compassionate, understanding, caring, and supportive. She recalls her father as energetic, entertaining, generous, and educationally stimulating. In early adolescence the only signs of impending trouble was a tendency to have wider swings in her mood and the start of some instability as evidenced by occupational changes, a tendency towards heavy drinking, and ultimately, marital estrangement.

Kay was fifteen when cracks began to form in her hitherto happy world, and by the time she was seventeen she had discovered that her energies and enthusiasms found expression at a pitch unusually higher than those of people around her. After some weeks of heightened sensibilities she would exercise thoughts and feelings darker and more brooding than those of others.

Of course, Dr. Jamison was never my patient and I have never done a mental status examination on her. I will use only the material from her book, *An Unquiet Mind*, that reports those symptoms that she has documented, for example:

I was fifteen years old when everything in my world began to crack apart.

By the time I was seventeen years old, it became clear that my energies and enthusiasms could be exhausting to the people around me, and after long weeks of flying high and sleeping little, my thinking would take a turn downward toward the really dark and brooding side of life.

She dates her first attack of manic-depressive illness to her senior year in high school, and her skill in recalling the experience and describing her symptoms as so great that it can only be done justice by quoting her at length:

The world was filled with pleasure and promise. At first everything seemed incredibly easy. I raced around like a crazed weasel, bubbling with plans and enthusiasm, immersed in sports, and staying out night after night, with friends, reading everything that wasn't nailed down, filling manuscript books with poems and fragments of plays, and making expansive, completely unrealistic, plans for my future: I felt great, I felt really great. I felt I could do anything, that no task was too difficult. My mind seemed clear, fabulously focused, and able to make intuitive mathematical leaps that had up to that point totally eluded me. Indeed they elude me still. At the time, however, not only did everything make perfect sense, but also it all began to fit into a marvelous kind of cosmic relatedness. My sense of enchantment with the laws of the natural world caused me to fizz over.

I found myself buttonholing my friends to tell them how beautiful it all was. They were less than transfixed by my insights into the webbings and beauties of the universe, although, considerably impressed by how exhausting it was to be around my enthusiastic ramblings; you're talking too fast, Kay. Slow down, Kay. When they didn't say it I could see it in their eyes.

I did finally, slow down. In fact, I came to a grinding halt. Unlike the very severe manic episodes that came a few years later and escalated wildly and psychotically out of control, this first sustained wave of mild mania was a light, lovely tincture of true mania; like hundreds of subsequent periods of high enthusiasms it was short lived and quickly burned itself out: tiresome to my friends, perhaps; exhausting and exhilarating, definitely; but not disturbingly over the top.

My thinking, far from being clearer than crystal, was tortuous. I would read the same passage over and over again only to realize that I had no memory at all for what I had just read. Each book or poem I picked up was the same way. Incomprehensible, nothing made sense. I could not begin to follow the material presented in my classes, and I would find my self staring out of the window.

Now all of a sudden, my mind had turned on me: it mocked me for vapid enthusiasms; it laughed at all of my foolish plans; it no longer found anything interesting or enjoyable or worthwhile. It was incapable of concentrated thought and turned time and again to the subject of death: I was going to die what difference did it make?

I dreaded having to talk with people, avoided my friends whenever possible, and sat in the school library in the early mornings and late afternoons, virtually inert, with a dead heart and a brain as cold as clay.

This serious first attack, in her senior year in high school, led to a rapid and terrifying development of the disease. For the first two years when she was an undergraduate at UCLA, her symptoms were primarily exquisite euphoria, a racing mind, and pressured speech, and then a crash into a deep depression, with her mind grinding to a total stop. Within these two years she became wildly and psychiatrically out of control, and then moribund, depressed, and without energy to concentrate. She later ruefully reflected on her college years, contrasting the common experience of acquaintances who believed them to be the best years, to her own sense of them as a terrible struggle, a recurrent nightmare of "violent and dreadful moods." She cannot understand how she survived those years without being locked up.

Of course the pattern set in her first attack was repeated, so that these periods of utter dread and blankness were broken intermittently by weeks or sometimes even months of preternaturally high enthusiasm and long runs of hard but enjoyable work as a student. (She was also, in all moods, working many hours a week to earn the means of putting herself through school.) The enthusiastic periods were passionate and filled with fun, and very seductive. She describes them as the following:

...quite extraordinary, filling my brain with a cataract of ideas and more than enough energy to give me at least the illusion of carrying them out. My normal Brooks Brothers conversation would go by the board; my

> hemline would go up and my neckline would go down, and I would enjoy
> the sensuality of my youth. Almost everything was done to excess; instead
> of buying one ticket to a Beethoven symphony, I would buy nine; instead
> of enrolling for five classes, I would enroll for seven; instead of buying
> two tickets for a concert, I would buy eight or ten.

Kay Jamison applied for and was granted a federal award abroad for her
third undergraduate year. She studied zoology at St. Andrews University in
Scotland, her happiest year as a college student. Freed from the pressure of
having to work for her room and board, and caught up in her studies and in
reading poetry, she describes the year as the "Indian Summer" of her life. Her
disease seems somehow to have gone into remission, and her moods leveled
out; despite the harshness of the winter, she was to look back on the year
abroad as thoroughly pleasant and fulfilling.

When she returned to UCLA for her senior year, she became once again
acquainted with the exaggerated euphoria and deadly depressions of her illness.
She decided during this year that she did not have the temperament nor the
desire to submit herself to the rigor and rigidity of medical training (her
original ambition and plan), but that she wished nevertheless to pursue graduate
studies. Having an interest in psychology, and having been influenced by
William James' *The Varieties of Religious Experience,* read at St. Andrews, she
applied for and was accepted in the doctoral program in psychology at UCLA
in 1973, when she was twenty-two.

Her own mood swings focused her attention irrevocably on the study of
moods. She goes on to say, "I became both by necessity and intellectual inclination a student of moods. It has been the only way I know to understand,
indeed to accept, the illness I have; it also has been the only way I know to try
and make a difference in the lives of others who also suffer from mood disorders." Here Dr. Jamison, consciously or unconsciously, shows that she has,
directly or indirectly, experienced *The Spirituality of Imperfection* as described
by Ernest Kurtz in his book by that same name.[1] She adds, "The disease that
has, on several occasions, nearly killed me does kill tens of thousands of people
every year: most are young, most die unnecessarily, and many are among the
most imaginative and gifted that we as a society have." She goes on to say, "I
have found it [manic-depressive disorder] to be seductively complicated, a
distillation both of what is the finest in our natures, and of what is the most

dangerous. In order to contend with it, I first had to know it in all of its moods and infinite disguises, and understand its real and imagined powers."

I find it intriguing that Dr. Jamison used the words "infinite disguises" (masquerades?) in the above paragraph to describe her changing moods.

From the Prologue of *An Unquiet Mind:*

When it's two o'clock in the morning, and you're manic, even the UCLA Medical Center has a certain appeal. The hospital—ordinarily a cold clotting of uninteresting buildings—became for me that fall morning not quite twenty years ago, a focus of my finely wired, exquisitely alert nervous system. With vibrissae twinging, antennae perked, eyes fast-forwarding and fly faceted, I took in everything around me. I was on the run. Not just on the run but fast and furious on the run, darting back and forth across the hospital parking lot trying to use up a boundless, restless, manic energy. I was running fast but slowly going mad.

The man I was with, a colleague from the medical school had stopped running an hour earlier and was, he said, impatiently, exhausted. This, to a saner mind, would not have been surprising: the usual distinction between day and night had long since disappeared for the two of us, and the endless hours of scotch, brawling, and falling about in laughter had taken an obvious, if not fatal toll. We should have been sleeping or working, publishing not perishing, reading journals, writing in charts, or drawing tedious scientific graphs that no one else could read.

Suddenly a police car pulled up. Even in my less-than-totally lucid state of mind I could see that the officer had his hand on his gun as he got out of the car. "What in hell are you doing running around the parking lot at this hour?" he asked. A not unreasonable question. My few remaining islets reached out to one another and linked up long enough to conclude that this particular situation was going to be hard to explain. My colleague, fortunately, was thinking far better than I was and managed to reach down into some deeply intuitive part of his own and the world's collective unconscious and said, "We're both on the faculty in the psychiatry department." The policeman looked at the two of us, smiled, went back to his squad car, and drove away.

Being professors of psychiatry explained everything.

Now, given the scenario described above, there are at least four diagnoses that could explain the entire behavior witnessed by that police officer:

1. They could be two young people intoxicated on alcohol and perhaps on the faculty in psychiatry.
2. They could be two people abusing cocaine or amphetamines.
3. They could be two young psychiatric doctors, one of them exhausted trying to keep up with the second doctor.
4. The second doctor has a manic-depressive disorder and is in the manic phase.

A police officer on his regular beat would have suspected number one, a plain-clothes detective on the narcotics squad would have suspected number two, and a seasoned psychiatrist—hopefully—would have diagnosed it as numbers three and four.

Dr. Jamison then goes on to tell us how insidiously her mood disorder started and how easy it was to rationalize that it was almost normal. She says, "Because my illness at first seemed simply to be an extension of myself—that is to say, of my ordinarily changeable moods, energies, and enthusiasms—I perhaps gave it at times too much quarter. And, because I thought I ought to be able to control my increasingly violent mood swings by myself, for the first ten years I did not seek any kind of treatment."

She then explains why she was resisting treatment. "Even after my condition became a medical emergency, I still intermittently, resisted the medication that both my training and clinical research expertise told me was the only sensible way to deal with the illness I had." But she still resisted because she thought she could handle it. She says, "My manias, at least in their early and mild forms, were absolutely intoxicating states that gave rise to great personal pleasure, an incomparable flow of thoughts, and ceaseless energy that allowed the translation of new ideas into papers and projects. Medications not only cut into these fast-flowing, high flying times, they also brought with them seemingly intolerable side effects." She later says that, "It took me far too long to realize that lost years and relationships cannot be recovered, that damage done to oneself and others cannot always be put right again, and that freedom from the control imposed by medication loses its meaning when the only alternatives are death and insanity."

Even though at this time Kay Jamison had begun weekly appointments with a psychiatrist, she resisted pharmacological treatment and refused to take the effective medication, lithium. She says, "I simply did not want to believe I needed to take medications. I had become *addicted* to my high moods; I had become dependent upon their intensity, euphoria, assuredness, and their infectious ability to induce enthusiasms in other people." The brief periods of observations that she had as a feature of her manic-depressive illness made her feel the euphoria of intoxication, and she was hopelessly addicted to that feeling of intoxication.

I distinctly remember a question asked me by one of the examiners when I was taking the oral boards part for my certification for the American Boards of Psychiatry and Neurology: "What is the hardest thing about treating a patient with manic-depressive disorder?"

I answered from experience with such patients, giving the correct answer and one borne over and over again with subsequent experience: "Keeping them on their medication."

Patients with this illness will offer many reasons or rationalizations for not taking their medications: forgetfulness, misunderstanding, intolerable side effects, quasi-philosophic objections, holding onto the belief that they should be able to make it on their own, among many others. Yet they rarely admit to what surely should be among the most potent reasons, which is addiction to the euphoria of their manic phases, as Kay Jamison describes above.

Dr. Jamison knew that in her deliberate refusal to take lithium on a consistent basis, she was putting everything at risk. She says:

> The war that I waged against myself is not an uncommon one. The major clinical problem in treating manic-depressive illness is not that there are not effective medications—there are—but those patients so often refuse to take them. Worse yet, because of the lack of information, poor medical advice, stigma, or fear of personal and professional reprisals, they do not seek treatment at all.

Jamison's description of her symptoms probably cannot be improved upon because she has lived it, so I will quote her:

> Manic-depression distorts moods and thoughts, incites dreadful behaviors, destroys the basis of rational thought, and too often erodes the desire and will to live. It is an illness that is biological in its origins, yet

one that feels psychological in the experience of it; an illness that is unique in conferring advantage and pleasure, yet one that brings in its wake almost unendurable suffering and, not infrequently, suicide.

Jamison learned a hard lesson:

...a floridly psychotic mania was followed, inevitably, by a long and lacerating black, suicidal depression; it lasted more than a year and a half. From the time I woke up in the morning to the time I went to bed at night, I was unbearably miserable and seemingly incapable of any joy or enthusiasm. Everything—every thought, word, movement—was an effort.... Over and over and over I would say to myself, if I can't move, if I can't think, and I can't care, then what conceivable point is there in living?

Her psychiatrist wrote in his office record, "Patient is intermittently suicidal." And so she was: she did make a very serious attempt at suicide by using a massive overdose of lithium. Her brother called from Paris, discovered her acute drugged state, and called her personal psychiatrist, who, with a psychiatrist friend arrived at her bedside just in time to save her life. Even after this experience it took some time before she finally became convinced to take lithium as it was prescribed; when she did, her moods slowly stabilized and her private and professional life flourished.

Because Kay Jamison lived out her own life in the war with manic-depressive disorder and its mandatory treatment experienced by so many patients with this illness, and because her own account of the struggle is brilliant in its acuity and precision, I quote at length now crucial passages form her book. She tells first of her sense of desolation when she realizes she must surrender her manic moods—not unlike the alcoholic bidding farewell to the bottle:

I had a horrible sense of loss for who I had been and where I had been. It was difficult to give up the high flights of mind and mood, even though the depression that inevitably followed nearly cost me my life.

Psychological issues ultimately proved far more important than side effects in my prolonged resistance to lithium. I simply did not want to believe that I needed to take medication. I had become addicted to my high moods; I had become dependent upon their intensity, euphoria, assuredness, and their infectious ability to induce high moods and enthusiasms in other people. Like gamblers who sacrifice everything for the fleeting but ecstatic moments of winning, or cocaine addicts who risk their families, careers, and lives for the brief interludes of high energy and mood. I found my milder manic states powerfully inebriating and very conductive to productivity. I couldn't give them up. More fundamentally, I genuinely believed—courtesy of strong-willed parents, my own stubbornness, and a WASP military upbringing—that I ought to be able to handle whatever difficulties came my way without having to rely upon crutches such as medication.

I was not the only one who felt this way. When I became ill, my sister was adamant that I should not take lithium and was disgusted that I did. In an odd reversion to the Puritan upbringing she had raged against, she made it clear that she thought I should "weather it through" my depressions and manias, and that my soul would wither if I chose to dampen the intensity and pain of my experiences by using medication. The combination of her worsening moods, along with the dangerous seductiveness of her views about medication, made it very difficult for me to maintain a relationship with her.

One evening, now many years ago, she tore into me for "capitulating to Organized Medicine" by "lithiumizing away me feelings." My personality, she said, had dried up, the fire was going out, and I was but a shell of my former self. This hit an utterly raw nerve in me, as I imagine she knew it would, but simply enraged the man I was going out with at the time. He had seen me very ill indeed and saw nothing of value to preserve in such insanity. He tried to deflect the situation with wit—"Your sister may be just a shell of herself," he said, "but her shell is as much or more than I can handle"—but my sister then took off after him, leaving me sick inside, and doubtful, yet again, about my decision to take lithium.

What on earth could I have been thinking? I also had been taught to think for myself. Why, then, didn't I question these rigid, irrelevant notions of self-reliance? Why didn't I see how absurd my defiance really was?

Part of my stubbornness can be put down to human nature. It is hard for anyone with an illness, chronic or acute, to take medications absolutely as prescribed. Once the symptoms of an illness improve or go away, it becomes even more difficult. In my case, once I felt well again I had neither the desire nor the incentive to continue taking medication.

I didn't want to take it to begin with; the side effects were hard for me to adjust to; I missed my highs; and, since I felt normal again, it was very easy for me to deny that I had an illness that would come back. Somehow I was convinced that I was an exception to the extensive research literature, which clearly showed not only that manic-depressive illness comes back, but that it often comes back in a more severe and frequent form.

It was not that I thought lithium was an ineffective drug. Far from it. The evidence for its efficacy and safety was compelling. Not only that, I knew it worked for me. It certainly was not that I had any moral argument against psychiatric medications. On the contrary, I had, and have, no tolerance for those individuals—especially psychiatrists and psychologists—who oppose using medications for psychiatric illness, those clinicians who somehow draw a distinction between the suffering and treatability of "medical illness" such as Hodgkin's disease or breast cancer, and psychiatric illness such as depression, manic-depression, or schizophrenia. I believe without a doubt that manic-depressive illness is a medical illness; I also believe that with rare exceptions, it is malpractice to treat it without medication. All of these beliefs aside, however, I still somehow thought that I ought to be able to carry on without drugs, that I ought to be able to continue to do things my own way.

My psychiatrist, who took all of these complaints very seriously— existential qualms, side effects, matters of value from my upbringing— never wavered in his conviction that I needed to take lithium. He refused, thank God, to get drawn into my convoluted and impassioned web of reasoning about why I should try just one more time, to survive without taking medication. He always kept the basic choice in perspective. The issue was not whether I missed my highs or that it was some idealized notion of my family background. The underlying issue was whether or not I would choose to use lithium only intermittently, and thereby ensure a return of my manias and depressions. The choice as he saw it—and as is now so painfully clear to me—was between madness and sanity, and between life and death. My manias were occurring more and more frequently and increasingly, were becoming more "mixed" in nature (that is, my predominantly euphoric episodes, that I thought of as my "white manias," were becoming more and more overlaid with agitated depression): my depressions were getting worse and far more suicidal. Few medical treatments, as he pointed out, are free of side effects, and, all things considered, lithium causes fewer adverse reactions than most. Certainly, it was a vast improvement on the brutal and ineffectual treatments that preceded it—chains, bloodletting, wet packs, asylums, and ice picks through the frontal lobes—and although the anticonvulsant medications now work very effectively, and often with fewer side effects, for many people who have manic-depressive illness, lithium remains an extremely effective drug. I knew all of this, although it was with less conviction than I have now.

In fact, underneath it all, I was actually secretly terrified that lithium might not work: What if I took it and I still got sick? If, on the other hand, I didn't take it, I wouldn't have to see my worst fears realized. My psychiatrist very early on saw this terror in my soul, and there is one brief observation in his medical notes that captured this paralyzing fear completely: "Patient sees medication as a promise of a cure and a means of suicide if it doesn't work. She fears that by taking it she will risk her last resort."

When Kay Jamison looks back upon her resistance to treatment, she regrets that it took her so long to yield—so many years lost and so many relationships, so much damage done to her and others.

Her own experience makes her especially aware of the fact that persons with this illness are frequently at war with themselves, and that the major clinical problem in treatment is not that medication is ineffective. We now have thoroughly effective ones, but patients often refuse to take, or neglect taking them. The availability today makes all the more tragic the fact that some suffering with the illness never get to the point of treatment at all, whether through lack of information, poor medical advice, or fear of stigma or of personal or professional reprisal.

Even in recovery, Kay Jamison was personally aware of this last motive for concealing the presence of her illness from others. After attaining tenure at

UCLA, she left to take a position at Johns Hopkins University and had to take anew the period of probation customary before the granting of tenure. She worried about the effect upon her chances for tenure if it were to be known that she had a mental illness. She had heard her chairman say on many occasions that doctors are there to treat patients, and patients should never have to pay—literally or medically—for the problems and suffering of their doctor. Dr. Jamison agreed completely with this sentiment, but still worried that her illness, though now well under control, might somehow prevent her attaining tenure. She made an appointment to discuss the issue with the chairman, and told him about her manic depression. She says that his response was suddenly to reach across the table, put his hand on hers, and smile:

> "Dear Kay," he said, "I know you have manic-depressive illness." He paused, and then laughed. "If we were to get rid of all the manic-depressives on the medical school faculty, not only would we have a much smaller faculty, it would be a far more boring one."

The chairman was certainly correct. One of the most intriguing and perplexing facts about manic-depressive disorder is that it seems to confer advantages as well as disadvantages upon the individual and society. When biographies of great artists and scientists, and histories of the arts and sciences, are reviewed back as far as recorded history permits, there appears to be a definite relationship between the illness, in both its severest and less severe forms, and artistic temperament and creativity. The association is found not in artists alone, but also in eminent scientists as well as leaders in business, politics, and the military. It is as yet ill understood, but probably arises from a commonality in the genes; one that we hope may someday soon be clarified. Meanwhile, there is no doubt as to the definiteness of the relationship and we are aware of some of the complexities involved.

We have already seen in the story by Kay Jamison how seductive the manias of the milder sort can be, both because they carry pleasurable euphoria and because they provide creative people with a flow of ideas and energies. Even in her total recovery, with her illness under complete control, she writes movingly and elegantly in the following passage about the remembered past of these moods and their sweet privileges, despite the sometimes dreadful moods and memories of the more psychotic, violent manias and the desperate depression that followed:

Yet however genuinely dreadful these moods and memories have been, they have always been offset by the elation and vitality of others; and whenever a mild and gentlish wave of brilliant and bubbling manic enthusiasm comes over me, I am transported by a pungent scent into a world of profound recollections—to earlier, more intense and passionate times. The vividness that mania infuses into one's experiences of life creates strong, keenly recollected states, much as war must, and love and early memories surely do. Because of this, there is now, for me, a rather bittersweet exchange of a comfortable and settled present existence for a troubled but intensely lived past.

There is for me, a mixture of longings for an earlier age; this is inevitable, perhaps, in any life, but there is an extra twist of almost painful nostalgia brought about by having lived a life particularly intense in moods. This makes it even harder to leave the past behind, and life on occasion, becomes a kind of elegy for lost moods. I miss the lost intensities, and I find myself unconsciously reaching out for them, as I still now and again reach back with my hand for the fall and heaviness of my now-gone, long, thick hair; like the trace of moods, only a phantom weight remains. These current longings are, for the most part, only longings, and I do not feel compelled to re-create the intensities: the consequences are too awful, too final, and too damaging.

Still, the seductiveness of these unbridled and intense moods is powerful and the ancient dialogue between reason and the senses is almost always more interestingly and passionately resolved in favor of the senses. The milder manias have a way of promising—and then for a very brief while, delivering—springs in the winter and epochal vitalities. In the cold light of day, however, the reality and destructiveness of rekindled illness tend to dampen the evocativeness of such selectively remembered, wistful, intense, and gentle movements. Any temptation that I now have to re-capture such moods by altering my medication is quickly hosed down by the cold knowledge that a gentle intensity soon becomes first a frenetic one and then, finally, an uncontrolled insanity. I am too frightened that I will become morbidly depressed or violently manic—either of which would, in turn, rip apart every aspect of my life, relationships, and work that I find most meaningful—to seriously consider any change in my medical treatment.

Among persons with this illness, the question, must inevitably rise: what if one might have mild manias and pleasant euphoria without having to pay the price of the violent and insane ones and the crash into depression? For persons devoted to the making of art, such as the three literary masters surveyed in chapters 4, 5, and 6, the question is why so many of them are willing to tempt fate by rejecting effective medication and by trying every conceivable means to bring about a state of happiness? Those, who in the early stages of manic-depressive disorder discover that alcohol may well be a temporary, but nonetheless satisfactory means of reducing and holding manias to a manageable proportion, acting as the depressant it is, are among the most unfortunate. Addicted to their manias, they now run the risk of a second, perhaps more complicating addiction. One devil has been cast out only to have the house now harboring two. The added difficulty of dealing with life's consequential problems is only compounded by the equally difficult task of obtaining a correct diagnosis and treatment.

Fortunately, for those with both afflictions who have made a decision to recover and get well, the means of treatment are simple and clear, provided they fall into the hands of an informed diagnostician—AA for alcoholism and effective medication for manic depression is readily available.

Kay Jamison does not seem to be among those with the additional disease of alcoholism. She writes in her book that she did not or does not have a problem with alcohol or sedative drugs. One must believe that this is so, because she has been so honest, detailed, and thorough in her account of her experiences with manic-depressive disorder. It remains true, however, that in most cases of this disorder, alcohol and sedative drugs are incompatible and strongly to be discouraged. Also, all patients with any illness have to be very careful about using alcohol or addictive drugs (lithium is not one) if there is a history of addiction in the family. Addictions and manic-depressive illness frequently masquerade as each other, with an identical set of symptoms, and often the severity of the symptoms and a longitudinal medical, surgical, psychiatric, and addiction history is the only way to tell them apart. In addition is the fact that two or more of these four diagnostic categories coexist in any event.

This likeness to the inebriation of alcohol and sedative drugs and to the "euphoria" or "highs" of cocaine and amphetamines (speed) should not be surprising. When blood levels are too high the same three neurohormones of the brain are the cause of most of the symptoms of manic-depression disorder.

In other words, the highs from cocaine and amphetamines mimic the highs of mania and the lows of alcohol, and sedatives mimic the lows of depression. In all cases, the mood swings are the result of changes in brain levels of the three neurohormones, serotonin, norepinephrine, and dopamine, that result either from pathological changes that occur in the brain as a result of mental disorders, or from the effects of mind-altering drugs on the brain as a result of drug abuse. Other related phenomena are the hallucinations, paranoia, and delusions that can occur following withdrawal from alcohol and other sedative drugs (*delirium tremens*) or from the adverse effects of high blood levels of cocaine and amphetamines or LSD-like drugs. Excessive sleeping (hypersomnia) and the painful inability to sleep (insomnia) are symptoms of addictions to alcohol as well as the above-mentioned addicting drugs.

When alcoholics in recovery read Kay Jamison's account of her resistance to treatment for her manic-depressive disorder, they may find that many of the same reasons she gives for refusing or postponing lithium are thoroughly similar to their own experiences before surrender to the First Step of AA. The pleasures of early drinking, the euphoria induced, the sense of magic, confidence and omnipotence in planning projects, the flow of ideas and insights, the apparent experience of insight and enlightenment—these are all fondly recalled by alcoholics and the grief and regret over their loss are as keenly felt.

Then, too, are the alcoholics imbued with a strong sense of self-reliance, who feel they ought to be able to handle their own problem with drinking by the use of their own resources, their strength of will, high intelligence, and ability (real ability, amply demonstrated in other areas) for self-control. These sentiments have been known to deter many from joining AA—even to the extent of fearing it might work, thus taking control of their lives out of their own hands, which is, ironically, precisely what needs to happen for recovery to begin.

We know that manic-depressive disorder affects about 1.0 to 1.5 percent of the population the world over, and that the incidence is about equal in males and females.

I firmly believe, along with Dr. Jamison and most of the scientific community, that manic-depressive disorder is a genetic illness. The exact gene has not yet been localized, but there can be little doubt that discovery is at hand and inevitable. This will indeed be a great blessing or breakthrough, but the discovery will not be without many ethical, moral, and legal questions in consequence.

A second, and even more troubling, deeper question arises from what Dr. Jamison and others have called "advantages" of the disease, including its known (if mystifying) association with creativity in the arts and sciences and indeed in many of the great endeavors of human life. If genetic research, localizing the gene or genes or genetic dynamic, results in better and earlier diagnosis of the illness and better indications for treatment, the benefits to patients, their families, to society in general could be extraordinary. But an immediate danger will present itself in the form of prenatal diagnostic testing.

Meanwhile, the terror and suffering of bipolar disorder patients remain to be treated, and the misfortune of the uninformed and the folly of the instructed neglecting medications takes its toll daily on thousands upon thousands. Kay Jamison includes in her book an account of the cost of defiance in a patient of hers:

> Unfortunately, this resistance to taking lithium is played out in the lives of tens of thousands of patients every year. Almost always it leads to a recurrence of the illness; not uncommonly it results in a tragedy. I was to see this, a few years after my own struggle with lithium, in a patient of mine. He became a particularly painful reminder to me of the high costs of defiance.
>
> ...Then came an absolutely blood curdling scream from one of the examining rooms—a scream of terror and undeniable madness—and I ran down the corridor; past the nurses, past a medical resident dictating notes for a patient's chart, and past a surgical resident poring over the PDR with a cup of coffee in one hand, a hemostat clamped and dangling from the short sleeve of his green scrub suit, and a stethoscope draped around his neck. I opened the door from where the scream had begun, and my heart sank. The first person I saw was the psychiatry resident on call, which I knew, he smiled sympathetically. Then I saw my patient, strapped down on a gurney, in four-point leather restraints. He was lying spread-eagled on his back, each wrist and ankle bound with a leather cuff, with an additional leather restraint across his chest. I felt sick to my stomach. Despite his restraints, I also felt scared. A year before this same patient had held a knife to my throat during a psychotherapy session in my office. I had called the police at that time, and he had been involuntarily committed to one of the locked wards at UCLA's Neuropsychiatric Institute.

Seventy-two hours later, in the impressively blind wisdom of the American justice system, he had been released back into the community. And to my care. I noted with some irony that three police officers who were standing by the gurney, two of whom had their hands resting on their guns, evidently thought he represented a "threat to himself or others" even if the judge hadn't. That he would get well again, I had no doubt. How long it would last was another question. Lithium worked remarkably well for him, but once his hallucinations and his abject terror stopped, he would quit taking it. Neither the resident nor I needed to see the results of the lithium blood level that had been drawn on his admission to the emergency room. There would be no lithium in his blood. The result had been mania. Suicidal depression would inevitably follow, as would the indescribable pain and disruptiveness to his life and to the lives of the members of his family. He had a particularly bad, although not uncommon form of the illness, lithium worked well, but he wouldn't take it. Over the years, I asked several of my colleagues to see him in consultation, but they, like me, could find no way to reach him, no chink in the tightly riveted armor of his resistance. His attacks of mania and depression became more frequent and severe. No breakthrough ever came. No happy ending ever materialized. Lithium worked, but he would not take it; our relationship worked but not well enough. He had a terrible disease and it eventually cost him his life—as it does tens of thousands of people every year. There were limits on what any of us could do for him, and it tore me apart inside. We all move uneasily within our restraints.

I tried to encourage our clinic doctors to see that this was an illness that could confer advantage as well as disadvantage, and that for many individuals these intoxicating experiences were highly addictive in nature and difficult to give up.

We all build internal sea walls to keep at bay the sadness of life and the often overwhelming force within our minds. In whatever way we do this— through love, work, family, faith, friends, denial, alcohol, drugs, or medication—we build these walls, stone by stone, over a lifetime. One of the most difficult problems is to construct these barriers of such a height and strength that one has a true harbor, a sanctuary away from crippling turmoil and pain, but yet low enough, and permeable enough, to let in fresh sea water that will fend off the inevitable inclination toward brackishness. For someone with my cast of mind and mood, medication is an integral element of this wall: without it, I would be constantly beholden to the crushing movements of a mental sea; I would, unquestionably, be dead or insane.

The darkness is an integral part of who I am, and it takes no effort or imagination on my part to remember the months of relentless blackness and exhaustion, or the terrible efforts it took in order to teach, read, write, see patients, and keep relationships alive. More deeply layered over but all too readily summoned up with the first trace of depression are the unforgettable images of violence, utter madness, mortifying behavior, and moods savage to experience, and even more disturbingly brutal in their effects upon others.

There is always a part of my mind that is preparing for the worst, and another part of my mind that believes if I prepare enough for it, the worst won't happen.

DEVELOPMENTAL HISTORY

Kay Jamison's nuclear family consisted of herself and an older brother and sister and her parents. It was a close-knit family, at least while she was young, and her parents were able to provide her with a very stimulating childhood. Jamisen's parents were graduates of the University of Chicago and her mother was a schoolteacher, her father a Navy pilot. As children, Kay's parents encouraged her and her siblings to pursue their creative and intellectual interests. Because of her father's job with the Navy, the family moved around frequently. Kay attended four different elementary schools in four different cities. This was perhaps the only negative effect on her as a child.

FAMILY HISTORY

Dr. Jamison's family was well educated, and on the paternal side of the family there were two scientists, her father being a Navy meteorologist and her grandfather being a college professor in physics. Her mother was a schoolteacher, and the maternal side of the family was compassionate, understanding, and supportive, and that included her maternal grandmother and her older brother. The only signs of impending trouble was a tendency for her to have mood swings, and the instability of her father as he grew older as evidenced by occupational changes and marital estrangement as well as a tendency towards heavy drinking.

EDUCATIONAL HISTORY

Kay did her first two years of undergraduate education at the University of California in Los Angeles, where she had to work in order to support herself. She received a federal grant and completed her third year as a zoology major at St. Andrews in Scotland, which she found exhilarating and memorable. She was very happy devoting all of her time to her studies and to poetry without having to work nights to pay her room and board. She was still twenty-one years old when she returned from Scotland and re-entered UCLA for her final year of undergraduate studies. She decided that her temperament was not suited for the rigors and rigidity of a medical school curriculum that was her original vocation. She decided to continue on at UCLA and give in to her intuition and forgo medical school.

In 1971 she began her doctoral studies in psychology at UCLA. Kay started her doctoral work in experimental psychology but switched to clinical psychology, and for a time concentrated on psychoanalytic psychiatry that "emphasized treatment being related to understanding early experiences and conflicts, dreams, symbols, and their interpretation." She decided to pursue a more medical approach to diagnosis, symptoms, illness, and medical treatment only after she started her internship at the UCLA Neuropsychiatric Institute. Throughout most of her professional training she has concentrated her research and clinical work on the study and of major affective disorders that include emphasis of her own illness, manic-depressive disorder.

OCCUPATIONAL HISTORY

Dr. Jamison started her professional career at the UCLA's Department of Psychiatry as an assistant professor. She became a tenured professor after struggling with her mental illness during the process. She also attained a teaching position at Johns Hopkins and worried about tenure there because of the knowledge that she had a mental illness.

MARITAL HISTORY

Dr. Jamison has been married once, and that ended in divorce after ten years. She was engaged once and her psychiatrist husband-to-be died suddenly of a massive heart attack at forty-four years of age. She now has a long-term relationship with her third significant other that is working well and she describes his tranquillity and imperturbability as equal to 300 mg of lithium a day to her emotional stability. Dr. Jamison has no children.

As Dr. Kay Jamison writes, "If love is not a cure, it certainly can act as a very strong medicine." As John Donne writes about love, "It is not so pure and abstract as one might once have thought and wished, but it does endure, and it does grow."

MEDICAL AND PSYCHIATRIC HISTORY

Kay Jamison was a senior in high school when she had her first attack of manic-depressive illness. She said, "Once the siege began I lost my mind rather rapidly." For the first two years, her symptoms were primarily exquisite euphoria, a racing mind, and a pressured or rapid speech. Within two years she was wildly and psychotically out of control and then moribund, depressed, and without energy to concentrate. She cannot understand how she survived without being locked up. Periods of hypomania and depression cycled through her first two years at UCLA. Her year at St. Andrews in Scotland was so aesthetic on a daily basis that she was unaware of her illness. Just three months after completing her doctorate at UCLA, she became Dr. Jamison and was hired as an assistant professor at UCLA. She became, she said, a "raving psychotic." That was when she first began seeing a psychiatrist as an out-patient at UCLA once a week, and it was when she first started taking lithium. She resisted taking the lithium. She says about that period of time, "I simply did not want to believe I needed to take medications. I had become *addicted* to my high moods; I had become dependent upon their intensity, euphoria, assuredness, and their infectious ability to induce enthusiasms in other people." In other words, the brief periods of mania that she had as a result of her manic-depressive illness made her feel the euphoria of intoxication, and she was hopelessly addicted to that feeling of intoxication.

Dr. Jamison learned a hard lesson from her refusal to take her lithium on a consistent basis. She says, "...Over and over and over, I would say to myself, if I can't move, if I can't think, and I can't care, then what conceivable point is there in living?" Her psychiatrist wrote in his office record, "Patient is intermittently suicidal."

She was definitely suicidal. Jamison made a very serious attempt at it by ingesting a massive dose of lithium. Her brother called from Paris and discovered her drugged state and he called her personal psychiatrist. He and a psychiatrist friend arrived in time to save her life. Finally, she was convinced to take the lithium as she was prescribed and she slowed her moods, and her private and professional life began to stabilize.

ALCOHOL AND SUBSTANCE ABUSE HISTORY

In her book, Dr. Jamison says that she did not and does not have a problem with alcohol and/or sedative drugs. Because she has been so honest and forthcoming with her admission of her manic-depressive disorder, I believe her. However, in most cases of manic-depressive illness, alcohol and sedatives are incompatible with the illness. Also all patients have to be very careful about using alcohol or drugs if there is a history of addiction in the family. There may be a history of both manic-depressive illness and addiction in Jamison's family. As a matter of fact, addictions and manic-depressive illness frequently masquerade as each other and the severity of the symptoms is frequently the only way to tell them apart, and they frequently co-exist anyway.

Dr. Jamison writes: "I tried to encourage our clinic doctors to see that this [manic depression] was an illness that could confer advantage as well as disadvantage, and that for many individuals these intoxicating experiences were highly addictive in nature and difficult to give up."

MENTAL STATUS EXAMINATION

Normally, a mental status examination is done on a patient within a certain time frame and the results of that mental status examination refer to that particular time frame only. In other words, in one time frame a person may be manic, and in another time frame they may be depressed. Another example is a person's orientation. On one occasion a patient may be oriented as to person, time, and place, and at another time they have been confused and totally disoriented. Dr. Jamison knows this fact all too well:

> I was a senior in high school when I had my first attack of manic-depressive illness.
> College, for most people I know, was the best time of their lives. This is inconceivable to me. College was, for the most part, a terrible struggle,

a recurring nightmare of violent and dreadful moods spelled only now and again by weeks, sometimes months, of great fun, passion, high enthusiasms, and long runs of hard but enjoyable work. This pattern of shifting moods and energies had a very seductive side to it, in large part that I had enjoyed in high school....

...I was working twenty to thirty hours a week in order to pay my way through college, and there was no margin at all for the expenses. Unfortunately, the pink overdraft notices from the bank always seemed to arrive when I was in the throes of the depression that inevitably followed my weeks of exaltation.

But then as night invariably follows after the day, my mood would crash, and my mind again would grind to a halt.

Decreased sleep is both a symptom of mania and a cause, but I didn't know that at the time, and it probably would not have made any difference to me if I had.

PSYCHIATRIC AND SUBSTANCE ABUSE FORMULATION

The usual psychiatric and substance abuse formulation is a synopsis of the history, physical, and mental status examination for reason of coming to a logical conclusion of the patient's diagnosis and planned treatment. In the case of Kay Redfield Jamison, these two goals are unnecessary because she gave her own irrefutable diagnosis and conclusions. She, along with most of the scientific community, is convinced that it is a genetic illness. Although we know it affects about 1 percent of the population the world over and the incidence is equal in males and females, the exact gene has not yet been localized. I believe that the inevitable discovery is at hand. There will be many ethical, moral, and legal issues that will need to be addressed in the near future. It is also appropriate to point out that if we eliminate the gene or genes that can cause manic-depressive disorder, and eventually we will be able to, we most likely should not do so. Also, there are the various mood disorders due to general medical conditions that have almost identical symptoms, many of which are not hereditary in nature. I am referring to the phenomenon that can produce syndromes difficult to distinguish from manic-depressive disorder (masquerades), but their cause or etiology are from trauma or toxicity such as traumatic brain disorder and toxic brain disease from medication side effects, drug addiction, and other diseases and endocrine imbalances.

I certainly share with Dr. Jamison her concerns about what may result from finding the gene for manic-depressive disorder. If a better and earlier diagnosis of the disorder results with better treatment, the benefits to the patients and their families and to society could be extraordinary. But there is also a danger in prenatal diagnostic testing. Will prospective parents choose to abort fetuses that carry manic-depressive disorder even if it proves to be a treatable disease and the treatment has no side effects? A recent study at Johns Hopkins University that asked patients with manic-depressive disorder and their spouses whether or not they would abort an affected fetus found that the majority would not. Do we run the risk of making our planet a blander, more homogenized place if we get rid of genes that carry both advantages and disadvantages? This is admittedly an impossibly complex scientific and moral problem. What is the risk to the risk takers, those energetic, creative, and gifted individuals who join with others in our society to propel the arts, business, politics, and science? Are manic-depressive individuals like spotted owls or dolphins that are in danger of becoming an endangered species?

These are very difficult ethical and moral issues especially because manic-depressive disorder can confer advantages and disadvantages on both the individual and society. If the biographies and history of the arts and sciences are reviewed as far back as recorded history permits, the disorder, in both its severe and less severe forms, appears to have a definite relationship to the person's artistic temperament and creativity. This association can also be found in eminent scientists, as well as leaders in business, religion, the military, and among politicians. More subtle effects, probably due to the same gene, can be seen in the personality (cyclothymic personality), thinking styles, and energy levels of affected individuals. This situation is further complicated by the fact that additional genetic, biochemical, and environmental factors (seasonal affective disorder), severe insomnia, childbirth (Post Partum Depression), and drug and alcohol use may be at least in part responsible for both the illness and the cognitive and temperamental characteristics associated with great achievement, as well as underachievement. These scientific and ethical issues are real ones. Fortunately, they are being addressed by our federal government's Genome Project as well as other groups of scientists and ethicists. But they are still immensely troubling problems and will continue to be so for many years to come.

FINAL DIAGNOSIS

AXIS I:
1.   Bipolar Disorder Unspecified, *DSM-IV* (296.7)

AXIS II:
1.   None

AXIS III:
1.   None

AXIS IV:
1.   Deferred

AXIS V:
1.   Deferred

DEFINING THE DUAL DIAGNOSIS CONCEPT

When speaking of a Dual Diagnosis or a Multiple Diagnosis, we are referring to any psychiatric patient that has any one or more of the following of the four basic psychiatric episodes, in any possible combination, in addition to any of all of the same four basic psychiatric episodes as a result of a substance-induced disorder. These basic four episodes are:

- Mood change episodes
- Impaired perception of reality (Hallucinations or Delusions Episodes)
- Episodic changes in personality
- Episodes of anxiety, panic, compulsions, and/or obsessions

The question is are these symptoms caused by a single psychiatric illness, including a substance-abuse disorder or, is there the possibility of this individual having more than one illness, causing a conglomeration of these symptoms? In other words, do they have either a Dual Diagnosis or a Multiple Diagnosis causing episodes of similar psychiatric symptoms from more than one disorder?

George E. Woody, M.D., summarized seventeen research papers in the January 2003 *Psychiatric Times* that confirms my hypothesis that medication, psychotherapy, and counseling can be combined for patients with substance-abuse and other psychiatric disorders with additional benefits and few adverse events. Evidence from the perusal of these studies indicate that patients who have one or more psychiatric disorders in addition to their substance-abuse disorder are those most likely to benefit from combined therapy for both their psychiatric disorder and their substance-abuse disorder. This is especially true for those that include Alcoholics Anonymous or Narcotics Anonymous within the same treatment program. The findings of these studies are consistent with clinical experience and common sense. Patients with substance-use plus an additional psychiatric disorder benefit most if both disorders are treated simultaneously in the same facility or program.

Any one or all of these psychiatric episodes of symptoms may occur singly or in any combination under different classifications of psychiatric or substance-induced groups. They are:

I. Psychiatric Disorders with Unknown Cause or Etiology
    A. Functional psychiatric disorders with four groups of symptoms:
- Mood change episodes
- Impaired perception of reality (Hallucinations or Delusions Episodes)
- Episodic changes in personality
- Episodes of anxiety, panic, compulsions, and/or obsessions

II. Psychiatric Disorders with a Known Cause or Etiology
    A. Psychiatric disorders due to a known medical condition with symptoms of:
- Mood change episodes
- Impaired perception of reality (Hallucinations or Delusions Episodes)
- Episodic changes in personality
- Episodes of anxiety, panic, compulsions, and/or obsessions

B. Psychiatric disorders due to a known surgical condition with symptoms of:
- Mood change episodes
- Impaired perception of reality (Hallucinations or Delusions Episodes)
- Episodic changes in personality
- Episodes of anxiety, panic, compulsions, and/or obsessions

C. Substance-induced psychiatric episodes with symptoms of:
- Mood change episodes
- Impaired perception of reality (Hallucinations or Delusions Episodes)
- Episodic changes in personality
- Episodes of anxiety, panic, compulsions, and/or obsessions

Notice that the episodes of psychiatric symptoms appear alike and are repetitive, which emphasizes how similar the symptoms can be in all of the four very different categories above.

PATIENT ADVANTAGE

The advantages for patients who can understand and accept their Dual or Multiple Diagnosis are many. Most importantly, with treatment for all of their disorders simultaneously and appropriately, patients can exchange a life of chaotic misery for one of happiness and freedom. Patients can enjoy true control over the events and circumstances of their lives, including economic security, as well as stability, despite their mental, emotional, and behavioral illnesses.

The rewards for patients, their families, and their physicians for learning about and utilizing the concept of the Dual Diagnosis or the Triple Diagnosis are many and important for maintaining life, liberty, and the pursuit of happiness.

The primary advantage to the struggling patient is that it will bring an end to the "revolving door" of relapses and recidivism. When patients are treated for only one of their illnesses at a time, the relapse of the other illness will mostly likely occur from the untreated part of the Dual Diagnosis or Multiple Diagnosis. This then will precipitate a relapse of all the Dual or Triple Diagnoses.

A research paper by LeClair Bissell, M.D., in the early 1970s revealed that the cost of treating ninety-nine physicians for their future combined medical, surgical, and addiction illnesses were reduced by two-thirds after their first, but not necessarily only, in-patient treatment for alcoholism and other addictions. This success in recovery would project to billions and billions of dollars being saved if treatment of those with a Dual or Multiple Diagnosis was to reduce the numbers of repeat admissions to alcohol and drug rehabilitation facilities and to psychiatric hospitals for treatment of mental illnesses. In addition, they would enjoy their own personal economic progress as a result of being able to join the work force and return to a position of value within their families. They would also be eliminating painful and costly confrontations with the law and other social agencies.

With this new concept they would receive treatment for both conditions during one admission for a Dual Diagnosis or Multiple Diagnosis. The savings would not only benefit the patients and their families, but also their employers, government agencies, insurance companies, and all types of charitable organizations.

I have learned from my personal and professional experiences that the quality of life changes so dramatically that only other recovering addicts and recovering mentally and emotionally ill members of a treatment group and/or fellowship can fully understand that full recovery is possible until they experience it for themselves.

The symptoms experienced by the four writers and poets I have studied are similar, if not identical, to the suffering and struggling of individuals that have an untreated Dual Diagnosis. Of those four writers, only Jamison is alive and able to describe what happened with treatment and medications and what it is like now following her remarkable recovery.

Both mental disorders and addiction disorders can cause impairment in brain function and therefore, seemingly diminish the patient's individual intelligence. What a horrible price to pay for having a *treatable* disorder and not seeking or accepting treatment. I cannot emphasize strongly enough that things have radically changed in the fields of psychiatry and psychopharmacology. The Dual Diagnosis approach has made a tremendous difference. However, another factor that is equally important has been the development of the newer psychotropic and antipsychotic medications, the new uses of older medications, and the relative nontoxic effects of both with much fewer side effects. There are also new generation neuroleptics, antidepressants, antianxiety agents, mood stabilizers, thought simplifiers, anger inhibitors, impulse inhibitors, nonaddicting attention stimulators, and even memory energizers that can be used in smaller doses and targeted to specific symptoms with better symptom relief with fewer side effects than ever before.

How do these medications cause changes in intelligence? Mood disorders, perception disorders, personality disorders, and anxiety disorders can all have components that can affect interest, energy, involvement, attention, impulsiveness, concentration, executive functioning, anger, simplification of thoughts, and if protracted, can cause decreased intelligence, pseudo-dementia, and dementia if they are not alleviated by early, proper, and specific treatment.

This need for early, proper, and specific treatment should clarify why it is crucial to diagnose and treat *all* diagnoses that an individual has. It should be noted that alcoholism and all types of addictions are mental disorders and can cause all of the impairments under discussion. The fact is that all substance-abuse disorders, including alcoholism, are mental disorders by definition. At the same time, alcohol is both a food containing calories and a lethal toxin when the blood level is above 0.8 percent. Nevertheless, it is a mind-altering drug with a high addiction potential and at the same time is the only mind-altering drug, except for tobacco, used as a legal social substance and social beverage in most Western cultures, which gives it a unique status.

Alcohol causes deaths by accidents and chronic illnesses, insanity from brain damage, suicides from depression, social breakdown problems, physical diseases of the heart, lungs, liver, pancreas and digestive system, inflammatory diseases, cancer, muscle and bone disease, blindness, endocrine disorders such as diabetes and malnutrition, as well as many other lethal physical and mental conditions. The litany of social problems caused by intoxication and physical illness is just as long and includes divorce, estrangement from friends and family, unemployment, legal problems ranging from driving violations and public intoxication to thefts, felonies, violent crime, overcrowded jails, and long prison sentences. It is the single most common cause of human misery both for alcoholics and their families.

Impairment in brain function can be either temporary or permanent and can range from poor concentration to frank dementia. Prior to the *DSM-IV* of the American Psychiatric Association, a diagnosis of dementia always meant it was permanent and there was no chance for recovery. Non-invasive studies like the CT Scan and MRI of the brain show that dementia can be reversible and brain function can be restored with early diagnosis and treatment.

Finally, you must consider the effects of mental disorders and addiction disorders on some of our most promising geniuses in poetry, literature, music, and in all of the arts. I am referring to people like Poe, Fitzgerald, and Berryman. Can you picture the tremendous productivity and creativity that these individuals would have contributed to our society had there been a way of arresting their mental illnesses and their addictions as there is available now?

CLINICIAN ADVANTAGES

The advantages to the clinician for learning about and utilizing the concept of Dual Diagnosis or Multiple Diagnosis are many. It provides a system for diagnosis and treatment that is more helpful than the old concept of *Differential Diagnosis*. This does not imply that one category of diagnosis is more important than any other category because when a Dual or Multiple Diagnosis is present they cannot and should not be separated because each diagnosis modifies or exacerbates the other(s). This system emphasizes the importance of combining different types of treatment and different classes of medication for each separate illness making up the Dual or Multiple Diagnosis.

Utilizing the Dual Diagnosis concept eliminates, or at least changes the use of the terms *Primary* and *Secondary*. With Dual Diagnosis or Multiple Diagnosis the words Primary and Secondary should not imply chronology because this usually cannot be inferred at the time the diagnosis is made unless there is a single traumatic event or medical condition that precipitated all components of a Dual or Multiple Diagnosis sequentially. Examples would be a psychiatric diagnosis, a surgical diagnosis, and a chemical-dependency diagnosis that all occurred as a result of a traumatic brain injury or open-heart surgery. Also untoward psychiatric symptoms (depression or mania), medical (diabetes mellitus with insulin shock or ketosis), and atypical alcohol withdrawal after the prescribing medications like cortisone or disulfiram can occur. These are neither common nor rare illness combinations.

If a physician or psychiatrist uses the Dual or Multiple Diagnosis concept in diagnosing a patient with psychiatric and/or addiction symptoms, he has not completed a review of the diagnostic possibilities until he has considered if the patient had mood, psychotic, behavior, or anxiety episodes. He could have a diagnosis of either/and:

I.   A psychiatric disorder with an unknown cause or etiology:
    A.   Functional Psychiatric Disorders; or
II. A psychiatric disorder with a known cause or etiology:
    A.   Psychiatric Disorder Due to a Known Medical Condition;
    B.   Psychiatric Disorder Due to a Known Surgical Condition;
    C.   Substance-Induced Psychiatric Disorder with a Known Substance as Cause or Etiology.

With the Dual Diagnosis discovery, the clinician of today has been given the opportunity and the tools necessary to prevent patients from deteriorating into a state of chaos as a result of mental disorders or addiction disorders that could eventually cause a dementia, pseudodementia, or disability as a result of an inadequately treated Dual Diagnosis or Multiple Diagnosis. Not to mention the possibility of preventing one of the world's geniuses like Poe, Fitzgerald, or Berryman from dying prematurely or deteriorating into such a state of madness that it would totally inhibit his or her creativity.

RESOURCES FOR HELP AND INFORMATION

ORGANIZATIONS FOR DEPRESSION, MANIC-DEPRESSIVE DISORDERS, SCHIZOPHRENIA, AND OTHER MENTAL AND EMOTIONAL DISORDERS:

American Psychiatric Association
(for psychiatrists)
1000 Wilson Boulevard, Suite 1825
Arlington, VA 22209-3901
1-888-35-PSYCH (7-7924)
(703) 907-7300
www.psych.org

APA Books and Journals
American Psychiatric Publishing, Inc.
1-800-368-5777
Fax: (703) 907-7322
www.appi.org

American Psychological Association (APA)
(for psychologists and mental health therapists)
750 First Street, NE
Washington, DC 20002-4242
www.apa.org

The Juvenile Bipolar Research Foundation
49 S. Quaker Hill Road
Pawling, NY 12564
info@bpchildresearch.org
www.bpchildresearch.org

Child and Adolescent Bipolar Foundation (CABF)
(Important interactive Web site offers online support group including Tomie Burke's PB Parents, chat rooms, message boards, learning center, database of professional members and local support groups, resource page with information on Social Security, drug database, and international resources.)
111 Wilmette Ave, #PMB 331
Wilmette, IL 60091
(847) 256-8525
www.bpkids.org

National Depressive and Manic-Depressive Association (NDMDA)
730 N. Franklin Street, Suite 501
Chicago, IL 60610
1-800-82-NDMDA (6-3632)
www.ndmda.org

The National Alliance for the Mentally Ill (NAMI)
200 N. Globe Road, Suite 1015
Arlington, VA 22203-3754
(703) 524-7600
Fax: (703) 524-9094
1(800) 950-NAMI (6264)
www.nami.org
(For *Because Kids Grow Up* newsletter, contact Monique Lewis monique@mani.org)

The Stanley Foundation Bipolar Network
5430 Grosvenor Lane, Suite 200
Bethesda, MD 20814
1-800-518-7326
www.bipolarnetwork.org

The National Mental Health Association
2001 N. Beauregard Street
Alexandria, VA 22314
1-800-969-NMHA (6642)
www.nmha.org

Federation of Families
1021 Prince Street
Alexandria, VA 22311
(703) 684-7710
www.ffcmh.org

Emotions Anonymous International
P.O. Box 4245
St. Paul, MN 55104-0245
(651) 647-9712
info@EmotionsAnonymous.org

Family Voices
3411 Candelaria NE, Suite M
Albuquerque, NM 87107
1-888-835-5669
kidshealth@familyvoices.org
www.familyvoices.org

Depression: A Serious But Treatable Illness
All Family Resources
4286 Redwood Highway, Suite 401
San Rafael, CA 94903

Lithium Information Center
c/o Madison Institute of Medicine
P.O. Box 626365
Middleton, WI 53562-8365
(608) 827-2470
Fax: (608) 827-2479

The Bipolar Child
(Web site of Demetri Papolos, M.D. and Janice Papolos)
www.bipolarchild.com

Bipolar Support Organization (BPSO)
Internet support group
www.BPSO.org (click children and adolescent icon)

Pendulum Resources
For people in relationships with someone who has a bipolar disorder, i.e., children parents, siblings, spouses, etc.
www.pendulum.org

ORGANIZATIONS FOR ALCOHOLISM AND OTHER ADDICTIONS:

Alcoholics Anonymous (AA)
15 E. 26th Street, Room 1810
New York, NY 10010
(212) 683-3900
Mailing address:
Grand Central Station
P.O. Box 459
New York, NY 10063

Adult Children of Alcoholics (ACOA)
P.O. Box 862
Midtown Station
New York, NY 10010
(212) 302-7240
1-800-344-2666

American Counsel for Drug Education
204 Monroe Street, Suite 110
Rockville, MD 20850
(301) 294-0600
1-800-244-8948

American Academy of Addiction Psychiatry
7301 Mission Road, Suite 252
Prairie Village, KS 66208
(913) 262-6162
(913) 262-4311
info@aaap.org
www.aaap.org

**Mothers Against Drunk Driving
(MADD)**
511 E. John Carpenter Freeway,
Suite 700
Irving, TX 75062
(214) 744-6233

Nar-Anon Family Groups
302 West 5th Street, #301
San Pedro, CA 90731
(310) 547-5800

Narcotics Anonymous (NA)
P.O. Box 9999
Van Nuys, CA 91409
(818) 780-3951

**National Association for Children
of Alcoholics (NACOA)**
31582 Coast Highway, Suite B
South Laguna, CA 92677
(714) 499-3889

**National Council on Alcoholism
and Drug Dependence (NCADD)**
12 W. 21st Street
New York, NY 10010
(212) 206-6770

Women for Sobriety
P.O. Box 618
Quakerstown, PA 18951
(215) 536-8026

CHAPTER ENDNOTES

Chapter 4

1   A.M. Ludwig. "Creative Achievement and Psychopathology, Comparisons Among Professions," *American Journal of Psychotherapy* 46 (1992): 330–335.

2   Ibid.

3   It may be noted here that a similar condition can occur after traumatic brain injury when the brain trauma causes a decreased tolerance for alcohol or sedative medication and the same head injury precipitates a mood disorder due to a general medical condition (head injury).

Chapter 5

1   Irving Thalberg was a key executive at Universal Studios and was in a position to delegate choice work to Fitzgerald for movie scripts. Fitzgerald used Norma Shear's dog as a prop to perform a ludicrous song called "Dog! Dog! Dog! Dog!" He also insulted a guest, Robert Montgomery, who arrived in riding gear, asking him, "Why don't you bring in your horse?"

Chapter 6

1   A revision of Francis T. Vincent, JR's *Definition of Spirituality* by Ernest
     Kurtz: "Spirituality teaches us, or has taught most of us, how to deal
     with failure. We learn at a very young age that failure is the norm in
     life...errors are part of the game, part of its rigorous truth."

ABOUT THE AUTHOR

D R. RICHARD A. MORIN graduated from the University of Michigan Medical School in 1958 and completed his internship at Toledo Hospital. After twenty years in practice in general medicine and addiction medicine in Michigan and California, he completed a formal three-year psychiatric residency at Wayne State University Lafayette Clinic in 1983.

Prior to his semi-retirement in 1995, Dr. Morin had numerous hospital, professional, and teaching appointments. He was chairman of the Department of Psychiatry and Substance Abuse at the Sisters of Mercy's Samaritan Health Center in Detroit, medical director of Samaritan's Health Center Dual Diagnosis Unit and medical director of Detroit Riverview Hospital's traumatic brain injury unit. He also had faculty appointments at Wayne State University Medical School, Lafayette Clinic, and the University of Michigan Medical Schools as director of the Department of Alcoholism and Substance Abuse at the University of Michigan.

Dr. Morin served on international, national, and state boards and committees to assist in ongoing quality education and treatment for his peers and co-workers in the field of substance education and treatment for his peers and co-workers in the field of substance abuse and psychiatry. His other publications include: *The Alcoholic Man; Too Much/Too Little,* and *Sexual Dysfunction and the Alcoholic Male;* an interview with Dr. Morin in the initial issue of *Alcoholism,* a national magazine, and an educational movie entitled *Sex, Booze, Blues, and the Drugs You Use,* an FSM Production film.

In addition, Dr. Morin is a national and international lecturer in Chemical Dependency, sexual dysfunction, Dual Diagnosis, and traumatic brain injury. He has spoken in Greece, England, Spain, and British Columbia, as well as at Rutgers University School of Alcoholism and the Southeastern Conferences on Alcohol and Drug Abuse in Georgia. He also organized and co-sponsored his own successful Midwest Addiction Conference in Michigan during 1988, 1989, and 1990.